High School Transition that Works!

High School Transition that Works!

Lessons Learned from Project SEARCH®

by

Maryellen Daston, Ph.D.

J. Erin Riehle, M.S.N.

and

Susie Rutkowski, M.A.

Cincinnati Children's Hospital Medical Center
Cincinnati, Ohio

·P·A·U·L·H·
BROOKES
PUBLISHING CO®

Baltimore • London • Sydney

Paul H. Brookes Publishing Co.
Post Office Box 10624
Baltimore, Maryland 21285-0624
USA

www.brookespublishing.com

"Paul H. Brookes Publishing Co." is a registered trademark of
Paul H. Brookes Publishing Co., Inc.

Typeset by Spearhead Global, Inc., Bear, Delaware.
Manufactured in the United States of America by
Versa Press Inc., East Peoria, Illinois.

The individuals described in this book are composites or real people whose situations are masked and are based on the authors' experiences. In some instances, names and identifying details have been changed to protect confidentiality. Real names are used by permission.

Photos by Rick Norton Photography.

"To be of use" from CIRCLES ON THE WATER by Marge Piercy, copyright © 1982 by Middlemarsh, Inc. Used by permission of Alfred A. Knopf, a division of Random House, Inc.

Library of Congress Cataloging-in-Publication Data

Daston, Maryellen.
  High school transition that works! : lessons learned from Project SEARCH / by Maryellen Daston, Ph.D., J. Erin Riehle, M.S.N., and Susie Rutkowski, M.A., Cincinnati Children's Hospital Medical Center.
    pages   cm
  Includes bibliographical references and index.
  ISBN-13: 978-1-59857-249-0
  ISBN-10: 1-59857-249-0
  1. Project SEARCH (1996–)   2. People with disabilities—Employment—United States.   3. School-to-work transition—United States.   4. Vocational guidance—United States.   I. Riehle, J. Erin.   II. Rutkowski, Susie.   III. Title.
  HD7256.U5D38 2012
  362.4'0484—dc23   2012008826

British Library Cataloguing in Publication data are available from the British Library.

2016   2015   2014   2013   2012

10   9   8   7   6   5   4   3   2   1

Contents

For the Reader

If you have an interest in promoting meaningful employment for people with intellectual and developmental disabilities, this book is for you. You can expect to gain an in-depth understanding of the philosophy and practices that form the foundation of the Project SEARCH® model and learn from the numerous anecdotes and examples that illustrate how our program works. We have also revealed some of the mistakes that we've made along the way and how these errors have ultimately strengthened the program model. We hope that these stories will add to your personal and professional growth, and help you envision an expanded range of possibilities for the young people in your life.

The book also includes many practical resources, such as classroom activities to promote independent living skills, roles and responsibilities of Project SEARCH partner organizations, a student selection rubric, and internship evaluation tools. These resources may inspire a fresh outlook and new approaches in many settings, and reading this book can be a first step in exploring a Project SEARCH start-up. However, to ensure model fidelity and consistent quality of programming across sites, Project SEARCH is a licensed, trademarked model. To establish an official Project SEARCH program site, it is necessary to secure individualized technical assistance and a licensing agreement with Project SEARCH. Please visit our web site, http://projectsearch.us, for more information on how to get started.

About the Authors

Maryellen Daston, Ph.D., Consultant, Grants and Communications, Project SEARCH®; Medical Writer and Editor, Department of Cancer and Cell Biology, University of Cincinnati College of Medicine; Cincinnati Children's Hospital Medical Center, 3333 Burnet Avenue, MLC 5030, Cincinnati, OH 450229

Dr. Daston has a background in biomedical research and technical writing. As a researcher, she specialized in developmental neuroscience. However, when she started working for Project SEARCH®, her focus shifted from cells in a dish to the development of the whole person.

When she joined the Project SEARCH team, Maryellen expected to be the in-house grant writer. But her role has evolved beyond that, and she has since become the written voice of the Project SEARCH program. As such, she is responsible for editing and writing content for the Project SEARCH web site, articles for professional journals, and other communications—including this book. She also identifies state and federal funding opportunities and prepares grant applications.

Maryellen lives in Cincinnati, Ohio, with her husband, George, two charming sons, Char and Jack, and their very lovable dog, Winnie. In her spare time, Maryellen enjoys yoga and reading. She is looking forward to someday having the time to make jewelry and knit.

J. Erin Riehle, M.S.N., Founder and Senior Director, Project SEARCH, Cincinnati Children's Hospital Medical Center, 3333 Burnet Avenue, MLC5030, Cincinnati, OH 450229

Ms. Riehle is a recognized authority and national leader in promoting employment opportunities for people with disabilities and other barriers to employment. She is a founder and Senior Director of Project SEARCH, an employment and transition program that has received national recognition for innovative practices.

When she started Project SEARCH, Erin was a nurse manager at Cincinnati Children's Hospital Medical Center with no particular expertise in disability issues beyond the strictly medical. Her motivation was to offer people with disabilities—who made up a significant portion of the hospital's patient volume—the same opportunities for training and employment that were available to everyone else. She brought a business perspective to the field of disability education, as well as an ability to bring organizations together for a shared purpose.

Now, Erin is regularly invited to present at national and regional conferences, and has coauthored numerous publications and book chapters. She has served on many national committees and is a past board member for APSE, the Ohio Governor's Council on People with Disabilities, and the U.S. Business Leadership Network. Project SEARCH received the U.S. Department of Labor's 2004 New Freedom Initiative Award and was the inaugural recipient of Dartmouth-Hitchcock's 2010 James W. Varnum National Quality Award.

Erin lives in Terrace Park, Ohio, with her partner, Judy, and their inimitable dog, Molly. When Erin grows up, she wants to be a master gardener.

Susie Rutkowski, M.Ed., Cofounder and Codirector, Project SEARCH, Cincinnati Children's Hospital Medical Center, 3333 Burnet Avenue, MLC5030, Cincinnati, OH 450229

Ms. Rutkowski is Codirector and Educational Specialist for Project SEARCH. She is a nationally recognized transition expert with specific experience in program development in career technical education and job development for young adults with disabilities. She served as Manager for Disability Education at Great Oaks Career Campuses for more than 12 years. During that tenure she, along with Erin Riehle, cofounded Project SEARCH. Susie has been instrumental in designing the Project SEARCH Training Institute modules and leading replication efforts for new Project SEARCH sites. She speaks and writes on transition-related topics.

Susie's degree in special education was received from Bowling Green State University. Her masters in educational administration was received from the University of Dayton, and she did postgraduate work at Wright State University and Xavier University. In addition to her other positions, she taught young students with multiple disabilities for 8 years and worked for 10 years as Job Placement Coordinator at Great Oaks for students and graduates with disabilities.

Susie lives in Loveland, Ohio, with her husband, Joe, and is the proud mother of five children: Sharon, Noah, Kurt, Kevin, and Lucas. Most important, she is the proudest Mimi ever to Gallagher, Sofie, and Jack. In her spare time, Susie dotes on her grandchildren, volunteers at her church, and creates beautiful handmade greeting cards.

Foreword

It is my distinct pleasure to write the foreword to this long overdue book on Project SEARCH®. I have known the coauthors for many years, and it has been a thrill to watch the growth, the expansion, and the impact of Project SEARCH initially in Cincinnati, then spreading throughout the United States, and now the world. Project SEARCH is having an impact on hundreds of schools and thousands of youth with developmental and other disabilities, as well as their families, co-workers, professional educators, and rehabilitation specialists.

It seems that once every 10–15 years a new innovation or clinical practice comes along in special education or in the rehabilitation field that creates a tremendous amount of excitement and buzz. It then turns into a race to see who can most quickly learn and gain access to using the innovation. Project SEARCH is easily that innovation for this past decade. The Project SEARCH model is one that requires businesses to host 9-month internships for youth with significant disabilities in their last year of high school. The purpose of these internships is to provide real-life training in skills that will lead to employment. Project SEARCH is about competitive employment. It is not a work adjustment program; it is a not a shadowing program; it is a not an evaluation program. This is a program that is directly related to and measured by the ability of its interns to gain competitive employment.

Project SEARCH often takes place in large hospitals in highly interdisciplinary health care settings. These environments require good work behavior, the capacity to navigate the hospital environment, and a serious ability to become sensitive to the customer relations perspective that modern-day hospitals must have to be competitive. Project SEARCH is funded through different sources that come from participating schools, local community rehabilitation programs, and usually the federal–state vocational rehabilitation program in the area.

It is time consuming and requires a lot of careful thought to follow the guidelines in the Project SEARCH model as well as to organize the many personalities that are necessary to launch a new Project SEARCH site. I know this because my colleagues and I have initiated programs in Richmond, Virginia, in several hospitals; additionally, two of my colleagues, Jennifer McDonough and Elizabeth Getzel, have worked closely with the Virginia Department of Education and Marianne Moore to create numerous other Project SEARCH sites in Virginia. In conjunction with local providers and the Virginia Department of Rehabilitative Services, we have all learned firsthand the power of Project SEARCH but at the same time realize the hundreds of planning and coordination hours necessary to get started.

The brilliance of Project SEARCH is that it builds on the knowledge of the host business and combines that with the best we know about community-based instruction, mentoring, on-site behavioral assessments, assistive technology, and supported employment. All of these practices are integrated into a real-time, real-life set of rotations in a 9-month internship. Sometimes interns are employed before the end of the 9-month period, sometimes at the end of the internship, but usually within 3–6 months after the completion of the program. According to national Project SEARCH data, positive employment outcomes run in the neighborhood of 70%, an incredibly high rate for a group of young people who traditionally go to adult activity centers, sheltered workshops, or sit at home. Our own data on Project SEARCH participants with autism show 94% employed after 3 years; in other words, 25 individuals with autism are now fulfilled, productive contributors to our society.

So who does Project SEARCH have an impact on in these different business sites? Well, for starters, the individual student now has a real-time work plan, starting with an internship leading into competitive employment. This creates a sense of dignity and purpose and better economic well-being—not to mention new friendships. Second, parents' and siblings' perceptions are altered dramatically from "can't do" to "can do." Each Project SEARCH graduation ceremony (and we now have had three of them in Richmond) brings together more people from throughout the workplace, which means that more people have been touched, and more hopes and aspirations have been raised. Department heads from, for example, ambulatory surgery, OB-GYN, or the Diabetes Treatment Center are in attendance. Co-workers, as well as people who have just met Project SEARCH interns during their 9 months and become close to them, all come to cheer them on.

Thanks to the dedication and efforts of people like Erin, Susie, and Maryellen, Project SEARCH programs will be appearing in more and more cities and states because it is a results-oriented program that has a history of outcome data. Our project here in Richmond is a randomized clinical trial comparing Project SEARCH students with those who have not had the experience, and to date the Project SEARCH students are having much richer employment outcomes. We would anticipate that more and more state agencies will be looking to fund this program because it does work and it is highly integrative within a community.

This book is critical. It is the right book for right now. People are eager to understand more about how this successful program works, what its guidelines and framework are, and how to maximize the opportunities it offers. The authors have done an outstanding job of filling the vacuum that currently exists in the published literature about Project SEARCH.

Readers of this book will want to go directly to Erin Riehle, Susie Rutkowski, and Maryellen Daston at Cincinnati Children's Hospital Medical Center to get the specific help that is necessary to get a Project SEARCH program started in their locality.

Paul Wehman, Ph.D.
Professor of Physical Medicine and Rehabilitation, Virginia Commonwealth University
Chairman, Division of Rehabilitation Research, Medical College of Virginia
Director, Virginia Commonwealth University Rehabilitation Research and Training Center
(VCU-RRTC)

Preface

When Susie Rutkowski, Jennifer Linnabary, and I started Project SEARCH® in 1996, we had no idea that one day we'd be writing a book to tell our story. What we *have* known all of these years is that nothing we have done would have been possible without the people and work that came before us. We are grateful to Wolf Wolfensberger, who pioneered the concept of normalization; Marc Gold, who developed the method of systematic instruction; John and Connie O'Brien, who articulated the concept of person-centered planning; Paul Wehman and Tom Bellamy, who developed the concept of supported employment; Lou Brown, who advocated for inclusive education; all of the parents, educators and politicians who crafted and championed Public Law 94-142; the leaders of APSE, who initiated the Employment First movement; and many, many others who have paved the way.

We are very proud to be one small part of the chain leading to integrated, gainful employment and richer lives for people with intellectual disabilities. Project SEARCH is a unique approach to the critical transition from high school to adult life. It is a 1–school-year internship program for students with intellectual and developmental disabilities in their last year of high school eligibility. It is targeted to students whose goal is competitive employment. A central concept of the program is total immersion in the workplace, which facilitates the teaching and learning process as well as the acquisition of employability and marketable work skills. Another innovative aspect is the idea of transformational collaboration among the various agencies that play a role in preparing young adults with disabilities for the working world. We believe that people with disabilities deserve a full continuum of choices related to training, education, employment, and quality of life, and we see Project SEARCH as one item on this rich and varied menu.

This book is not meant to be a comprehensive overview or an exhaustive reference resource on the fields of transition to work and disability employment. While we have made an effort to describe Project SEARCH in the context of current thinking and trends and to honor the work of others, the primary purpose of this book is to tell the story of Project SEARCH. We are delighted to share what we have learned and are still learning on this amazing journey. And to keep ourselves and our readers focused on the real purpose for Project SEARCH, we have interspersed throughout the book photos and stories that spotlight Project SEARCH graduates who have found success in meaningful, rewarding jobs.

Our intention in writing this book was to spark interest, provoke new thoughts, and invite comments. The book on its own does not replace the licensing and technical assistance required to begin a Project SEARCH program. We do, however, hope that this book will be a useful resource for families, teachers, job coaches, employers, and anyone else who works with or has an interest in helping young people with intellectual and developmental disabilities to achieve competitive employment. We have included multiple examples of tools, lesson plans, rubrics, and other best practices that we have developed centrally and that have been contributed by Project SEARCH practitioners in many of the over 200 program sites in the United States, England, Scotland, Canada, and Australia.

This entire journey has been a labor of love. We are better for every young adult with a disability who has come into our program and has gone on to become a valued employee, and for all of the educators, family members, rehabilitation professionals, and employers who work together to make Project SEARCH possible. As long as we share high aspirations with and for young adults with disabilities, we succeed.

Differing perspectives keep us honest and evolving; please let us know what you think!

J. Erin Riehle
Cofounder and Senior Director of Project SEARCH
Director of the Division of Disability Services at Convalescent Hospital for Children
Cincinnati Children's Hospital Medical Center, Cincinnati, Ohio

Acknowledgments

Project SEARCH® is built on the strength of collaboration. Likewise, this book would not have been possible without all the student interns, program graduates, family members, teachers, job coaches, business liaisons, and other Project SEARCH partners who shared their stories, insights, and unique perspectives. Although you are too numerous to name individually, please know that we are deeply grateful to all of you for your generous contributions.

We would also like to personally thank the dedicated staff in the Project SEARCH Cincinnati office for their part in making this book a reality and for their heroic efforts in keeping the ball rolling when Erin, Susie, and Maryellen were deeply enmeshed in writing: Michael Behrman, Sandy Fritz, Greg Lynch, Charee Partee, Art Patrick, Gina Surgener, and Anne Wendell.

Any success that we have achieved in building our network of Project SEARCH program sites is, in large part, because of our dedicated international team of Project SEARCH consultants: Lyn Andrews, Linda Emery, Paula Johnson, Teri Johnson, Sara Murphy, Anne O'Bryan, Karen Quammen, and Debbie Robinson. We thank you all for sharing your expertise and leading us to compelling, illustrative stories from Project SEARCH sites throughout the United States and around the world. We would also like to extend a special thank you to Linda Emery who pitched in during the final stages of writing this book and cheerfully took on the task of creating and editing some of the most complicated tables and figures.

We are also indebted to our Ohio partners who were instrumental in pioneering the Project SEARCH model with us. These include Cincinnati Children's Hospital Medical Center, Great Oaks Career Campuses, the Ohio Rehabilitation Commission, Hamilton County Board of Developmental Disabilities, and the Ohio Developmental Disabilities Council.

Finally, we would like to thank our families:

Maryellen is grateful to George, Char, and Jack for their patience and support throughout the long and arduous process of writing this book and to her sister, Kassie, who encouraged her to take on this project from the very beginning.

Erin is grateful to Judy for her continuous love and support. Being a million-miler means being away from home for many of the activities that define partnership, and yet, you still love me. I am fortunate beyond words. Thank you, LOML Lou, thank you!

Susie wants to thank Joe and the boys—Noah, Kurt, Kevin, and Lucas—who not only supported the book but also put up with all the time and travel that went into creating and developing Project SEARCH. They believe in the program and its goal of employment. Thanks for always showing it with grace and a positive spirit!

High School Transition that Works!

1 | Obstacles to Meaningful Employment for People with Disabilities

> *A pitcher cries for water to carry,*
> *and a person for work that is real.*
>
> Marge Piercy (Piercy, 1982)

THE IMPORTANCE OF MEANINGFUL WORK

It's a simple fact of life—if you have a job, it's a near certainty that you will, at times, be heard complaining about it. The exasperated sighs, the eye rolling, and the competition over who has the most tyrannical boss or the most incompetent co-workers can be therapeutic, and frankly, it's what's expected in a social setting. But it only takes a moment of reflection to know that, on a deeper level, you truly need your work. More than that, you probably need it more than it needs you. Ask anyone who has recently retired, lost a job, or just spent too much time between jobs—a fulfilling career is more than a way to pay the rent and keep food on the table. Our work defines us, gives our lives structure and meaning, and establishes our place in the world. Indeed, it's the first question we ask a new acquaintance, "What do you do?" The answer puts us in a context. It gives us a social framework.

The desire for meaningful work is not unique to driven professionals: the physicians, lawyers, engineers, and college professors among us. Rather, it is a fundamental human need that applies to everyone. Clearly, the income that a job provides is necessary to meet the basic needs for food and shelter. An adequate income also provides a safety net that contributes to our sense of security. But, in addition to that, there

The Right Job for the Right Person—The Difference It Can Make

Meaningful work has an enormous impact on a person's ability to reach contentment and life satisfaction. This point is beautifully illustrated in a moving story that Veronica Chater told about her younger brother, Vinnie, in an episode of the radio program, *This American Life* (Chater, 2002). Vinnie, the fifth child in a family of 11, was born with a rare developmental disability that involved significant cognitive impairment. Vinnie's parents—strong people with a positive outlook—were undaunted by the prospect of raising a child with a disability. They provided a loving home for Vinnie and, when he became a young man, found employment for him in a workshop where he spent his days in a warehouse, stuffing envelopes and doing light assembly alongside other people with developmental disabilities. Vinnie's parents and siblings clearly knew and appreciated him as an individual. Nonetheless, they were all completely mystified when, after 12 contented years at the workshop, he abruptly started to become irritable at work. He began to snap at his co-workers and even

(continued)

1

(continued)

to threaten them with bodily harm, and he would often retreat to the restroom for hours at a time. After an on-the-job outburst that resulted in his parents being called in, Vinnie abruptly quit his job and refused to go back. What's more, he retreated from everything—basketball, his Special Olympics team, socializing of any kind—and spent more and more time alone in his bedroom. His parents, confused and worried, took him to see his doctor. The doctor suggested that there might have been a shift in his brain chemistry and prescribed Prozac. Nonetheless, Vinnie continued to withdraw while his family cast about for ways to draw him out of his shell. Around this time, his mother decided to start raising chickens on their property—an idea that had been in the back of her mind for many years. Vinnie's mom asked one of her sons to build a chicken coop in the back-yard and asked Vinnie to take on the responsibility for the chickens' daily upkeep. Serendipitously, it turned out that Vinnie was a natural at chicken husbandry. He was meticulous about keeping the chickens' quarters clean and maintained his charges on a precise schedule of feeding, water-ing, and exercise. But most critically, he clearly delighted in being around the chickens, naming them all after important people in his life. And the best news of all was that the fulfillment he found in his new responsibilities had a positive impact on all aspects of his life: He became interested in his social life again, he went back to basketball practice, and he once more started training for the Special Olympics.

are deeper spiritual, nonmaterial needs that are addressed when we take our place in the workforce: our needs for belonging, self-esteem, and self-actualization. We gain a sense of belonging when we share ease and familiarity, inside jokes, and common goals with a community of co-workers. And by contributing our particular expertise as an essential part of a functioning team, whether that skill is brain surgery or short-order cooking, we gain a feeling of self-worth and self-esteem. And, by doing work that suits our talents, work that we feel we were "meant to do," we achieve self-actualization. This idea was beautifully stated by Siegel, Robert, Greener, Meyer, Halloran, & Gaylord-Ross (1993), who wrote,

> Those who have failed to achieve a gainful career are also missing out on the richness of having an economic life, the self-respect that comes from being able to earn a decent wage, and the sense of community and personal growth that comes from being part of a work culture. (p. 3)

THE DISAPPOINTING STATE OF EMPLOYMENT FOR PEOPLE WITH DISABILITIES

Sadly, meaningful employment is a route to fulfillment, independence, and maturity that is too often denied to people with disabilities. In 2008, the employment rate for people of working age (18–64 years) with disabilities was 39.1%, but for the same age group without disabilities, the employment rate was 77.7%. That's a gap of 38.6 percentage points. Not surprisingly, people with disabilities are also more likely to live in poverty. In 2007, among individuals with disabilities, 24.9% lived in poverty, whereas the poverty rate of individuals without disabilities was 10.0%—a gap of 14.9 percentage points. Moreover, for people with mental disabilities, the poverty rate was even higher, at 31.2% (Rehabilitation Research and Training Center on Disability Statistics, 2009). Over the years, this gap in employment and income has stubbornly persisted regardless of the economy and the availability of jobs. In good times when work is plentiful, and in times of recession when work is scarce, the employment rate for people with disabilities lags around 30% behind that of the population without disabilities (Kessler Foundation/NOD, 2010). Moreover, in an economic downturn, people with disabilities are laid off in the highest numbers and are the last to be rehired when the economy improves (Diamant, 2010; Kaye, 2010). In fact, during good economic times when money for disability employment programming increases, the result is more jobs for people who work in the disability industry, but this does not necessarily add up to more jobs for people with disabilities. Many individuals who could be working end up in sheltered work-shops (Rogan & Rinne, 2011), and for the people with disabilities who are employed, most still work in food service or custodial work (Hill, 1998). Indeed, the National Longitudinal Transition Study-2 found that nearly half of the young people with disabilities in the survey who were employed were working in food service or maintenance (Carter, Austin, & Trainor, 2011). Although this can be honorable and rewarding work, the disproportionate numbers of people with disabilities in those jobs suggest that a number of them are not there by their own choice.

For people with disabilities, barriers to employment persist despite an increasing aware-ness of the value of diversity in the workforce as well as a growing commitment by the federal government to increase opportunities for people with disabilities to participate in all aspects of society. Twenty years after the Americans with Disabilities Act (PL 101-336) was signed into law, with millions of federal, state, and local dollars spent each year to address the issue, and with mandatory diversity training de rigueur at most workplaces, the problems of unemployment and underemployment for people with disabilities are still with us. In August of 2011, President Obama signed an executive order (EO13583) mandating an emphasis on increasing the employment of people with disabilities within the federal government. Moreover, there is another pending order for federal contractors that requires 7% of their workforce be employees with disabilities. It seems that, as much as we as a society want to do the right thing, the employment statistics for people with disabilities stubbornly remain the same. This vexing problem has nothing to do with a lack of ability or desire among people with disabilities. In fact, surveys and personal narratives have shown that employment is a high priority among young adults with disabilities (Walker, 2011; Wright, 1996). Moreover, employment was an even higher priority for young people than access to health care—a telling statistic, especially in light of the fact that this population has more than the usual share of health problems.

WHAT ARE THE OBSTACLES AND WHY ARE THEY THERE?

There are a number of logistical difficulties that get in the way of employment for people with disabilities. A lack of reliable transportation is a common one. Many people with disabilities are unable to drive, and others require cars with significant adaptations. For those who can't drive or can't afford a specialized vehicle, or for a person who is uncomfortable navigating public transportation independently, or who lives in an area that lacks adequate public transportation, it is nearly impossible to consistently show up on time for work. Many communities have specialized or paratransit systems designed for the elderly and people with disabilities; however they are not able to guarantee consistent arrival and departure times. Another common factor that can hamper successful employment is the need for extra time for self-care or medical appointments. In addition, many people with disabilities, and their families, worry about losing eligibility for the public disability income that they receive in the form of Social Security Disability Insurance (SSDI) or Supplemental Security Income (SSI).

These logistical barriers to employment can often be circumvented with the appropriate support, flexibility, and knowledge, and in the pages ahead, we go into more detail on the ways that this can be achieved.

Competitive Employment versus Sheltered Workshops

There is increasing recognition of the inherent right of people with disabilities to pursue complete and fulfilling lives. Indeed, the guiding principles of the Employment First movement (Niemiec, Lavin, & Owens, 2009), recently established by the APSE, state that "individuals with disabilities, including those with the most significant disabilities, should enjoy every opportunity to be employed in the workforce, pursue careers, advance professionally, and engage actively in the economic marketplace" and that they should "be empowered to attain the highest possible wage with benefits consistent with their interests, strengths, priorities, abilities, and capabilities" (Kiernan, Hoff, Freeze, & Mank, 2011, pp. 300–301). It follows that people with developmental and intellectual disabilities should be encouraged to work in inclusive, integrated, and competitive work environments rather than in enclaves, sheltered facilities, or day programs. In 2007, Patricia Rogan wrote, "Sheltered facilities and day activity centers that serve adults with disabilities represent an outdated model of service delivery that congregates and segregates people" (p. 253).

In 2001, the same year that the New Freedom Initiative was unveiled, the Rehabilitation Services Administration (RSA) published a final rule that eliminated placement in a sheltered workshop as a successful outcome. With this rule, work in an integrated setting became the sole defining criterion for successful case closure in the vocational rehabilitation (VR) system. According to this rule, the only allowable exceptions are circumstances in which placement in a sheltered setting is considered a temporary training situation on a pathway toward integrated employment. The rationale for the rule came out of an increasing recognition of the limitations of sheltered employment settings that included "a lack of effectiveness in achieving employment outcomes or in improving vocational skills, social skills or psychological function; the demonstrated potential for financial exploitation of workers; and a failure to employ sound business practices or simulate a genuine work environment" (Rogan, 2001, p. 3).

Indeed, the U.S. General Accounting Office (2001) found that more than half of individuals in sheltered workshops earn less than $2.50 per hour and nearly a quarter earn less than $1.00 per hour. Moreover, it was found that only about 3.5% of individuals in sheltered workshops ever move to competitive employment (Rogan & Rinne, 2011).

(continued)

(continued)

Despite a clear national commitment, as well as the well-documented benefits of competitive employment, there is still a surprising level of reliance on sheltered employment. In fact, a recent national survey of community rehabilitation partners (CRPs) that provide sub–minimum-wage employment revealed some of the outdated beliefs that are still guiding practices in these organizations. Nearly all of the respondents (89%) agreed that sheltered employment was a necessary service; a surprising majority (69%) did not even believe that people with intellectual disabilities would be able to earn minimum wage, and less than half (47%) said that their agencies had a strategic plan to increase competitive employment for their clients (Butterworth, Smith, & Hall, 2009).

Project SEARCH is a business-led model, and, as such, sheltered workshops and enclaves have no role in the process. The core fidelity components of the model state that a successful outcome for a Project SEARCH participant is solely defined as competitive employment in an integrated work setting. We define that employment as a job in which employees work 20 hours or more each week in jobs that involve complex and systematic work. Moreover, the employees must be directly hired by the business and earn the prevailing wage for a given job.

But the more intractable obstacles are the ones that are due to the deeply entrenched attitudes that we hold as a society, and these are more difficult to overcome. Such attitudes are rarely verbalized, but occasionally, under the right circumstances, they will bubble to the surface in revealing ways. Indeed, among the respondents in a national survey of private employers, about 20% agreed that the most important barrier to employment for people with disabilities was discrimination and prejudice among employers, and they even admitted that attitudes and stereotypes limited opportunities for people with disabilities in their own companies (Dixon, Kruse, & Van Horn, 2003). Moreover, the actual figures are very likely to be higher than those reported because of the natural reluctance to admit to attitudes that are, at least on a conscious level, considered socially unacceptable by most people. Another interesting example came in response to an online article in a rural Ohio newspaper. The article described a newly established Project SEARCH® program site where students with disabilities were receiving training in health care–related jobs at a hospital. The commentary by readers was overwhelmingly positive and enthusiastic. But among the supportive words, there was a lone reader with a dissenting point-of-view. This reader felt that it was unrealistic to expect people with disabilities to compete in a period of economic downturn when even "normal" people were having trouble finding jobs. The commenter went on to suggest that employment for typically-abled people was a higher priority than employment for those with disabilities and, moreover, that it was wasteful to spend tax dollars on vocational training for individuals with special needs. Our sensibilities have advanced to the point where it is shocking for most people to see this opinion voiced so overtly and unapologetically.

But it is interesting that, concealed by the anonymity of the Internet, this person felt free to reveal what is probably, as the employment statistics belie, a fairly common conception. In a sense, what the commenter is saying is that, whereas employment for people with disabilities may be a noble goal, it is somehow an entirely different thing than employment for "regular people." That is, it relegates employment for people with disabilities to the status of either a burden on society and the workplace or a luxury that should be addressed only once all the so-called normal people are taken care of. Even though this idea strikes us as outrageous when stated in this way, it is an attitude that arises naturally from viewing employment for people with disabilities from a philanthropic framework. Although well intentioned, this perspective tends to set people with disabilities apart from other prospective employees and results in the perception among employers that they are an obligation rather than an asset to the business. On close examination, it seems that it is exactly this attitude that, in many ways, has subtly informed the policies and practices of the entire employment system, from the schools to the agencies to the human resources (HR) departments.

SYSTEMIC BARRIERS WITHIN THE REHABILITATION INDUSTRY

Resistance, low expectations, and misunderstanding come into play on both sides of the employment equation—the employers and the job seekers—to hinder people with disabilities in their search for meaningful employment. And, for this group of prospective employees, there is a third element in the hiring equation—the rehabilitation industry. By this, we mean the private and government agencies that train and advise people with disabilities as well as the educational institutions that serve them. These groups are charged with assisting people with disabilities in finding and gaining employment. But, often, the well-intentioned policies and practices that have been put into place over the years actually have the effect of reinforcing and perpetuating the very attitudes that get in the way of meaningful employment. For example, businesses that hire people with disabilities may be eligible for tax credits under government programs. Moreover, in certain cases, they may even be granted permission, through special provisions in the Fair Labor Standards Act (PL 75-718), to pay less than the prevailing wage. It is possible to see the logic behind programs like these and how they might be expected to encourage the hiring of people with disabilities. But, in practice, they can actually have the opposite effect of stigmatizing a prospective employee. Such programs can backfire by turning the usual hiring scenario on its head and setting up an expectation of failure. That is, an employer is used to seeking the best possible job candidates, and with the expectation that that employee is going to add value to their company, they offer the best possible salary and benefits to attract them. But if an employer is offered monetary incentives to hire a certain candidate, it can leave the impression that the potential new hire is a high-risk proposition and, at the outset, raise doubts about that individual's ability to perform in the job. All in all, unless they are very carefully presented to the employer, such incentives feed into the deeply ingrained perception that people with disabilities will not be an asset to the workplace and, in general, cannot compete effectively in the job market. Moreover, many employers who have set out to hire people with disabilities are discouraged from following through by unpleasant experiences with an intractable government bureaucracy. One business owner who opted to take advantage of tax credits and other incentives found the paperwork to be onerous—"a nightmare," as he put it (National Council on Disability, 2007).

Another rehabilitation industry habit is the tendency to use "deficit marketing" (see Appendix 1.1). This refers to the practice of using terms to "sell" a potential employee that—to someone with a business mind-set—seem like negative attributes (Riehle & Daston, 2006). This unintentional effect is a by-product of rehabilitation industry jargon, which has a certain meaning among insiders but can have bad connotations to an outsider. For example, when a job description is altered to accommodate a particular job candidate, the practice is called *job carving* among rehabilitation professionals. Whereas this term is never used in a business context, in actuality, it describes a scenario that is common in the working world. For example, a group of employees in an office might all have the title "administrative assistant," but the actual duties of individuals within this group may be quite different. One might spend most of her time keeping the departmental web site up to date while another is responsible for filing and scheduling. In the development department of a not-for-profit organization, two development specialists might work side-by-side in the same office and share the same title, even though one specializes in maintaining relationships with major donor families while the other does the work of an event planner. This division of labor happens naturally in many work environments because of the differing skills and interests of the individuals involved, and in a healthy work environment, two employees can make equal contributions while doing very different work. But when the same phenomenon is called *job carving*, it suggests that the "carved" position is not as valuable, that it is something less than whole and, again, leaves the impression that the person with a disability is making a lesser contribution or, worse, is a drain on departmental resources. And when job carving is part of the discussion at the outset of employment, it sets the stage for underestimating an employee's capabilities and can deprive the person of the opportunity to prove himself or herself on the job.

Another example of counterproductive jargon is the term *job coaching*, which is used to describe the assistance that a person with disabilities receives when learning a new job. But this is also something that can easily be translated into conventional business language. It is usually simply called "training" or "orientation"—processes that are standard practice for nearly all new employees. For example, a newly hired nurse will work under the guidance of a preceptor for as long as 6 months. Likewise, new managers in the banking or finance sectors are usually required to spend up to a full year in training. This sort of training is viewed by the business as a worthwhile investment that will result in a productive employee. Clearly, there is no need to have a special term for people with disabilities and, in fact, it is worse than a benign redundancy. When the training of a person with a disability is called *job coaching*, it can be perceived as a burden and is yet another way that people with disabilities are set apart from "regular" employees.

MAKING THE BUSINESS CASE FOR HIRING PEOPLE WITH DISABILITIES

Regardless of what happens in the rehabilitation industry, substantial gains in the employment of people with disabilities will happen only when businesses, in large numbers, start seeing it as a sound business practice. But, to get businesses to see this, it is necessary to present disability in the right framework (Dembo, Leviton, & Wright, 1975). Indeed, cognitive science has shown that, regardless of the hard evidence, it is the framework surrounding that evidence that drives decision making. The neural circuitry of the human brain is hardwired to think in terms of frames and metaphors. The result is that—when faced with facts that don't fit these conceptual structures—those facts are often discarded while the frames are left intact (Lakoff, 2006).

Politicians, lobbyists, and others in the political arena are well aware of this effect and use it masterfully to drive public opinion. Think of the extremely different connotations of "estate tax" versus "death tax" or "exemptions for the wealthy" versus "tax relief," and the very different conclusions that a person might make when they accept one term or the other.

Likewise, the framework in which the business world views disability informs the reception that people with disabilities receive when they present themselves as job applicants. According to Dembo et al. (1975), there are four common frames through which disability is perceived: deviance, deficiency, tragedy, and diversity. Although it is no longer usual to view disability as deviance, most people approach disability as a shifting blend of deficiency, tragedy, and diversity that depends on context and personal experience. When disability is viewed as deviance, the response is marginalization, segregation, avoidance, and aggression. In this framework, people with disabilities are isolated at home or in sheltered workshops. At best, they might be employed in enclaves doing busywork.

When disability is viewed as a deficiency, the response is rehabilitation and remediation. This is the framework that is presented, deliberately or subliminally, through traditional rehabilitation practices. The result is the current state of employment, in which work for substandard wages, underemployment, and limited choices persist. This point of view is supported by tax breaks and other hiring incentives as well as counterproductive jargon (such as job carving and job coaching).

The framing of disability as tragedy may have the positive effect of generating a desire to help. However, the philanthropic motivation ultimately leads to paternalism and a patronizing attitude. People with disabilities may become token employees with lower standards of performance. They may be allowed to ignore workplace rules and have exceptions made for them. Although the immediate effect might be increased employment, it will not be employment that is sustainable. The only way that people with disabilities can be employed on equal footing is to consider disability as a form of diversity. Within this framework, the response is support, innovation, and understanding. People with disabilities are more likely to be valued, respected, accepted, and appreciated, and the chances for a mutually beneficial relationship are maximized.

These four frames were delineated in 1975, and they introduced the framework of diversity, which was revolutionary at the time. Although they are still useful, a renaissance in our appreciation for the gifts, talents, and potential of people with disabilities has brought us to an era in which it is time to add an additional frame—a framework in which hiring people with disabilities is routine because it is recognized as a sound business practice.

THE BOTTOM LINE: EMPLOYING PEOPLE WITH DISABILITIES IS SMART BUSINESS

The societal benefits of employment for people with disabilities are obvious. Every adult who is working and earning wages contributes to society through the work that they do as well as through the taxes that they pay. It is clearly a better deal for the taxpayer if a person with disabilities is employed as opposed to being supported in a day program or sheltered workshop. Indeed, the federal government spends four times more on segregated adult day programs than on supported employment, and only 2% of the costs of the entire disability system are spent on programs that provide employment services (Wittenberg, Rangarajan, & Honeycutt, 2008). In addition to the monetary benefits, when we encounter people with disabilities in positions of responsibility on a regular basis, we grow and improve as a society by gaining greater acceptance for people with disabilities and a more complete understanding of their varied gifts and talents.

Whereas the societal benefits of employing people with disabilities are important, it is equally true that it is a practice that simply makes good business sense. First of all, people with chronic illnesses and disabilities represent the fastest growing market segment in the United States. Recent estimates of aggregate spending among this group set the value at around $1 trillion. If you include the families and other significant people in the lives of these individuals, that estimate grows to $3 trillion (Katherine McCary, Managing Partner, C5 Consulting, LLC, personal communication). And the best way for a business to attract these dollars is to hire people with disabilities.

In addition to the spending that it might attract, a commitment to hiring people with disabilities is a good way to enhance a business's image. Indeed, a 2005 Gallup poll showed that 87% of Americans, if given a choice, would prefer to do business with a company that hires people with disabilities (Siperstein, Romano, Mohler, & Parker, 2006). This was true regardless of whether the respondents had a disability themselves or had a family member with a disability. The opinion was based on the perception that a business that employed people with disabilities was a kinder and gentler business that would give better treatment to all its employees as well as to its customers. Clearly, the presence of people with disabilities, wearing the business's uniform and engaged in useful work, speaks volumes to consumers, and does so with far greater impact than any advertising campaign could ever achieve. Recent surveys show that business owners are increasingly aware of this effect, and this is a sign that bodes well for the future of employment for people with disabilities. Indeed, the same surveys revealed that businesses value the positive feedback that they receive in response to a visible commitment (Dixon et al., 2003; Bruyère, 2000).

Nonetheless, some business owners and managers are reluctant to hire people with disabilities because of a fear that they might get in the way and slow things down (Luecking, 2011). But, on the contrary, the actual effect is often the exact opposite. The presence of people with disabilities in the workplace can require a rethinking of the way things are done. And when businesses make use of the principles of universal design, which simply refers to "the design of products and environments to be usable by all people, to the greatest extent possible, without the need for adaptation or specialized design" (National Council on Disability, 2007, p. 43), they often experience increased efficiency for all workers. In many cases, the increased efficiency that they achieve can result in significant cost savings.

PROJECT SEARCH AS AN AGENT FOR ACHIEVING SYSTEMIC CHANGE

Project SEARCH is an organization dedicated to challenging the status quo of low expectations and poor employment outcomes for young people with intellectual and developmental disabilities. We have developed a model for high school transition that promotes competitive employment for these young people.

The Project SEARCH High School Transition Program is a unique, 1-year, school-to-work program that takes place entirely at the workplace (Rutkowski et al., 2006). This innovative, business-led model features total workplace immersion, which facilitates a seamless combination of classroom instruction, career exploration, and on-the-job training and support. The goal for each student is competitive employment. Real-life work experience combined with training in employability and independent living skills to help youths with significant disabilities make successful transitions from school to productive adult life.

Interagency collaboration is a critical element of the Project SEARCH model. Specifically, Project SEARCH operates as a partnership between a business, education, vocational rehabilitation, a long-term supported employment agency, a community rehabilitation provider, and other organizations as needed. The program requires an unprecedented level of coordination among agencies, and this is what makes Project SEARCH effective in driving systems change. Agencies are motivated to reduce inefficiencies and counterproductive policies that can create barriers for people with disabilities. Moreover, Project SEARCH creates a significant positive presence of people with disabilities in the workplace, which is an effective way to promote culture change in the business world. As stated by Rob McInnes (2006), Project SEARCH is "by design, massaging and changing corporate culture and the receptivity of those workplaces to employing people with disabilities."

Deficit Marketing
Good Intentions, Bad Results*

Imagine that you were out of work and in urgent need of a job. In this situation, you might seek a career counselor with the reasonable expectation that this individual's expertise would maximize your chances for a successful job search. Now, imagine that your counselor started in on your case by randomly calling businesses, with no clear idea of what sort of work went on in those businesses or what jobs were available. What if your counselor then described you as someone who could do only the easiest jobs and would probably not be able to manage all the tasks associated with those jobs? What if they suggested that you start out as a volunteer? What would you think of the service you were getting if the counselor went on to say that you were willing to work for less than the standard wage and tried to entice the business into hiring you with promises of tax credits or salary subsidies? Naturally, you would consider this to be totally unacceptable. Yet, this is exactly how professionals in the rehabilitation industry—with the best of intentions—approach job placement for people with disabilities.

Deficit marketing, that is, using negative descriptors to "sell" a potential employee, is an approach that is totally at odds with the business mind-set. Indeed, it seems downright absurd when applied to an able-bodied person. Yet, it is firmly ingrained in rehabilitation practices, not by design, but rather as a sort of organic by-product of the structure of the rehabilitation industry. In some cases, the programs and procedures put into place to help people with disabilities get jobs end up stigmatizing them or setting them apart. It's no wonder that rehabilitation professionals repeatedly come up against skeptical or unwilling employers, and they can hardly be blamed for concluding that business has no interest in hiring people with disabilities. Certainly, there is more that business could do, but it is equally important that the rehabilitation industry take a hard look at entrenched and self-defeating practices.

Let's start with the initial contact with the employer. Rehabilitation counselors often make cold calls to businesses. Unless you are an unusually skilled talker, this is a sure way to get the relationship off to a bad start. A cold call immediately sets the counselor apart as a nonbusiness person with a nonbusiness approach. That is, someone who does not understand business culture, rules, or procedures. Further, it gives the impression that this is not a serious or well-considered request. An equally unproductive, but commonly used approach—particularly in school-to-work programs—is to suggest that an individual enter the workplace as a volunteer. Without doubt, volunteering at a hospital or other not-for-profit organization is a worthwhile activity that should be considered by everyone in the position to do so, but it is not a pathway to employment. Anyone hoping to gain employment through an unpaid work experience needs to enter the workplace through the "student intern door," not the "volunteer door."

In some cases, it is the jargon of the rehabilitation industry that undermines a job candidate's chances. Take the term "job carving"; it makes sense to a rehabilitation professional. It simply refers to the modification of job duties to fit the particular skills of a job candidate. This is something that happens routinely in the workplace. For example, an individual might be hired as a social worker but, once on the job, might display a particular aptitude for computers. That person might end up spending more time working on the department web site and database than seeing clients. They're not doing the exact same thing as the other social workers, and they're not doing what was expected at the time of hiring; but they are making an equal contribution to the department, nonetheless. This sort of scenario might seem entirely logical to a manager when it is described in this way, but when it is framed in terms of "job carving," it connotes a job performance that is incomplete or lacking rather than simply different. When rehabilitation agencies initiate the conversation by bringing up job carving, not only do they send a negative message to the employer, they may also be underestimating their consumers. By making too many a priori assumptions about job candidates' capabilities, they rob potential employees of the opportunity to prove themselves.

Another example of self-defeating industry jargon is the term, "job-coaching." Why is it that a person with a disability needs a special word for something that is known as "orientation" for all other employees? Businesses routinely spend a great deal to orient new staff. In a hospital, for example, a new nurse often works with a preceptor for as long as 6 months. In a bank, it is not unusual for newly hired managers to spend a good part of their first year of employment in training. Job coaching is a necessity, but it is a necessity for everyone, not just

In *High School Transition That Works: Lessons Learned from Project SEARCH®* by Maryellen Daston, J. Erin Riehle, and Susan Rutkowski. (2012, Paul H. Brookes Publishing Co., Inc.)

Project | SEARCH

people with disabilities. If we simply refer to it as orientation or training, it is transformed from a special accommodation for the person with a disability—and a nuisance to the business—to a familiar concept that is understood and valued by business.

Employers that hire people with disabilities may be eligible for tax credits and, in some cases, may be granted permission, through special provisions in the Fair Labor Standards Act, to pay less than the prevailing wage. Employers should be informed of these programs where applicable, but they should never be used as a selling point for a job candidate. Although intended to provide incentives, these programs actually have the paradoxical effect of being a disincentive for hiring—setting up an expectation of failure and giving the impression that the candidate is a high-risk hire or a known poor performer. On a larger scale, it feeds into the erroneous perception that people with disabilities, in general, will not make a positive contribution to the workplace and are not capable of true competitive employment.

Funding for disability issues continues to grow, and the disability industry grows along with it. But so far, although this growth has had a positive impact on employment for rehabilitation workers, it has not translated into a better employment outlook for people with disabilities. Certainly, this is a complex issue, and many factors enter into this outcome, but the habit of deficit marketing is one clear barrier that is within the power of the rehabilitation industry to change. It is a habit that can be rooted out only when we start to look at job placement, not from a traditional rehabilitation perspective, but from the perspective of employers and of people with disabilities. The key to doing this is to look at every practice and ask two simple questions: Is this consistent with normal business hiring procedures? Would I want to work or be hired under these conditions? Such reflection leads to the surprisingly simple conclusion that what works for people without disabilities also works for people with disabilities:

1. Look for a job that matches the interests and skills of the job candidate.

2. Learn as much as you can about a business before you make a call.

3. Focus on the skills and the good attitude that the job candidate would bring to the business.

4. Don't give the business the impression that hiring the candidate would be a philanthropic gesture. Instead, make them feel lucky to be getting this person!

*Reprinted from *Journal of Vocational Rehabilitation,* Vol. 25, J. Erin Riehle and Maryellen Daston, Deficit Marketing: Good Intentions, Bad Results, Pages 69–70, Copyright (2006), with permission from IOS Press.

In *High School Transition That Works: Lessons Learned from Project SEARCH®* by Maryellen Daston, J. Erin Riehle, and Susan Rutkowski. (2012, Paul H. Brookes Publishing Co., Inc.)

page 2 of 2

Project | SEARCH

Meet Vander

Vander is a graduate of the Project SEARCH program at the U.S. Department of Education in Washington, D.C. He is a young man with cerebral palsy who has achieved remarkable things despite formidable obstacles. At the age of 9, he was put into foster care and separated from his mother and four brothers. Moreover, Vander was somehow allowed to fall through the cracks and didn't attend school until he was 10 years old. Considering his difficult start in life, it is all the more impressive that Vander made history by becoming the first Project SEARCH student to land a full-time, permanent job in the U.S. Department of Education.

The early educational neglect that Vander experienced set up a pattern of low expectations that could have derailed a young person who didn't have Vander's intense determination and drive. "I was quiet," he said. "A lot of people used to say things about me and they didn't think I understood. They didn't ever think I would be anything." But as Vander grew up, he sought independence and ways to show his potential, "I started taking initiative for myself, learning stuff like how to wash my clothes, tie my shoes, and how to compensate for things I couldn't do by finding other skills. My reading wasn't good, so I learned to speak real well." In high school, Vander reached a turning point when he became a member of the hip hop club: "I realized that I really like expressing myself in a powerful way, and being able to vent and let the frustration out, and help people understand who I really am and what I stand for, finding a way to reach people my age with a disability and other young people. That's when people started to respect me."

The next important milestone for Vander was when his occupational therapist (a school employee who provided related services specified in his individualized education program) encouraged him to fill out the application for Project SEARCH. He was accepted to the program and describes his experience there in this way: "We learned how to escort guests, how to express ourselves in an appropriate way for the workplace, how to answer the telephone in the proper manner, fit for the workplace, and I learned how to put my personality together with a workplace personality to make one personality appropriate for the workplace."

Vander did two rotations in the Federal Student Aid ombudsman's office, which handles correspondence from people about their loans. His co-workers and manager liked working with him so much that he stayed on for a second rotation. Eventually, he was offered the full-time job in that department, and his hiring was approved near the end of his year in Project SEARCH.

(continued)

Now, as a regular employee, Vander's main task is to scan incoming correspondence and match it with case numbers. When he started in the office, there was a 1-year backlog that he was able to clear within 6 months on the job.

Vander's long-term goal is to become a public speaker and inspire other people with disabilities who "gave up on their life or are headed down that path." The message he would like to deliver is that "even though I have a disability, I can still fit in with regular employees and interact in a normal way and do all the things they can do. I realize having a disability in the workplace, a lot of people, they just see you, they don't know who you are, so they make all these assumptions in their mind that you can't do anything or that you always need help with something, or they talk to you like you're special. It's an everyday thing to prove yourself."

2 The Project SEARCH Model

A Business-Driven Approach

> *Far and away the best prize that life offers is*
> *the chance to work hard at work worth doing.*
>
> Theodore Roosevelt

THE ORIGINS OF PROJECT SEARCH

The seeds for Project SEARCH® were planted in 1996, when Erin Riehle was nursing director of the Cincinnati Children's Hospital Emergency Department. An important part of her job was hiring and managing personnel to stock examination room supply carts with gloves, diapers, syringes, and so forth. To fill these essential positions, Erin did what is done in most hospitals around the country: She turned to the most readily available pool of job candidates, that is, undergraduates who were hoping to get into medical school, nursing students, and others who saw the job as a stepping stone and not as a career. These were, of course, competent, bright people, but as examination room supply stockers, they lacked any real interest in the work they were hired to do. For most of them, their primary reason for being there was to add hospital experience to their resumes. As a result, she was frustrated by chronically high turnover and lackluster performance.

Around this same time, Cincinnati Children's had introduced a major diversity initiative that focused on race, religion, and gender but did not address disability. Erin was well aware that young people with chronic illnesses and disabilities were a major source of revenue for the hospital; in fact, she learned that 10 of the top 20 revenue generators for the hospital were related to providing treatment for this population. In addition, she noticed that the hospital often featured children with disabilities in its promotional materials to project a caring image. With this in mind, it seemed to her a simple matter of justice that children with disabilities should have the opportunity to grow up and be employees of the hospital. Another important inspiration for these ideas was a policy statement adopted in 1995 by the American College of Healthcare Executives (ACHE) that reads, in part, "Healthcare executives must take the lead in their organizations to increase employment opportunities for qualified persons with disabilities and to advocate on behalf of their employment to other organizations in their communities." With these two issues coming to a head at the same time—her staffing problems and the hospital's diversity initiative—and converging with the influence of the ACHE statement, the stage was

13

set. Erin's mind was receptive to the idea that occurred to her one day while she was off work and running errands. In the grocery store, she saw a young man with a developmental disability bagging groceries and asked herself, "If he can do this job, why couldn't he stock exam rooms?" She wondered if training and hiring people with disabilities might be an idea worth pursuing. It seemed like it might be a good way to hire and retain valuable support staff while at the same time contributing to and broadening Cincinnati Children's diversity objectives.

Erin knew what she wanted to do, but she didn't know where to start. When she talks about these early days, she readily admits that she had no firsthand experience with disability; she had no family members or friends with significant disabilities, she knew nothing of the services or supports available to people with disabilities, and most importantly, she had no idea whether her idea was realistic. Not knowing where else to turn, she simply looked in the telephone book to find help and advice. Given this random approach, it seems a tremendous stroke of luck that led her to Susie Rutkowski, the manager of disability education at Great Oaks Institute of Technology and Career Development, the largest career and technical school system in the Greater Cincinnati area, and Jennifer Linnabary, an employment coordinator with the Hamilton County Board of Mental Retardation and Developmental Disabilities (now called Hamilton County Developmental Disabilities Services). She asked Susie and Jennifer if they'd be willing to talk with her about whether someone with an intellectual disability could do the job of stocking emergency room supply shelves, and whether they had any prospective job candidates. Much to her surprise, although probably not surprising to anyone who works in rehabilitation services, Susie and Jennifer were in Erin's office by that afternoon. Jennifer and Susie recall being surprised and somewhat skeptical when Erin proposed doing complex work in the emergency department. To them—at the time—her ideas seemed unrealistic and somewhat naïve. Nonetheless, they were impressed by Erin's enthusiasm and could see the potential in a working relationship with her. But it was not without trepidation that Jennifer and Susie agreed to work with the hospital. Even with their many years of experience in the disability world, they could not say with any certainty whether or not a person with a significant cognitive disability could do the jobs that Erin needed to fill. Still, they were eager to give it a try, and Jennifer ultimately recommended Gretchen, a young woman with Down syndrome; Kirk, who has a brain injury; and Eric, who has autism. After an initial adjustment period, the three made it clear that they were competent and dedicated employees, and the program took off from there. Encouraged by the positive experience with the first cohort to be hired, Erin saw that there was plenty of room in the hospital to expand on this success. Indeed, she recognized that, although 70% of positions in the hospital required professional qualifications, 30% of jobs were support positions that required short- or moderate-term on-the-job training that could potentially be filled by people with cognitive disabilities.

Early on, Erin, Susie, and Jennifer recognized the critical role that training played in the successful employment of people with disabilities in complex jobs. In response to this new understanding, a training program was developed within months of the first round of hiring. This shift in focus, from employment to training, turned out to be the key to achieving a rapid expansion of the program. Within a year, 35 people with significant disabilities were employed at Cincinnati Children's. And after 2 years, in 1998, the hospital officially recognized its commitment to promoting employment for people with disabilities by creating a department to house the program, the Department of Disability Services, with Erin in charge.

The change in strategy came at a time when Susie was becoming increasingly aware that the vocational training programs offered through Great Oaks were not always appropriate for her students with the most significant disabilities. She recognized that this group needed new options, and thus, she was highly motivated to initiate a program at Cincinnati Children's to specifically meet their needs. She, Erin, and Jennifer worked together to establish a program for students with significant disabilities who were transitioning from high school to adult life. By combining their different perspectives, they established a win-win scenario by considering the needs of the students while at the same time keeping in mind the actual job skills required for employment in the health care industry.

When the high school transition aspect of Cincinnati Children's employment initiative was developed, it was given the name Project SEARCH, with "SEARCH" standing for "students exploring alternative resources at Children's Hospital." The name didn't adequately describe the scope and intent of the newly formed Department of Disability Services because it was meant to specifically refer to the high school transition program. But it was a pleasing title that caught on quickly and stuck tenaciously, despite some attempts over the years to adopt a new name. At one point, a consultant came up with, "Collaborative Center for Specialized Workforce Development at Cincinnati Children's Hospital." Although this was a fairly accurate description at the time, the new name could not dislodge the firmly entrenched "Project SEARCH" because it was simply too long and not at all conducive to acronyms or convenient abbreviations. However, the need for a more descriptive title is no longer a pressing issue because, over time, "Project SEARCH" has lost its original meaning entirely and has become a convenient, all-encompassing, term that denotes the whole of the philosophy and practices of the Project SEARCH model for training and supported employment.

THE EVOLUTION OF THE PROJECT SEARCH MODEL

A defining aspect of the Project SEARCH model is that it arose from a real business need rather than a strictly philanthropic motive and that it was business-led from the beginning. Certainly, the issues of justice and fairness entered into the decision making and design, but the primary motivation in the beginning was to improve retention and performance in critical support positions that were beset by chronically high turnover. These origins informed and shaped the program at the outset and have continued to do so over the years.

The Project SEARCH philosophy grew from a series of interactions with the rehabilitation system in which Cincinnati Children's, in effect, probed the practices of rehabilitation agencies and learned empirically what was effective from a business perspective, and what was not. For example, after the initial experiment hiring cart stockers in the Emergency Department, Erin, Jennifer, and Susie lobbied the hospital to reconsider a plan in which the hospital was to purchase a robot to transport laboratory specimens. Instead, Erin wrote a business proposal asking for a 3-month trial period during which she would hire 13 people with significant disabilities to do the job. She believed the people with disabilities could provide better service at a competitive cost. The hospital agreed to the proposal and a call went out to all of the rehabilitation agencies in the Cincinnati area to recruit candidates to fill the new positions. At the culmination of the selection process, the hospital was delighted with their new employees but dismayed to find that each of the 13 new hires was receiving services through a different community agency. This meant that each new employee came with his or her own job developer, job coach, and follow-along case manager. With the hospital's critical focus on security and infection control, not to mention limited parking, accommodating these 39 extra people was a logistical nightmare. All 13 new employees had been interviewed by the hospital. They had all completed their drug screens, felony background checks, and tuberculosis tests, and had been issued hospital identification badges. None of this was true for the 39 support staff. Moreover, they all had different methods of documentation, followed different dress codes, and worked according to schedules that were not necessarily compatible with hospital routines. Furthermore, news of the hirings spread through the rehabilitation community and the hospital was inundated with job inquiries from agencies and other organizations that served people with disabilities. This experience brought into focus the disconnect between the established procedures of service-providing agencies and the needs of employers and led to the conclusion that, although businesses and agencies both have an interest in improving employment prospects for people with disabilities, their different motivations and styles of operation often lead to inefficiency or worse—obstruction—in realizing shared goals.

The Project SEARCH team also learned that the traditional model (in which every agency in a given area sends job developers to every employer in that area) not only leads to logistical problems for the business but can also result in certain disadvantages for the newly hired employees with disabilities, such as support that is fragmented and sporadic because the service provider is not familiar with the employer. Furthermore, they found that it does not promote a real understanding of the internal workings of the workplace on the part of agency personnel. In response, Project SEARCH developed the "single-point-of-entry" principle, which the hospital found to be more compatible with business practices. What this meant was that Project SEARCH would provide a single conduit for organizing and delivering employment services in an effective and accountable way as an integrated part of the worksite, and this practice has been a cornerstone of the Project SEARCH model ever since. The approach was readily adopted by Cincinnati Children's because it was consistent with standard business practice, that is, the "preferred vendor" model whereby businesses contract with a single supplier to provide a given commodity or service. In this way, businesses reap the benefits of a predictable, efficient, consistent, and trusting relationship. In turn, for Project SEARCH, the practice allowed the training and follow-along staff to form a more in-depth relationship with the employer and, thus, to acquire a more thorough understanding of their operations, culture, and workforce needs.

CORE COMPONENTS OF THE PROJECT SEARCH MODEL

Project SEARCH began with the simple intention of hiring people with disabilities. From there, as the need arose, the program tackled issues such as finding the most effective training methods, maximizing employee retention, designing efficient adaptations and accommodations, and facilitating the transition from school to employment. As a result, Project SEARCH has become a large, multifaceted program. In fact, Project SEARCH has grown from 1 original program site at Cincinnati Children's to over 200 programs across 39 states and 4 countries. Project SEARCH business partners include, but are not limited to, Fifth Third Bank, Medtronic, the Department of Labor, the Miami Metro Zoo, the City of Miami, Kaiser Permanente, Chesapeake Energy Corporation, and the University of Rochester Medical Center. This list gives some idea of the diverse set of industry sectors and the wide variety of geographic, demographic, and political contexts in which Project SEARCH operates. But through years of experience and refinement, a cohesive philosophy and a corresponding set of practice standards have emerged so that all of the services that Project SEARCH provides are rooted in 10 core elements that are critical to the success of the model. Strict adherence to these core elements ensures model fidelity for this growing program as it is adapted to new locations and new industries. The components are listed below, where they are described briefly, and discussed in more detail in subsequent chapters.

1. **The outcome of the program is integrated employment for each participant.** This means that day programs, sheltered workshops, or other specialized circumstances, such as supplemented employment, that marginalize the employee with disabilities are not acceptable outcomes. The only acceptable outcome is integrated, meaningful work for which the employee is paid the prevailing wage.

2. **True collaboration among agencies is essential.** Each Project SEARCH site is a partnership with support and resources from the education community, the vocational rehabilitation system, a long-term support agency, and a community rehabilitation provider. It might also include constituent organizations such as the Down Syndrome Association or the National Autism Association. The specific partners will vary according to the specifics of agency structure in different states and countries. However, the important point is that Project SEARCH is not a program that can be overlaid onto an existing bureaucracy. Rather, it requires systemic change from all the partners so that their functions and funding are truly integrated.

3. **Project SEARCH is a business-led program.** It is critical that the business partner participates without a subsidy; that is, the business must have "skin in the game." For example,

in situations in which a service organization receives grant funding to hire a business liaison, the project is likely to fold after the grant runs out.

4. **Project SEARCH partners must provide a consistent on-site staff in the business place.** Employment support services are delivered as an integrated part of the worksite. This facilitates a more thorough understanding of the operations, culture, and workforce needs of the employer, which, in turn, allows Project SEARCH consumers access to a greater variety of complex and rewarding jobs. It also provides an opportunity for the business to gain coherent insight into the disability perspective including education, employment, Americans with Disabilities Act (ADA) of 1990 (PL 101-336), Individuals with Disabilities Education Act (IDEA, PL 108-446), adaptations and accommodations, and funding.

5. **The primary focus of Project SEARCH is on serving young adults with significant disabilities.** Project SEARCH is a resource-intensive program that is meant for those with significant disabilities who require basic training in employability skills and who have few other training options. Within this population, Project SEARCH has chosen to focus on youth as they transition from the education system to adult life. The purpose for this is to maximize impact at a programmatic level by reaching individuals at a life stage at which adult patterns begin to be established. It is possible for older adults to benefit from Project SEARCH practices, and exceptions are made in the right circumstances.

6. **Project SEARCH is sustainable because it relies on braided funding streams.** "Braided funding" means that Project SEARCH sites are funded by the redirection of existing funds from a variety of sources. Thus, it shouldn't require new funding or grants to sustain a Project SEARCH site. Grants can be useful for pilot programs or for covering costs during the start-up period, but they should not form the basis for long-term operations because a program that is built on soft money is difficult to sustain once the grant runs out. The concept of "braided funding" is integral to achieving true collaboration, as described previously (component #2).

7. **Project SEARCH requires total immersion in the work place.** Because Project SEARCH teaches competitive, marketable, transferable skills, it is critical that training takes place in real work settings. Student interns should be on site for at least 6 hours a day. This is critical not only to the progress of the person with a disability but also to effecting cultural change within the business.

8. **Data are submitted to a national Project SEARCH database.** The database uses clearly defined outcomes that match the goals of Project SEARCH. The database also addresses parameters that are relevant to the Federal Department of Education's 20 IDEA indicators and to the Rehabilitation Services Administration.

9. **Project SEARCH graduates will receive effective follow-along services to retain employment.** To achieve this, gaining eligibility for follow-along services must be a priority before entering the program or early in the program. Follow-along services should be customized to meet the needs of the individual.

10. **Each site has a licensing agreement signed with Project SEARCH Cincinnati through Cincinnati Children's Hospital Medical Center.** The licensing program is critical for maintaining integrity of the Project SEARCH model by ensuring quality control and model fidelity.

BUSINESS BENEFITS OF PROJECT SEARCH FOR CINCINNATI CHILDREN'S HOSPITAL

Approximately 10% of American people have some sort of disability, and as an organization that exists to serve the public, it is a high priority to Cincinnati Children's to have a workforce

---

THE EXECUTIVE DIRECTOR OF THE OHIO RSC WEIGHS IN ON PROJECT SEARCH

Project SEARCH is so successful because the entire program is embedded inside the sponsoring organization, in support of their mission. Time after time, business leaders tell us opening the door to Project SEARCH has improved productivity of their entire enterprise, as the innovative methods used to train Rehabilitation Services Commission (RSC) clients are actually at the forefront of the Lean process revolution. It is a joyful experience to see RSC clients have life-changing success through Project SEARCH while adding great value to the organizations that gave them an opportunity. The rapid expansion of Project SEARCH is testimony to the fact that people with disabilities can make a big contribution to business competitiveness as leaders in health care, financial services, government, logistics, and many other industries are now discovering.

Kevin Miller, Executive Director of Ohio Rehabilitation Services Commission
Presented at the Ohio Project SEARCH Quarterly Statewide Meeting, October 2011

---

that mirrors the public. Through Project SEARCH, the hospital has built a substantial and visible presence of people with disabilities. As a result of this presence, the program has gone far beyond its original goals of increased retention in chronically unfilled support positions and enhanced workforce diversity. The program has delivered an added bonus by setting off a ripple effect that has resulted in other unanticipated business benefits for the hospital.

Greater productivity and improved retention in high-turnover support positions is a clear and direct benefit of the work activities of employees with disabilities within Cincinnati Children's. But Project SEARCH has also had an indirect impact on the recruiting of high-level professionals. Over the past several years, the hospital has hired a new chief of surgery, a new chief of staff, and a new director of cardiac research. Naturally, it is a high priority for the hospital to hire the very best individuals to fill these critical positions, and it appears that Project SEARCH played an important role in each of these recruiting efforts. All three of the professionals who were ultimately hired had requested a meeting with the Project SEARCH staff as part of the interview process. It turns out that all three have children with disabilities, and on accepting their respective positions, they all stated that the hospital's commitment to training and hiring people with disabilities had influenced their decision to move to Cincinnati Children's. Likewise, when the Down syndrome clinic needed to hire a new staff physician, Project SEARCH was influential in the hospital's ability to attract an excellent physician to fill the post.

In addition to its positive impact on employee recruitment, Project SEARCH is also an effective tool for expanding the hospital's patient base and increasing patient satisfaction. It is a simple truth that children with chronic illnesses and disabilities are a major source of hospital revenue. They tend to be very loyal customers who form long-term relationships with their health care organizations. Because of this, it makes sense that Cincinnati Children's wants to be the provider of choice for this group, and it follows that anything that encourages the families of children and young people with disabilities to choose Cincinnati Children's is good business practice for the hospital. It is clear that the hospital's obvious and visible commitment to employing people with disabilities increases the loyalty of this important customer base. It has made a difference in the hospital's development efforts as well; since the inception of Project SEARCH there has been a noticeable increase in charitable gifts from the families of people with disabilities and chronic illnesses.

Employees with disabilities encourage patient loyalty because these workers serve as role models for patients and families at Cincinnati Children's. It gives a sense of hope to these families when they see people with disabilities as productive employees, and this effect is reflected in increased compliance with medical orders and in patient satisfaction surveys. A striking and moving example of this came in a letter to Erin from a mother of an infant with Down syndrome. In her letter, she explained that her baby experienced cardiac complications and was airlifted to Cincinnati Children's for surgery. She received excellent medical care for

A PHYSICIAN REFLECTS ON THE IMPACT OF PROJECT SEARCH

I see people every day who have the same names as patients I took care of years ago—but they're not the same. They're all grown up and working at real, important jobs. When we take care of babies and young children with health problems, we often don't get to see 'the rest of the story,' especially the really good endings. Project SEARCH reminds us of that. But it's also important to our new families. I tell them as they walk the halls here, or sit in the cafeteria, that they shouldn't stare, but they should **notice.** And what they should notice is that young adults who happen to look a little different, who use a speech board, who get around in a power chair are **working**, doing important jobs not just for themselves but for US. And that's what we expect to see their child able to do.

Dr. Nancy Leslie, MD, Professor of Clinical Pediatrics,
Division of Human Genetics, Cincinnati Children's Hospital Medical Center

her child, but that wasn't what made the biggest impression on her—after all, she *expected* excellent medical care. What she hadn't expected was a life-changing moment that came when she was with her baby in intensive care waiting for surgery. She was in tears, worrying about the surgery but, even more than that, fearing for her child's future. She was still adjusting to the reality of her child's disability and was feeling that the outlook for her family was dim. But then a young woman with Down syndrome walked into the room, looked into the crib and said, "That's a cute baby," and proceeded to stock every supply in the room. At that moment, the new mother's outlook changed completely. After seeing what this young woman could do, and how confidently she moved about the hospital room, she had new hope for her own child. She knew then that her baby could grow up and be productively employed, and she was intensely grateful to Cincinnati Children's for giving her that new perspective. For her, more than anything else that happened during her hospital stay, it was that experience that changed the outcome for her baby and for her family.

The presence of co-workers with developmental disabilities also has an important influence on staff perspectives. By working with them as colleagues, staff members at Cincinnati Children's have increasingly come to see people with disabilities as individuals who make unique contributions. Moreover, as workers with disabilities grow in their jobs and take on new responsibilities, the people around them gain new understanding of their potential.

Another outcome of Project SEARCH has been increased recognition for the hospital. This occurs naturally as a by-product of active dissemination of twwhe Project SEARCH model. In addition, Project SEARCH has attracted high-profile awards at a local, regional, and national level—most notably the U.S. Secretary of Labor's New Freedom Initiative Award in 2004. Under the Bush administration, this award was given to organizations that "recognize the value that persons with disabilities bring to the workplace" and reflect that wisdom in their daily actions and operations.

Naturally, Cincinnati Children's is most well known for its clinical and research excellence. But as Project SEARCH is replicated across the country and overseas, and the program is acclaimed for its success and innovative practices, the hospital gains recognition in new geographic regions, among new groups of people, and in different business sectors for a contribution that sets it apart from other hospitals.

Project | SEARCH

Meet Jill

Jill is one of the pioneers of Project SEARCH; she joined the original program site at Cincinnati Children's Hospital Medical Center in the very early days—even before the structure of the High School Transition Program was formalized. She came to the program from her home school—a K through 12 school operated by the Hamilton County Board of Developmental Disabilities.

Jill trained in the Sterile Processing department for about 5 months before she was offered a job in that area. She worked with a job coach to learn how to assemble surgical trays (kits including the specific instruments needed for a given operation) and how to prepare them for the sterilization process. For each tray that Jill learned, her job coach, along with the Project SEARCH team, created a notebook showing photographs of each instrument in that tray. These notebooks took the place of the text-only checklists of surgical instruments that were typically used. Initially, the Project SEARCH team had Jill focus on learning the trays that had the highest utilization rates and the fewest instruments such as ear tube, tonsillectomy, and laceration trays. Over time, she kept learning and increasing the complexity of the trays that she could prepare such that she is now able to do 30 or 40 different trays—some with more than 150 different instruments. According to her supervisor, Timothy Lyons, "Jill is excellent on trays. She's very thorough, she enjoys putting up trays, and she's really focused when she does it."

Jill's parents played an important supportive role in her success. While she was learning her job, they did homework with her every night—quizzing her on the names of instruments and discussing the subtle but important differences among them. To help her with the difficult "sterile field" concept, Jill's parents made the extra effort to train at the hospital in the process of maintaining a sterile area. They learned how to "suit up" to enter a sterile area, as well as the dos and don'ts of working in such areas, and used this knowledge to reinforce the procedures with Jill at home. Jill and her dad still do homework once a week to help keep her skills sharp.

Jill is continuously progressing in her job. At first, she worked part time but later changed to a full-time schedule. In addition, she continues to add new trays to her repertoire. Jill uses a photo book each time she learns a new tray but quickly memorizes the trays and no longer needs the book. In addition to her own personal progress, Jill has also been able to keep up with the constant changes that are inherent in the work she does—newly designed surgical instruments, changes based on doctors' preferences, and changes in policy and procedures. For example, the department instituted a system of bar codes so that each step in the sterilization process could be traced back to the responsible individual, and Jill seamlessly incorporated this change

(continued)

into all her work. Jill no longer needs a job coach to help her retrain in response to such changes. Instead, she goes through departmental in-service trainings along with her colleagues. She eats lunch with her co-workers every day, has an identical workspace to any other employee, and enjoys the same salary and benefits.

Jill recently celebrated her 10-year anniversary with Cincinnati Children's. When you ask Jill about her work at the hospital, she simply says, "I love my job!"

3 The Project SEARCH High School Transition Program

> *While freedom of choice is given,*
> *the right to work is earned.*
>
> Stephen Simon, 1998

When Jim D. finished high school, he knew he wanted a career, but like most teen-agers, he didn't feel ready to start navigating the vast and confusing world of work. Because Jim has autism, he was on an individualized education program (IEP) and, thus, eligible for 3 years of transition services through his school district, which he and his family hoped would help him in defining his goals. But it didn't turn out quite as they had expected. His first year consisted of 5-day weeks in the transition program, and in the second year, the program was offered 2 days a week. At the end of the first 2 years of transition, he wasn't any closer to knowing what he wanted to do or to having a real career plan in place. He had spent his mornings taking a class at a community college, and by mid-morning, he and the other students were bused back to the transition program where they spent the rest of the day in seminar classes on a variety of topics such as dating, social skills, and resume writing. The program was strongly focused on independent living skills, with the expectation that the students would independently find employment so that they could prac-tice their job skills. Jim's teachers showed him how to look for jobs in the newspaper and on the internet, and vocational rehabilitation (VR) services were available to him, but the job search and application process were pretty much left up to him. This was confusing for the students and their families. In some instances, the students were treated as if they had limited abilities, but at other times, the transition staff had expectations that seemed unrealistically high. The way Jim's mother, Sandy, described it, "They acted as if the transition students were capable, but just needed to be pushed." But she knew that her son needed more than just a push. He was trying his hardest to meet the goals put before him.

After 2 years of working on his independent living skills in a large group setting, it was time to see what else was out there. Jim needed a smaller setting in which he could build upon his skills and develop and practice them in order to reach his employment goals. It was in this context that Jim and his family learned about the Project SEARCH® program starting up at Medtronic, Inc., an international medical technology company in Minneapolis. From their first contact with the program at the Project SEARCH Open House, the family was impressed with the philosophy and atmosphere that was so positive and focused on the students' strengths. Sandy D. could see right away the effect it had on the participants, "It's building them up and helping them feel good about themselves—helping them feel capable and confident." And in that environment, with plenty of support coupled with high expectations, she could see that the students were thriving and surprising themselves and everyone around them with what they were capable of. Jim and his family knew right away that this was where they wanted Jim to be.

Jim applied for Project SEARCH at Medtronic and was accepted. He began Project SEARCH in the fall of his third year of transition, and his experience in the program was what he and his family had hoped for. Now that Jim has been able to train in several different types of jobs, his confidence has increased, he's gained new skills, and he has a good idea of the kind of work he wants to do. Moreover, he and his family have found that the way the school, the business, and VR all work together in Project SEARCH has made Jim's relationship with his VR counselor much more productive. Jim had been linked with VR at the end of high school, but although his VR counselor was equipped to help him prepare for and find a specific type of job, the counselor was lacking the resources to help Jim decide what sort of job interested him. There seemed to be a mismatch in the information that VR expected to get from the family and what the family was actually prepared to tell them. Without the opportunity for job exploration, Jim and his parents didn't know what he would enjoy or be good at—they didn't even know the names of the jobs. But after his time in Project SEARCH, Jim had three internships under his belt and knew exactly what sort of work he wanted to do, and he had the language and terminology to name those jobs in a way that his VR counselor could understand. In addition, he was able to tell his counselor exactly what skills he had that qualified him for those jobs. Jim's experience in Project SEARCH gave him new, marketable skills and helped him to define his career path. At the same time, it's helped him to get more out of his interaction with VR so that, shortly after he graduated from the program, he was offered and accepted a job in the human resources department of a local clinic. As his mother Sandy said, "This is what transition services should be!"

Project SEARCH is primarily focused on young people with disabilities, like Jim, as they transition from high school to adult life. We emphasize this age group because of the copious research and practical experience showing that this is a critical juncture for establishing lifelong patterns. For a young person with a disability, an unsuccessful transition can lead to lower self-esteem, diminished engagement in social activities, decreased life satisfaction, and lower income. On a societal level, unsuccessful transitions to adulthood are associated with reduced productivity, lower tax revenues, and higher rates of criminal activity and incarceration (Fraker & Rangarajan, 2009). Conversely, when young people are prepared to enter the work force, they gain a number of personal benefits as well as an increased likelihood that they will achieve financial independence and, thus, become less dependent on their families and on social services. Because of the high stakes, and the considerable costs of unsuccessful transition—to the young people themselves, to their families, and for society as a whole—interventions that target this transitional period are particularly effective in combating the chronic problems of unemployment and underemployment for people with intellectual and developmental disabilities (IDD).

The change from high school to adult life is a demanding time for everyone, and any young person can benefit from the guidance that an experienced adult can offer at this stage. But young people with intellectual and developmental disabilities face particular challenges that heighten that need for assistance. Disability research has provided decades of data documenting persistent low rates of participation in employment, postsecondary education, and other indicators of productive engagement for young people with disabilities in the years after they exit high school (Benz, Lindstrom, & Yovanoff, 2000; Peraino, 1992; Wagner, Blackorby, Cameto, Hebeler, & Newman, 1993; Wagner, Cameto, & Newman, 2003). Recognizing this problem, federal law now mandates transition assistance for students receiving special education services under the Individuals with Disabilities Education Act (IDEA, PL 108-446). However, although excellent

Table 3.1. Differences between a traditional school environment and a Project SEARCH® classroom/host business

	Traditional school environment	Project SEARCH
Social environment	Many social activities are available to students—such as dances, plays, and clubs—with the goal of developing more well-rounded people.	Students have team-building activities, staff meetings, and other work-related activities that are social but have work-specific purposes.
Performance	Many schools reward effort. They will look for alternative methods when a student is not learning or exhibits a bad attitude.	Employers reward results. They will look for alternative ways to give employees the skills to perform the job. Employers are looking for performance, ability, and a positive attitude.
Dress code	A more casual dress code is tolerated. More lenient dress standards are acceptable—tattoos, extreme hairstyles, and facial piercings are often tolerated.	Employers will have specific, formal, and uniform dress requirements, with strict rules about footwear, jewelry, and tattoos. In a business, the customers' perceptions are of extreme importance.
Support personnel	Various individuals—such as counselors, special needs coordinators, and nurses—are available on a daily basis to handle personal problems that may occur.	Most employers do not have a nurse or any other coordinator to help the employee with daily struggles. Project SEARCH partners can fill this need, but not always in person or on a daily basis. Job coaches are on site to teach the essential job functions and core skills.
Discipline	A principal or other administrator is available to address and enforce concerns that could lead to detentions, suspensions, or any other deterrent.	Managers and supervisors handle any discipline items. Documentation, performance improvement plans, or possible termination may result.
Environment	Loud voices, talking in the hallways, running, and bells indicating where one should be are all typical in school.	In a professional environment, there is no running or shouting, and there are no bells or other indicators to help students know when to take a break, go to lunch, return from break, or return from lunch.

services are available in many regions, there is no consistency in the quality or availability of such assistance throughout the United States (Larson, Goldberg, McDonald, Leuchovius, Richardson, & Lakin, 2011). Moreover, when transition services are available, they are often delivered with good intentions but in an unfocused manner with no clear pathway to employment. Consequently, youth with disabilities often miss out on opportunities to develop the specific competencies, work habits, communication skills, and attitudes that employers look for when making hiring decisions and that are critical to maintaining employment once hired.

OVERVIEW OF CONCEPTS IN TRANSITION

IDEA is the special education law mandating free and appropriate public education for eligible infants, toddlers, children, and youth with disabilities. It was originally enacted in 1975 and most recently amended in 2004. The law specifies how states, school districts, and public agencies are to provide early intervention, special education, and related services. With regard to transition, IDEA states that services should be based on the individual student's needs and interests [34 CFR 300.43 (a)] [20 U.S.C. 1401(34)]. Section 602 (30)(C) of the act specifies that transition services include "instruction, related services, community experiences, the development of employment and other post-school adult living objectives, and, when appropriate, acquisition of daily living skills and functional vocational evaluation." This is an all-encompassing mandate and effectively delivering on all seven of these broadly stated priorities is a lot to expect of the schools. Schools do a lot of things well, but considering that they are trying to incorporate so many elements, it's not surprising that transition programs sometimes lack focus. Some schools respond to this mandate by trying to cover all seven aspects of transition at once with no clear progression. But, in many cases, schools make an effort to break down the goals and address them in a logical sequence in their transition programs or in traditional career technical training.

FEDERAL DEFINITION OF TRANSITION SERVICES UNDER THE INDIVIDUALS WITH DISABILITIES EDUCATION ACT (IDEA, PL 108-446)

The term "transition services" means a coordinated set of activities for a child with a disability that

- Is designed to be within a results-oriented process, that is focused on improving the academic and functional achievement of the child with a disability to facilitate the child's movement from school to postschool activities, including postsecondary education; vocational education; integrated employment (including supported employment); continuing and adult education; adult services; independent living; or community participation
- Is based on the individual child's needs, taking into account the child's strengths, preferences, and interests
- Includes instruction, related services, community experiences, the development of employment and other postschool adult living objectives, and if appropriate, acquisition of daily living skills and functional vocational evaluation

---

Schools have developed different programs and practices to meet IDEA requirements and prepare students for employment. In traditional classroom models, employability training takes place strictly in a school setting with students in segregated special education classrooms. Work-study models combine classroom instruction with actual work experience, but usually, time at a community work setting is limited to a few hours a day or week. Students might participate in job-shadowing or tour worksites in groups. Many programs include a transition-to-community component that emphasizes social skills and independent living skills. Other programs use an adapted career and technical model in which job skills are taught in a laboratory environment with simulated or actual worksites that model different business sectors such as restaurants, hotels, or horticulture operations. Among the factors that distinguish the different options, the degree to which students are exposed to real work environments is one that seems to make the biggest difference in work readiness (Carter et al., 2011; National Alliance for Secondary Education and Transition, 2005; Test, Fowler, Richter, White, Mazzotti, Walker, et al., 2009).

Table 3.2. Project SEARCH® High School Transition contributes to Individuals with Disabilities Education Act performance indicators

IDEA indicator	Performance measure	Relevant Project SEARCH features
1. Graduation*	Percentage of youth with IEPs graduating from high school	• State-approved curriculum and lesson plans are used. • Formal assessments are performed. • All goals are focused on training and employment. • Students have completed high school graduation requirements before entering program.
5. Least restrictive environment	Percentage of children with IEPs served inside the regular classroom less than 40% of the school day	• Immersion in host business is 100% of time. • Ample opportunity exists to model work environment and culture in integrated environment. • Internships teach competitive, marketable work skills. • Curriculum reinforces business culture.
8. Parent involvement	Percentage of parents with a child receiving special education services who report that schools facilitated parent involvement	• Parents/families are an integral part of student's team and are expected to attend monthly progress meetings. • Parents/families receive training in transition topics and guidance on how best to support students. • Parents/families are active participants in the job development process.
13. Quality of IEPs and transition goals	Percentage of youth ages 16 and older with an IEP that includes coordinated, measurable, and annual IEP goals and transition services that will reasonably enable the student to meet the postsecondary goals	• Teachers receive training on quality transition goals. • Assessments measure career readiness and employability skills. • Regular meetings with team are designed to monitor progress toward goals.

(continued)

Table 3.2. *(continued)*

IDEA indicator	Performance measure	Relevant Project SEARCH features
14. Postschool outcomes	Percentage of youth who had IEPs, are no longer in secondary school, and who have been competitively employed, enrolled in some type of postsecondary school, or both, within 1 year of leaving high school	• Braided funding is used to create sustainability. • Students gain employability skills. • There is full immersion in an integrated work setting. • Three internships in an actual work setting that teach relevant marketable skills are completed. • It provides preparation for jobs that are complex and systematic, pay a prevailing wage. • Individualized job development and coaching are built into the program. • Program fidelity is ensured through licensing agreement and audits.

Note: Through IDEA and its specific recommendations regarding transition, schools have been given more responsibility for employment outcomes. State departments of education and local education agencies (LEAs) are held accountable to significantly improve their outcomes tied to federal IDEA indicators, with an emphasis on attaining higher outcomes as it relates to IDEA indicator 14, postschool outcomes. Schools benefit from their involvement in Project SEARCH because it helps them to satisfy 5 of the 14 federal student outcome–related performance indicators that show compliance with IDEA. Project SEARCH has a strong track record of working efficiently with LEAs to significantly increase their outcomes tied to federal IDEA indicators 1, 5, 8, 13, and 14. That is, whereas the ultimate objective for Project SEARCH is to secure competitive employment for its student graduates, the program's core model components and curriculum focus on the least restrictive environment, the development and implementation of IEPs with quality transition goals, family involvement, employment outcomes, and graduation.

*Participating in Project SEARCH, or any other transition program, promotes progress toward graduation but requires students to stay in high school longer than the traditional 4 years. Currently there are federal school performance measures that conflict with IDEA indicators in that they emphasize graduation in 4 years. However, IDEA and the need for students with disabilities to participate in critical training and employment programs should take priority over the emphasis on graduation in 4 years.

Key: IDEA, Individuals with Disabilities Education Act, PL 108-446; IEPs, individualized education programs.

OVERVIEW OF THE PROJECT SEARCH HIGH SCHOOL TRANSITION PROGRAM

Introduction

The Project SEARCH High School Transition Program is a school-to-work program for students with intellectual and developmental disabilities. Students in their last year of high school eligibility attend the program for 1 school year in which they are trained in a real-life work environment while also learning employability and independent living skills. What makes it unique is the extent to which it requires and fosters collaboration among businesses, education systems, VR, and other disability service agencies. Another important difference is that it takes place entirely within the workplace. This total immersion allows for the seamless integration of classroom instruction, career exploration, and supported job training in a relevant, business-based environment. It also sets the stage for embedded relationships between the teaching, the coaching, and the business staff that leads to culture change and employment opportunities.

Our difference in philosophy leads to differences in our approach to the details of transition. For example, the way we handle transportation issues and special services sets Project SEARCH apart from other special education programs. All of these differences are driven by our intense focus on achieving competitive employment and maximal independence for each student participant.

Another important part of the Project SEARCH program is our beliefs and overall philosophy. Once the students are accepted into the program, it is important that all the partners strongly believe and have the expectation that each student can achieve the goal of competitive employment. As the inventor and philanthropist Charles Kettering put it, we "believe and act as if it is impossible to fail."

The Project SEARCH program works best when it is offered as part of a continuum of transition services. In general, the most successful students are those who come to Project SEARCH after spending 1 or 2 years in more traditional career and technical education programs that allow for maturation, functional skill development, and career exploration. In this way, students can use the first part of their transition process to focus on the softer aspects of the section 602 definition of transition such as community experiences, adult living objectives, and daily living skills. Project SEARCH continues to reinforce those skills, but the context clearly shifts to a laser-like focus on the development of work skills and getting a job.

The Project SEARCH approach can be applied to supported employment for adults; this has been done successfully in several contexts. However, when working with prospective Project SEARCH sites, we strongly recommend that they initiate their program by introducing a High School Transition Program. There are two reasons for this: the first relates to the importance of reaching youth at this juncture, and the second relates to the powerful impact that the High School Transition Program has on business culture. As Erin Riehle put it,

> Instead of having a High School Transition Program, Cincinnati Children's could hire three adults with significant disabilities tomorrow. Those new employees could do fabulous work, but the difference is that they'd be scattered throughout the hospital and they wouldn't create a big enough presence to drive institutional culture change. In contrast, when you take 12 student interns and, over the course of a year, move each one of them through two or three departments where they are learning real skills—by the end of the school year you could potentially have 20 department heads that, for the first time in their lives, have worked with people with disabilities. And they now see those individuals through different eyes—as capable adults. You also have 20 or more groups of staff who now see people with disabilities as inherently capable people who are able to learn and perform complex tasks. Suddenly, you're not worried about them or afraid of them, but you see them as people who fit into your mix and you can see them as colleagues. The extensive presence that comes with a High School Transition Program makes a significant impact and, with that change, it becomes easier for everyone to envision a person with a significant disability becoming a permanent part of that environment.

This scenario has been played out time and again at Project SEARCH sites: Skeptical managers and co-workers become transformed by their experiences with young people with disabilities. And this transformation is possible because of the duration and extent of their interactions with

---

PROJECT SEARCH AND SPECIAL EDUCATION: DIFFERENT FOCUS, DIFFERENT RULES

To participate in a Project SEARCH program, students have to apply and be accepted. Part of the purpose of this application is to demonstrate an awareness of the Project SEARCH process and a willingness to move beyond the protections and entitlements of special education. Because we are an application-only program, and not the sole option for transitioning students, we have the flexibility to vary from some of the standard special education procedures when they are at odds with our goals of employment and independence. For example, independent travel is not just encouraged, but rather, it is required by Project SEARCH programs in most areas. That is, there is no school bus or van involved in transporting the young people to the worksite. Each young adult must complete travel training during the summer before entering the program or during the first internship. The goal is for each young adult to learn to travel as independently as possible. In some circumstances, this might mean that they are driven by a friend or family member, but ideally, the family and the young adult will begin to take advantage of the best options available in the community. This could mean public transportation, a taxi, ride sharing, or a variety of other options.

Another example in which Project SEARCH differs from school-based special education is in the approach to special services such as speech therapy, psychological services, or mobility training. We are supportive of students receiving the services that they need; however, we require that they have those needs met in the same way as others who are functioning in an adult world. That is, appointments must be scheduled so that they do not interrupt the skills training that is the raison d'être of Project SEARCH. For example, occupational therapy will be provided as a consultation rather than an ongoing service and occurs at the internship site to integrate recommendations directly into the work environment. With each internship, the providers of special services (such as occupational therapists) can return to the new internship, consult with the staff, and determine the scope of services. These specialists could also attend the monthly employment-planning meeting, consult with the team, address issues, and help solve problems.

the student interns. It would happen much more slowly, or not at all, in a business following the typical model of supported employment. First of all, in a typical job application process, an applicant with a disability would be less likely to get a job in the first place because they would be a complete unknown to the business and, without the internships, wouldn't have received the training or the opportunity to demonstrate their capabilities. Moreover, even if the applicant is successful in getting the job, the hiring of individuals with disabilities would be an isolated event. In these circumstances, the individuals with disabilities are likely to be scattered too widely to make an impact beyond their immediate surroundings, and they may not have received sufficient orientation or training to allow them to perform to their highest potential. In contrast, with the Project SEARCH model, students enter the business with the support of a job coach and a special education teacher, which ensures that students receive the guidance that they need to succeed. And it makes a powerful impression on managers and co-workers to observe the students as they grow in maturity, improve in accuracy and efficiency, and acquire new skills.

Target Population

The Project SEARCH High School Transition Program serves students with significant intellectual and developmental disabilities who are transitioning from high school to adult life. Most fall in the age range of 18 to 22 years, but more importantly, these are students who are on an IEP, have completed all of their high school credits and graduation or certification requirements, and have deferred graduation status. The most important eligibility criterion is a personal and family desire to achieve competitive employment.

FEDERAL DEFINITION OF DEVELOPMENTAL DISABILITIES

According to the Developmental Disabilities Act, section 102(8), "the term 'developmental disability' means a severe, chronic disability of an individual 5 years of age or older that

1. Is attributable to a mental or physical impairment or combination of mental and physical impairments;
2. Is manifested before the individual attains age 22;
3. Is likely to continue indefinitely;
4. Results in substantial functional limitations in three or more of the following areas of major life activity:
    i.   Self-care;
    ii. Receptive and expressive language;
    iii. Learning;
    iv. Mobility;
    v.   Self-direction;
    vi. Capacity for independent living; and
    vii. Economic self-sufficiency.
5. Reflects the individual's need for a combination and sequence of special, interdisciplinary, or generic services, supports, or other assistance that is of lifelong or extended duration and is individually planned and coordinated, except that such term, when applied to infants and young children, means individuals from birth to age 5, inclusive, who have substantial developmental delay or specific congenital or acquired conditions with a high probability of resulting in developmental disabilities if services are not provided."

From the web site "Real People, Real Jobs: Stories from the Front Lines" (http://www.realworkstories.org/dev-disability-definition)

DEFINITION OF INTELLECTUAL DISABILITY

"Intellectual disability is a disability characterized by significant limitations both in intellectual functioning and in adaptive behavior, which covers many everyday social and practical skills. This disability originates before the age of 18."

From the web site of the American Association on Intellectual and Developmental Disabilities (http://www.aaidd.org/content_100.cfm?navID=21)

PROJECT SEARCH HIGH SCHOOL TRANSITION PROGRAM ENTRANCE CRITERIA

- Is at least 18 years of age
- Has completed high school credits necessary for graduation or certificate
- Agrees that this will be the last year of student services and will accept diploma or certificate at the end of Project SEARCH
- Meets eligibility requirements for vocational rehabilitation
- Meets eligibility requirements for developmental disabilities services and other service providers as necessary for follow-along services *(This is preferred but not necessary.)*
- Has independent personal hygiene and grooming skills
- Has independent daily living skills
- Is able to maintain appropriate behavior and social skills in the workplace
- Is able to take direction from supervisors and modify performance or change behavior, as requested
- Is able to communicate effectively
- Can utilize public transportation *when available* and participate in travel training to maximize independence in travel
- Has previous experience in a work environment (including school, volunteer, or paid work)
- Is able to pass drug screen and felony check and have immunizations up to date
- Desires and plans to work competitively in the community at the conclusion of the Project SEARCH program

---

Deferred graduation is an IDEA provision that allows for education and transition services for young people with disabilities to continue until the age of 22. It is a policy that is implemented locally such that the specific structure varies regionally. But, regardless of the locale, the legislation provides students with disabilities the opportunity to gain additional skills training. This eligibility ends once a student accepts a regular high school diploma or special education certificate. Leveraging the option of deferred graduation is a key concept in funding the Project SEARCH High School Transition Program. Before entering Project SEARCH, students complete their academic requirements but do not accept their diploma until after completing the program. Alternatively, a student might participate with his or her peers in the important social ritual of the high school graduation ceremony. However, the student would receive a blank diploma and, thus, remain eligible for per-student education dollars from a combination of federal, state, and local sources, as well as special education-weighted funding. In the Project SEARCH High School Transition Model, those education dollars are used to support the special education teacher who has responsibility for supervising students in the program and planning and delivering the Project SEARCH curriculum in the worksite-based classroom.

Under certain circumstances, young adults who have already received a high school diploma or certificate of completion can also participate in the Project SEARCH High School Transition Program. Young adults who have aged out of high school can fill vacant slots in a Project SEARCH program if the recruiting team cannot identify enough eligible high school–aged students to fill a classroom or if a space opens up mid-year because a student intern is hired and leaves the program for regular employment. Either way, inclusion of these young adults can present certain challenges. First of all, if a young person is no longer school-eligible, she or he will not be accompanied by the per-pupil education dollars that helps to pay the instructor's salary, which can leave the program with a gap in funding that could be filled through funding from an adult disability employment agency, such as VR. The other challenge is that a large age difference among the students can disrupt the dynamics of the Project SEARCH experience. An important part of Project SEARCH's formula for success is the formation of a supportive cohort of similarly aged peers, and a student who is at a different life stage and mind-set may not identify with or interact well with high school students. We recommend that eligibility guidelines be set around age, typically limiting participation in the program to young adults ages 26 and younger. Adult candidates must be eligible for services from VR and, ideally, the local DD agency as well. Also, the young adults must go through the same application procedure as the high school students. That is, they should submit an application along with all supporting documentation; take part in an interview; and participate in a program site tour or hands-on assessment, or both. All or part of the selection committee should meet to interview and assess the young adult candidate and accept or decline the application.

Another way to include young adults in Project SEARCH is to create a program that is strictly for high school graduates. In this model, no school system would be involved and the instructor would not necessarily be a special education teacher. An experienced and strong rehabilitation professional, or possibly a community college instructor with special education training, could fill this role (many of our U.K. Project SEARCH sites follow this model). However, because there would be no school system involved in the program, arrangements would have to be made for a supported employment agency to cover the cost of instruction. Funding is a challenge for this type of program; some agencies have utilized "Day Rehab," Medicaid, and/or VR as funding sources. We continue to recommend the high school program as the best model for implementing Project SEARCH. If a "young adult–only" program is implemented, all other aspects of the typical structure and model should be maintained.

Program Overview

Students attend the Project SEARCH High School Transition Program for a full school year (see Figure 3.4). Each program site is based in a place of business. The host business provides an on-site classroom that can accommodate approximately 12 students. The specific number will vary from site to site from as few as 6 to as many as 15, based on the local minimum requirements for a full classroom (i.e., the number of students required to cover the expense of staffing the classroom with a teacher) and the capacity of the host business. Each site is staffed by a teacher and job coaches (a sufficient number to achieve a 4:1 student-to-coach ratio). The required credentials for teachers will vary from state to state, but in Ohio (where Project SEARCH originated), the requirements include a special education or vocational education certificate and a state-licensed transition-to-work endorsement. For continuity in the program, it is critical that each Project SEARCH site is staffed by a single teacher and that 100% of that teacher's work time is devoted to facilitating and coordinating the Project SEARCH program. Likewise, the job coaches should be consistent at a given site. Figures 3.1 and 3.2 show how the teacher's and the job coach's specific duties shift throughout the school year.

After an initial orientation period of 3 to 4 weeks, the students' day consists of a 1-hour morning classroom session in which they participate in activities designed to enhance employability and independent living skills, as shown in Table 3.3. The rest of the day is devoted to learning specific, relevant, and transferable job skills in an internship. Students rotate through two to three different worksite internships throughout the business over the course of the year. Throughout the week, the students participate in a minimum of 20 hours at their internship to learn work skills as well as social and communication skills. As they experience the culture and learn to function with support and guidance, they utilize classroom time at the end of the day to review their work and experiences, discuss different options, and plan for the next day. Figure 3.3 shows how the specific roles and responsibilities of the students evolve as they move from their last year of high school (the Project SEARCH planning year) into Project SEARCH and as they progress through the program year.

Each program site is guided by an Advisory Board that includes Project SEARCH teachers and job coaches, an additional special education administrator, VR counselors, employer representatives, family members, and Project SEARCH students or alumni with disabilities.

Role: Teacher

Student recruitment: organize school presentations, information sessions, tours, skills assessment days, student interviews, selection process and perform, associated tasks such as application process selection rubric and eligibility determination

Internships: identify and analyze potential internship locations, develop task designs for internship areas, provide job coaching, monitor and evaluate intern progress, provide education and communicate with internship site staff, and create job accommodations

Job development: analyze employment climate, connect with community employers, build vocational profiles for interns, provide individual job search activities, and facilitate supports for competitive employment

Meetings and marketing: develop and utilize marketing tools and facilitate Business Advisory Committee, intern employment-planning meetings, individualized education program (IEP) meetings, and other problem-solving team meetings

Teaching and curriculum: orientation to host business, individual, and group classroom instruction

Training and staff development: participate in Project SEARCH®–sponsored training, prepare and deliver family involvement curriculum, and prepare and deliver program information to internal and external partners

Technical assistance: work with the internal Project SEARCH team on program development and continuous improvement

Paperwork: process licensing agreement, intern attendance sheets, Commission on Accreditation of Rehabilitation Facilities (CARF) reports, intern progress reports, billing to funders, grant-related reports; create materials for interns and businesses

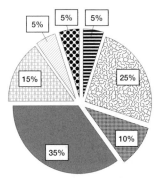

Program Phase: Planning Year (to start up new program site), 4th Quarter—June, July, and August

Assumption: The teacher will need to be hired in June and have 20 contracted days during this quarter. Contract days will be needed before the program begins so that the teacher can complete the host business orientation, receive training related to Project SEARCH® programming, and develop initial internship sites within the host business.

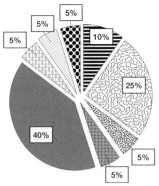

Program Phase: Year 1, 1st Quarter—September, October, and November

Assumption: The program year begins in late August and the interns are in the classroom for the majority of the day through early September for orientation activities. Job development activities, such as analyzing local employment needs, begin early in the year.

Figure 3.1. Teacher responsibilities.

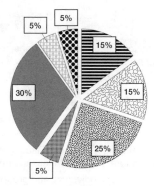

Program Phase: Year 1, 2nd Quarter—December, January, and February

Assumption: A focus on teaching the curriculum remains strong, but it shifts from general employability skills to lessons directed toward job-seeking skills. Student recruitment activities for next year's students increase and there is a sharp increase in activities for job development and placement.

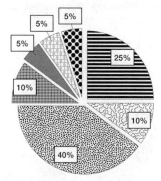

Program Phase: Year 1, 3rd Quarter—March, April, and May

Assumption: Activities for the current class shifts to job placement. If a community placement service is part of the team, the teacher focuses on placement in the host site and collaborates with the community placement service. The teacher also increases activities for recruitment and selection of next year's class.

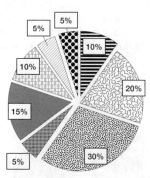

Program Phase: Year 1, 4th Quarter—June, July, and August

Assumption: The teacher will need to have 20 contracted days between June and August to finalize job placement activities for the current class, complete intake process for incoming class, set up new internships, and complete billing paperwork for funding agencies.

Role: Job Coach

▤ **Student recruitment:** organize school presentations, information sessions, tours, skills assessment days, student interviews, selection process and perform associated tasks such as application process selection rubric and eligibility determination

▦ **Internships:** identify and analyze potential internship locations, develop task designs for internship areas, provide job coaching, monitor and evaluate intern progress, provide education and communicate with internship site staff, and create job accommodations

▦ **Job development:** analyze employment climate, connect with community employers, build vocational profiles for interns, provide individual job search activities, and facilitate supports for competitive employment

▦ **Meetings and marketing:** develop and utilize marketing tools and facilitate Business Advisory Committee, intern employment-planning meetings, individualized education program (IEP) meetings, and other problem-solving team meetings

▦ **Teaching and curriculum:** orientation to host business, individual, and group classroom instruction

▦ **Training and staff development:** participate in Project SEARCH®–sponsored training, prepare and deliver family involvement curriculum, and prepare and deliver program information to internal and external partners

▧ **Technical assistance:** work with the internal Project SEARCH team on program development and continuous improvement

▩ **Paperwork:** process licensing agreement, intern attendance sheets, Commission on Accreditation of Rehabilitation Facilities (CARF) reports, intern progress reports, billing to funders, grant-related reports; create materials for interns and businesses

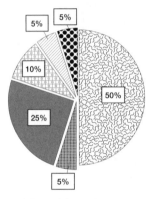

Program Phase: Planning Year, 4th Quarter—June, July, and August

Assumption: The job coach will need to be hired by July or early August and have 10–15 contracted days during this quarter. Some days will be needed before the program begins so that the Job Coach can complete the host business orientation, receive training related to Project SEARCH® programming, and assist the teacher to develop initial internship sites within the host business. Once the program begins, the job coach's primary responsibilities are internship training and teaching job skills.

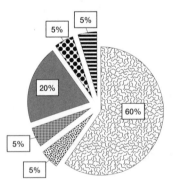

Program Phase: Year 1, 1st Quarter—September, October, and November

Assumption: The interns are placed in their first rotation (department worksite) by early to middle September. Job coaches use a majority of their time in late August and early September to prepare standard work (task designs) for internship departments.

Figure 3.2. Job coach responsibilities.

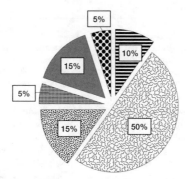

Program Phase: Year 1, 2nd Quarter—December, January, and February

Assumption: The job coach remains focused on internships and teaching job skills, including task designs, task analysis, and job accommodations. Other activities include assisting with job development and recruitment activities.

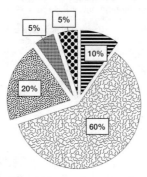

Program Phase: Year 1, 3rd Quarter—March, April, and May

Assumption: Activities related to successful internships continue. It is critical to identify teaching/coaching strategies for the intern as the job placement phase intensifies. Coaches also will assist with new student recruitment activities and job placement planning.

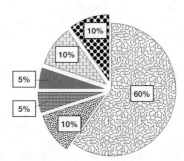

Program Phase: Year 1, 4th Quarter—June, July, and August

Assumption: The job coach for the program may also be the coach assigned to the community job. If so, that will be the focus of the work. The coach will need contracted days during this quarter to participate in Project SEARCH training and review internship task designs in August.

Table 3.3. A typical day for a Project SEARCH student

Time*	Activity	Comments
8:00 a.m.–9:00 a.m.	In the classroom: employability skills class	Students sign in. Lessons are based on an approved Project SEARCH® curriculum that focuses on daily living/employability skills (i.e., team building, workplace navigation, safety, technology, social skills, communication, interviewing skills, money management, health and wellness, resume and career passport, job search skills, and keeping a job). Instruction follows an approved Project SEARCH curriculum.
9:00 a.m.–11:30 a.m.	At internship sites: morning session	Students participate in nonpaid job internships in departments throughout the host business. They rotate through three different internships throughout the school year and learn the core skills of entry-level jobs.
11:30 a.m.–12:00 p.m.	Lunch	Students may purchase a lunch or pack their own. Students are encouraged to eat with their co-workers and peers at the internship sites.
12:00 p.m.–2:00 p.m.	At internship sites: afternoon session	Students return to sponsoring department to continue learning job-specific and employability skills.
2:00 p.m.–2:30 p.m.	Reconvene in the classroom	At the end of the day, students have time in the classroom for reflection on the day's events, planning, and working on communication skills (journaling, group discussion). Students sign out at 2:30 p.m. and, if available, take public transportation home.

*Project SEARCH follows the yearly calendar and daily start and dismissal schedule of the local school district. Make the host business aware of any holiday breaks, staff professional development days, and weather-related closures or days the students will be absent. This schedule can be flexible and responsive to the business's needs. For example, the curriculum could be taught at the end of the day if an earlier start time is needed to accommodate worksites at which mornings are particularly busy, as is often the case in hospitals and other health care settings. The "bookend" class times allow for maximum and immediate teaching opportunities. If one of the students has an issue with another co-worker or supervisor or a question arises regarding protocol or following the code of contact, the class can review the situation and have a discussion, role play, develop a T-chart, or use some other strategy to problem solve and address the new issue. The time spent on internships should equal 20 to 25 hours per week, which builds skills and stamina for a part- to full-time position.

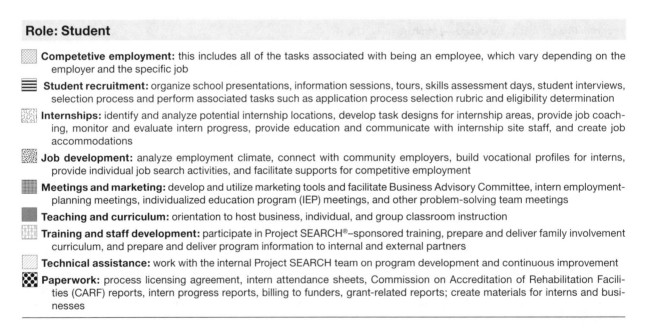

Role: Student

Competetive employment: this includes all of the tasks associated with being an employee, which vary depending on the employer and the specific job

Student recruitment: organize school presentations, information sessions, tours, skills assessment days, student interviews, selection process and perform associated tasks such as application process selection rubric and eligibility determination

Internships: identify and analyze potential internship locations, develop task designs for internship areas, provide job coaching, monitor and evaluate intern progress, provide education and communicate with internship site staff, and create job accommodations

Job development: analyze employment climate, connect with community employers, build vocational profiles for interns, provide individual job search activities, and facilitate supports for competitive employment

Meetings and marketing: develop and utilize marketing tools and facilitate Business Advisory Committee, intern employment-planning meetings, individualized education program (IEP) meetings, and other problem-solving team meetings

Teaching and curriculum: orientation to host business, individual, and group classroom instruction

Training and staff development: participate in Project SEARCH®–sponsored training, prepare and deliver family involvement curriculum, and prepare and deliver program information to internal and external partners

Technical assistance: work with the internal Project SEARCH team on program development and continuous improvement

Paperwork: process licensing agreement, intern attendance sheets, Commission on Accreditation of Rehabilitation Facilities (CARF) reports, intern progress reports, billing to funders, grant-related reports; create materials for interns and businesses

Figure 3.3. Student responsibilities. Pie charts at left indicate time spent on regular school-related tasks (gray) versus Project SEARCH tasks (black); charts at right break down the Project SEARCH tasks (see key above).

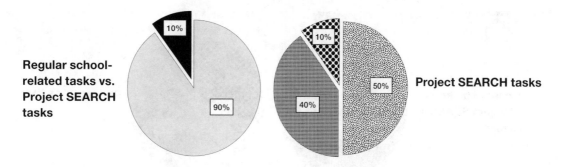

Program Phase: Preentry Year (when the student applies for entry into Project SEARCH), 1st Quarter—September, October, and November

Assumption: Potential students for Project SEARCH® are completing their academic credit requirements for graduation. Individualized education program (IEP) planning should include transition to work activities such as job shadowing, paid or unpaid work experiences, and career counseling. Students should have a vocational rehabilitation (VR) counselor in place and apply for developmental disabilities (DD) services. There are often work study, career tech or transition opportunities for students to prepare for a Project SEARCH program.

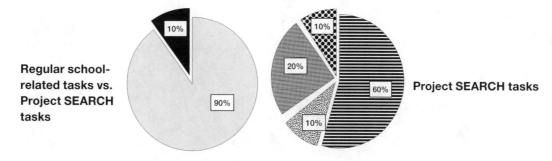

Program Phase: Preentry Year, 2nd Quarter—December, January, and February

Assumption: Students will receive information about Project SEARCH from teachers or vocational rehabilitation (VR) counselor and have access to the application process.

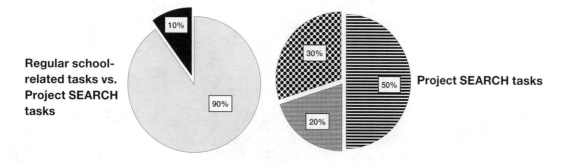

Program Phase: Preentry Year, 3rd Quarter—March, April, and May

Assumption: Students will complete the individualized education program (IEP) process and vocational rehabilitation (VR) planning process for participating in Project SEARCH in the fall.

(continued)

Figure 3.3. *(continued)*

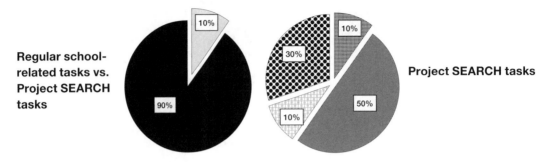

Regular school-related tasks vs. Project SEARCH tasks

Project SEARCH tasks

Program Phase: Preentry Year, 4th Quarter—June, July, and August

Assumption: Students will complete the host site entrance requirements, such as updated immunizations and background checks, and purchase work-related clothing. Travel training should be completed prior to beginning the program in August. Many students will participate in their school graduation but make arrangements to defer the acceptance of their diploma.

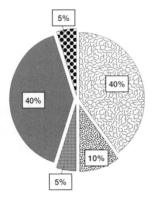

Program Phase: Program Year, 1st Quarter—September, October, and November

Assumption: Students will spend their entire day in orientation in the first 2 to 3 weeks of the program year. The first rotation will begin in early to mid-September.

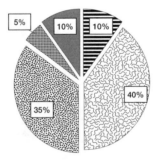

Program Phase: Program Year, 2nd Quarter—December, January, and February

Assumption: Students focus on successful internship completion. Classroom learning shifts from general employability skills to job-specific and job seeking skills. Students are valuable spokespersons for recruiting new students for the following year.

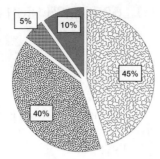

Program Phase: Program Year, 3rd Quarter—March, April, and May

Assumption: The students complete their final internship, which should be targeted to potential employment opportunities either in the host site or in a community business. The students work toward maximizing their skills and making the transition from intern to employee.

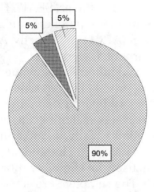

Program Phase: Program Year, 4th Quarter—June, July, and August

Assumption: The student completes processes for employment and works with a job coach to meet and exceed employer expectations. The student learns self-monitoring techniques to ensure maximum sustained performance. The student can be a useful team member for evaluating and improving the Project SEARCH program. If the student is not yet employed, job development replaces employment on the chart.

Monitoring Student Progress

Each student is carefully monitored throughout his or her time in the Project SEARCH program. This is achieved on a daily basis, through the student's regular contact with the teacher, job coaches, and worksite supervisors, co-workers, and mentors. In addition, the student's progress is tracked by a team that includes the student, family members, the teacher, the student's job coach, the student's VR counselor, the employment specialist, and others as appropriate. By interacting with this team, the student builds a network of people and resources to help in defining and reaching employment goals. Starting with an initial employment-planning meeting at the beginning of the school year, each student's team meets monthly or at least twice during each internship. At the meetings, the team reviews the student's progress on skill acquisition, discusses any challenges he or she may be encountering, and helps to plan for future internships. These meetings keep the focus on the goal of employment and ensure that each student has established realistic goals and that he or she is making steady progress toward those goals. The meetings also teach the students self-advocacy skills because they are expected to take over leadership of their team, invite the attendees, plan the agenda, present their progress, and facilitate the meetings as the year progresses.

THE ANNUAL TIMELINE FOR THE PROJECT SEARCH HIGH SCHOOL TRANSITION PROGRAM

Recruitment and Admissions

Each Project SEARCH site carries out its own independent recruitment program. One of the first methods of outreach is an information session for prospective students, families, and school special education staff. Other stakeholders who should be invited include the host business personnel involved in the program, VR staff, DD and supported employment agency staff, and representatives from any other agencies that might be involved or interested in becoming involved. Currently enrolled students should take part in the information session where they can act as greeters and, along with their internship manager or mentor, give firsthand information about their internships and other aspects of participating in Project SEARCH. This is a rewarding experience for the students, a way to engage the business departments, and a very effective way to communicate the value of the program.

Typically, students are referred to Project SEARCH through their schools, but they can also enter through other routes. Sometimes, parents learn about Project SEARCH through word of mouth and contact the Project SEARCH site directly. Alternately, VR counselors or other service providers might be the source of a referral.

Student applications are submitted in the winter and spring in the year prior to entering the program. The selection process is overseen by the local Project SEARCH teacher with extensive input from the Advisory Board or an ad hoc student-selection committee that represents all Project SEARCH partners including the host business. After the initial review of the applications, eligible candidates are invited to tour the program individually or in groups and participate in hands-on assessments. The students are then interviewed and scored by the members of the selection team using an eligibility rubric. A sample showing 2 of the 17 strands of the rubric are in Figure 3.5. The complete Project SEARCH Student Selection Rubric Guide is available in Appendix 3.1.

At this stage of selection, the process to determine VR eligibility should begin for prospective students. Once the applications are complete, the selection committee reviews the candidates and makes their selections based on the application, the tour, on-site assessment information, the interview, the rubric score, their VR eligibility status, and other pertinent observations. The rubric is not a tool to screen students out of the program but, rather, a vehicle for conversation about each applicant. Indeed, candidates with perfect scores generally do not need the program to gain skills and employment. However, to gauge the likelihood of success for a given candidate, teams should also consider important criteria such as prior work experi-

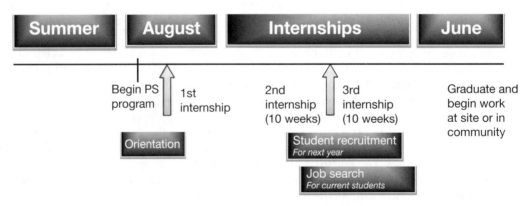

Figure 3.4. Time line of Project SEARCH® (PS) year.

Student name_____ **Date completed**_____ **Completed by**_____

TOTAL SCORE (out of a possible 85):

Criteria	1	2	3	4	5
Age and school status	Younger than 18 or older than 22 years of age.	Student has had 2 or more possible years of school eligibility, lacks maturity, and is working toward skills for employment.	Student needs one or two credit requirements for graduation and these can be fulfilled through participation in the Project SEARCH® High School Transition Program.	Student has had 2 possible years of school eligibility remaining but has agreed that this will be the last year and has the end goal of employment.	Student will be in last school year of eligibility and has all credits necessary for high school graduation.
Commitment to community employment	Student is unsure of interest in community employment.	Student is unsure of interest in community employment but parent is supportive and encouraging.	Student demonstrates commitment to work but has significant restrictions such as inappropriate work goal, location, type of work, and so on.	One member of the team— student or family member—may be noncommittal to the goal of community employment.	Student and family are committed, are appropriate, and will be flexible to meet the work goal.
The complete rubric, which is presented in its entirety in the Appendix 3.1., includes 15 additional scoring criteria.					
				TOTAL SCORE	85

Figure 3.5. Project SEARCH® Student Selection Rubric Guide High School Transition Program (excerpt).

ence, communication skills, attendance, family support, and most importantly, the desire to work competitively.

Like many other Project SEARCH tools, the Eligibility Rubric can be adapted for individual programs, states, and teams. The template has 17 components or strands and the student is scored on a scale of 1 to 5 for each of these, such that the highest possible score is 85. Most transition-age students with developmental disabilities (or even a typical youth) will not score an 85. If they did, it is likely that they could transition successfully from school to work on their own. Many Project SEARCH teams are looking for candidates who score in the 50 to 70 range and who have motivation and basic transition skills that can be developed during the program year.

Several things influence how the rubric might be adapted:

- Selection teams are sometimes uncomfortable with a total score of 85 instead of the traditional 100, so alter the rubric accordingly.

- The meaning and relevance of some rubric components (such as transportation) will vary depending on such things as the makeup of the program site team, the geography and culture, and host business priorities.

The rubric should be just one of several ways to evaluate a candidate's potential for success, and teams should feel free to adapt it to fit their situation. Many teams have added additional components to evaluate skills that are specific to the requirements of their host business. Other teams, after a year of operating a Project SEARCH program, will choose in the second year to give double weight to items that proved problematic in the first year. For example, an inner-city program that grappled with poor attendance in the first year gave double weight to this factor in the second year. Other groups have developed ways to evaluate certain skills through a hands-on assessment session at the host business. This eliminates the need for estimating the corresponding score on the rubric and allows the team to reduce the number of strands to include only those components that they did not directly observe during the hands-on assessments.

One example of a team using the rubric in tandem with other evaluation tools involved a new program at Grady Memorial Hospital in Delaware, Ohio. There were over 25 applicants for 9 Project SEARCH slots in Year 1 of the program. The program planning team, which doubled as the student-selection team, scheduled a skills assessment day in March, approximately 5 months before the program start date. Before that day, part of the group met to narrow the applicant pool from 25 to 16 candidates through a prescreening system based on age, work experience, and school attendance. The 16 candidates then came to the hospital for 3 hours (eight students in the morning and eight students in the afternoon) for the assessment day. During each 3-hour block, students participated in skills that mirrored tasks they might be doing as part of the internships. These skills were designed by one of the business liaisons. The students were coached and observed by half of the members of the planning team. Another business liaison from the human resources department led the other half of the team in interviewing the candidates individually. The hospital created a very welcoming environment with snacks and greetings from various staff members for all the students. After all the students left the hospital, the entire planning team convened and utilized an adapted rubric with 10 strands to rank the students. The resulting scores were combined with information gained from the skills assessments and interviews. By the end of the day, the team had identified a slate of students and two alternates.

When students are not accepted into a local Project SEARCH program, families can ask for an appeal. We recommended that implementation teams establish a formalized process for such appeals. First, the selection committee should establish a separate, objective appeal committee. It can be small, with as few as 3 members, and should consist of people who were not part of the original selection process or who are not familiar with the applicant in question. The following are some individuals who might be appropriate for the appeals committee:

- A guidance counselor or special education staff member from the high school sponsoring the Project SEARCH program site

- A VR counselor who is not presently serving the Project SEARCH program involved in the appeal

- A staff member from the local DD agency who is familiar with transition services

The appeals committee should receive information from the selection committee on the student applicant and the reasons she or he was not accepted into the program. The family involved with the appeal should then be scheduled to appear in front of the appeals committee at a time convenient for all involved. The next step is for the committee to interview the student and ask questions that address topics such as prior work experience, school activities, community involvement, and commitment to competitive employment. The parent or other family member should then have the opportunity to speak to the committee and address why the Project SEARCH program would be beneficial for his or her young adult. The committee can then ask the family members questions that may clarify issues that may be barriers to success in the program. Directly after these two interviews, the appeals committee should discuss the information and make a recommendation for acceptance or denial into the program. This recommendation, along with the documentation on which the recommendation is based, should be given to the selection committee so they can use it to make a final decision. If the final recommendation is to *not* accept the student into the Project SEARCH program, the members should list the reasons along with other transition options for the family to consider.

Summer

The selection process should be completed in time for new students to be notified of their acceptance into the program in the spring, allowing time to develop an IEP and ensure VR eligibility. This schedule also allows the summer before program entry to be used for preparation, orientation, assessment activities, and a Benefits Analysis (a tool usually provided through the local Social Security Administration or DD organization to help clarify the positive impact of competitive work and provide very specific information to each family about how their government benefits will be affected.

Summer orientation activities could include a home visit or meeting in which the teacher discusses the scope and goals of the program with the student and the family members. In turn, the teacher gets a sense of the student's home life through these visits. The Project SEARCH Family Involvement Curriculum should be introduced in the spring or summer before the program begins. This program gives transition information, helps families develop goals related to achieving employment, sets the tone, and establishes the expectation that families will be a critical part of each student intern's success in the program. The specific roles and responsibilities of the families during the application process and throughout the Project SEARCH program year are outlined in Figure 3.6.

Summertime family engagement activities, such as picnics or other informal gatherings, are important for team building and developing camaraderie among the cohort of students and their families. These get-togethers can also be opportunities to share expectations such as independent travel, attendance, behavior, dress, the goal of employment, the family's role in student progress meetings, and so on and to provide information such as advice on managing Social Security issues.

Transportation to the program site is an important issue that is addressed in the summer. The student's home school is ultimately responsible for facilitating travel training or making other arrangements if independent travel is not possible. Students are strongly encouraged to travel independently, and the teacher often will work with the student and family to begin travel training over the summer. VR is often involved and may financially support this activity in partnership with the school and supported employment agency.

Part of an incoming student's summer preparations will be to fulfill the host business's requirements for access to the worksite. These will vary with the specific business and industry sector but often include a criminal background check, updated immunizations and tuberculosis test (especially relevant in a health care environment), and a drug screen. Most businesses will also require that the Project SEARCH students wear an

The Project SEARCH Family Involvement Curriculum

Because parents and other caregivers play such a critical role in a student's success, Project SEARCH developed a Family Involvement Curriculum to accompany the High School Transition Program. The Project SEARCH Family Involvement Curriculum involves several sessions to be delivered throughout the school year. They are facilitated by a designated parent partner or team of designated parents (and often the Project SEARCH teacher). The parent partners could be alumni parents who have children who have completed the Project SEARCH program. These sessions should be attended by all parents or caregivers of students currently enrolled in the Project SEARCH High School Transition Program.

Session 1: Family Involvement Introduction

Families are prepared to understand the shared commitment and responsibility of the Project SEARCH program and their involvement in the employment process.

Session 2: Social Security Benefits

Local experts provide information on topics such as Supplemental Security Income, Social Security Disability Income, Medicaid, Medicare, Plan to Achieve Self-Support (PASS), impairment-related work expenses (IRWE), and work incentives planning and assistance (WIPA).

Session 3: Expectations of Employment

This session involves a discussion of family and student responsibilities in regard to seeking job opportunities. The goal is 100% employment for Project SEARCH interns so families and interns are encouraged to clarify their expectations in regard to job selection.

Session 4: Family Involvement Beyond Project SEARCH

This session can be customized to the current cohort to address their specific issues and circumstances. For example, some topics might be parenting, recreation options, and financial planning.

Role: Family Members

▨ **Competetive employment:** this includes all of the tasks associated with being an employee, which vary depending on the employer and the specific job

▤ **Student recruitment:** organize school presentations, information sessions, tours, skills assessment days, student interviews, selection process; perform associated tasks such as application process selection rubric and eligibility determination

▨ **Internships:** identify and analyze potential internship locations, develop task designs for internship areas, provide job coaching, monitor and evaluate intern progress, provide education and communicate with internship site staff, and create job accommodations

▨ **Job development:** analyze employment climate, connect with community employers, build vocational profiles for interns, provide individual job search activities, and facilitate supports for competitive employment

▨ **Meetings and marketing:** develop and utilize marketing tools and facilitate Business Advisory Committee, intern employment-planning meetings, individualized education program (IEP) meetings, and other problem-solving team meetings

■ **Teaching and curriculum:** orientation to host business, individual, and group classroom instruction

▦ **Training and staff development:** participate in Project SEARCH®–sponsored training, prepare and deliver family involvement curriculum, and prepare and deliver program information to internal and external partners

▨ **Technical assistance**: work with the internal Project SEARCH team on program development and continuous improvement

▨ **Paperwork:** process licensing agreement, intern attendance sheets, Commission on Accreditation of Rehabilitation Facilities (CARF) reports, intern progress reports, billing to funders, grant-related reports; create materials for interns and businesses

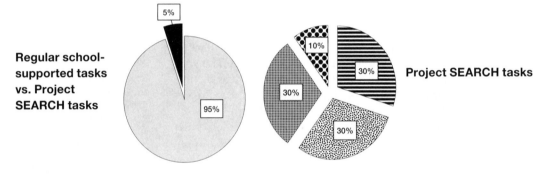

Program Phase: Year: Preentry Year, 1st and 2nd Quarters—September through February

Assumption: Family members of students who are interested in the Project SEARCH® program should make sure the student is referred for developmental disabilities services and vocational rehabilitation services. They also will be a valuable support in helping the student work on independence skills at home and in community volunteer settings.

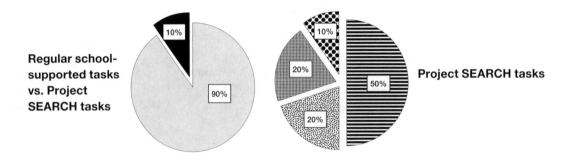

Program Phase: Preentry Year, 3rd Quarter—March, April, and May

Assumption: Families will receive program and application information from teachers, vocational rehabilitation, and developmental disabilities agencies.

Figure 3.6. Family responsibilities. Pie charts at left indicate time spent on regular school-supported tasks (gray) versus Project SEARCH tasks (black); charts at right break down the Project SEARCH tasks (see key above).

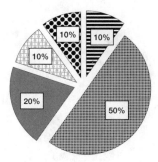

Program Phase: Preentry Year, 4th Quarter—June, July, and August

Assumption: Families will assist the student with travel training and meeting the requirements of the host business, such as updated immunizations, background checks, and proper attire.

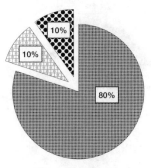

Program Phase: Program Year 1, 1st Quarter—September, October, and November

Assumption: Families are valuable partners as the program develops an individual training and employment plan for the intern. It is critical that families participate in monthly employment planning meetings, internship planning, and activities associated with building the intern's general employability skills.

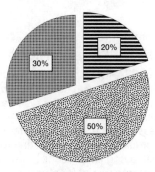

Program Phase: Program Year, 2nd Quarter—December, January, and February

Assumption: As job placement planning progresses, families are valuable resources for job placement leads. Families can also assist the program with recruitment of new students.

(continued)

Figure 3.6. *(continued)*

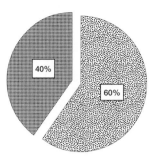

Program Phase: Program Year, 3rd Quarter—March, April, and May

Assumption: Families are vital to the job placement process. They provide job leads and work with the team to support the job goals.

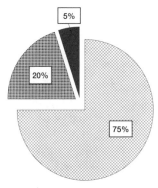

Program Phase: Program Year, 4th Quarter—June, July, and August

Assumption: As interns gain employment, families continue to be their strongest support. Their focus will be on activities to help the intern transition from intern to employee. If the intern is not employed, the focus will remain on job development activities.

PITFALLS IN OBTAINING THE BUSINESS IDENTIFICATION BADGE

Worksite immersion is critical to the Project SEARCH model, and it is the biggest factor in our success. However, there are logistical challenges that come along with having school transition take place in a business. For example, to issue an identification badge, most hospitals require a two-step tuberculosis test. This means scheduling four visits for each student over the course of 9 days. The timing is highly structured, and if any of the four visits are missed, the entire process must be started over from the beginning. Another common point of stress is drug screening. Urinalysis for drug screening can be an invasive and uncomfortable procedure for anyone, and especially so for someone with a cognitive disability who may not understand the reasons for the strict rules and lack of privacy. Another common barrier for students in gaining the business identification (ID) badge is the lack of a state-issued picture ID. Many Project SEARCH students do not drive and, therefore, don't have drivers' licenses. If their families or teachers haven't worked with them to make sure that they have a state-issued ID, they won't be able to even initiate the process of gaining access to the worksite.

Clearly, it's difficult to get all of these things done for all of the students, and it becomes even more difficult once the students are out of school and have gone their separate ways for the summer. But, with some advance planning, we have found that many things can be done to help things go more smoothly. It takes some coordination on the part of the teacher and job coaches, but it can make all the difference in terms of reducing stress and achieving an on-time start for all the students. Project SEARCH teachers should encourage and facilitate taking care of many of these items in the spring after students are accepted into the program but are still in school and, thus, are still a "captive audience." Another strategy is for the teacher or a job coach to arrange times for the students to come in and take care of these requirements as a group over the summer before the program begins. This is helpful with regard to simplifying the scheduling and also can reduce stress by allowing for some preparation and explanation for the young people as well as for the person who is administering these tests.

identification badge at the workplace. The badging process may be completed during the summer so that the student will have full access as soon as the program starts.

The Project SEARCH Annual International Conference takes place in a different U.S. city every summer. This is where the professionals and families involved in Project SEARCH sites around the country come together to share their successes, lessons learned, and insights gained through their work in administrating and participating in Project SEARCH programs. Although it is by no means necessary for incoming students and their families to attend, for those who are able to get there, it's an excellent venue for gaining a deeper understanding of Project SEARCH and networking with other families and disability professionals.

The summer is also a time of preparation for the Project SEARCH staff. The teacher, job coaches, and business liaison can use this time to identify new internship sites and develop job and task analyses for those internships and to think about potential adaptations that might be useful at those sites. It is also a convenient time to provide education to the host business about Project SEARCH on topics such as disability issues, supervision strategies, and the goal of internships. During the summer, the teacher might also choose to work with the Advisory Board to review the Project SEARCH classroom curriculum and to discuss how it can be customized for the host business.

Orientation and Assessment

The annual schedule of the Project SEARCH school year is governed by the local school calendar, but the students do not spend any time at the home school. At most sites, the program start date is mid-August or early September, and once the school year starts, the students come to the business every weekday for a full school day.

The first few weeks of the program are focused on student assessment and orientation to the work environment. Students undergo a specially designed vocational assessment with their teacher. The assessment explores functional math and reading skills that relate to the individual internships as well as basic job skills. The specific job skills will vary depending on the nature of the host business; however, certain core skills—such as filing, computer skills, telephone use, materials handling, and the ability to follow instructions and solve problems—are important in nearly any business setting.

To become oriented to the host business facilities and culture, the students participate in "way-finding" exercises; review the business's employee code of conduct; hear presentations by representatives of the host business on the mission and core values of the business and how the students contribute; learn about and practice communication protocols in use at the business; and complete any mandatory employee education, such as safety and confidentiality training.

After this more general orientation, the students become involved in activities that specifically prepare them for their internships, which will take place over three 10-week rotations at worksites throughout the business. These include touring the potential internship sites, creating a resume and cover letter, and practicing interviewing skills.

Classroom Activities

A typical day at a Project SEARCH High School Transition program site begins with a 1-hour classroom session. During this time, students work on lessons from a functional curriculum that stresses employability and independent-living skills. Classroom activities are designed around 12 major focus areas: team building, workplace navigation, workplace safety, technology, social skills, presentation skills, interviewing skills, money management, health and wellness, resume development, job search skills, and job retention skills. Some examples of specific lesson topics include beginning and more advanced computer skills; effective verbal, nonverbal, written, and electronic communication; and personal budgeting. In the beginning of the year, lessons are focused on general skills needed to function in the workplace, such as learning to navigate and get around within the business, making good choices in the cafeteria, and appropriate dress and grooming. The curriculum is flexible so that, as the year goes on and the teacher gets to know the students better, the teacher can customize the curriculum to accommodate the specific needs and interests of the students and the business as they arise. This flexibility helps to ensure a meaningful and successful experience for participants, as well as to provide responsiveness to the business. Even though we have an entire academic year with the students, the time goes quickly. In order to reach our goal of competitive employment for each intern, we must ensure that every activity, every lesson, and every skill gained contributes to reaching this important objective.

Linkages

In the Project SEARCH High School Transition model, linkages to adult services are established before high school eligibility ends and, ideally, before the students begin the program. This is important because young people with disabilities run the risk of "falling through the cracks" as they move from the consolidated support system of the school environment to the more fragmented world of adult services (Certo, Mautz, Pumpian, Sax, Smiley, Wade, et al., 2003; Certo & Luecking 2006). A relationship with a VR counselor is usually among the first linkages made for a Project SEARCH student because VR eligibility is typically a requirement for entry into the program. Moreover, Project SEARCH teachers are familiar with other community resources and are able to assist students in accessing those services as the need arises. These might include DD services; psychological services; or specific services related to hearing, speech, or visual impairments.

Linkages to appropriate services in the community are particularly important as students prepare to graduate from the program to ensure a successful transition to employment and adult life. Specific availability of services varies with the locale, but in most cases, assistance with necessary adaptations required to perform a specific job, job coaching, as well as job development and long-term follow-along can be arranged through the local VR Services Commission, the Administration on DD, or both. Locally based and disability-specific organizations are additional sources of needed services. The array of services and the way they are delivered can vary from state to state and often use a regional or county approach. In many states, VR does not provide direct services but instead vends with supported employment or community rehabilitation partners (CRPs). The vendor (CRP) provides consistent personnel in accordance with the provision of the Project SEARCH model concerning the need for "consistent, on-site staff."

Worksite Internships

The hallmark of the Project SEARCH model of high school transition is a series of supervised internships through which students build communication and problem-solving skills, as well as job-specific skills (for more detail, see Chapter 4). These are unpaid student internships—analogous to the clinical rotations that are part of every medical school curriculum and the internships that are often used to incorporate career-specific training and experience for undergraduate college students. The internships should be chosen strategically to ensure that the students learn marketable, competitive, transferable skills.

Potential internship sites are identified through a continuous collaborative process involving the teacher, the job coach, the business liaison, and specific worksite supervisors. For the students, work rotations begin after the orientation period, with staggered start dates so that each student has access to individualized attention from the teacher and a job coach on her or his first day of a new internship and beyond, as needed. Students usually participate in three different internships over the course of the program. The student and teacher work together to choose worksites based on that student's previous work experience, interests, specific career goals, and skills assessment.

Monthly Employment–Planning Meetings

Monthly employment planning meetings are an important aspect of the Project SEARCH High School Transition Program through which the core members of each student's team convene monthly to discuss the student's progress. In the beginning of the year, the focus is on the internships and the skills the student is acquiring. By the second internship, the focus should shift to employment goals and job development. Students should lead the meetings and could utilize technology, such as a PowerPoint presentation or a video, to demonstrate their progress.

Transition Weeks

Between each of the three 10-week rotations in internships, the students spend a week in the classroom. The names for these intervals vary from site to site, but they are often called "workshop" or "transition" weeks. These weeks fill a scheduling need by facilitating the staggering of internship rotation start dates. In addition, they give students the opportunity to regroup, review the skills they learned on their previous internships, update their resumes, add samples of their work to their portfolios, and start preparing for the next internship as the cycle begins again. These weeks also afford the time to present additional curriculum topics or to reinforce those that need to be revisited. It's also a good opportunity to host guest speakers to broaden the students' perspectives on topics related to employment or independent-living skills. This can be likened to the ongoing professional development and training that any employee might engage in to enhance job success and career advancement.

Job Development and Employment

Starting in the second half of the school year, the emphasis shifts to refining skills, finalizing the career goal, and carrying out an individualized job search. The provision of job development services vary from site to site and state to state. Because most supported employment agencies vend their services with VR, they can negotiate a rate and service delivery method on an individual basis. In some places, the job coach and job developer are the same person and share these duties. In other places, the job coach and job developer are separate people. In any case, each Project SEARCH team should design their job development plan in the summer before the program begins. That way, the roles and responsibilities can be sorted out and job

---

Monthly Employment–Planning Meetings

The monthly employment-planning meetings are a critical feature of the Project SEARCH model of high school transitions. They offer a level of communication, planning, and strategic thinking that is highly unusual among transition programs. The purpose is for each student's team members to exchange information regarding the internships, skill acquisition, and the job search process. They are meant to be short (30–45 minutes) and student-led. These individual meetings keep all team members "on the same page" and identify ways to support the intern to reach his or her end goal of competitive employment. Some Project SEARCH programs have the meetings during 1 day each month; others schedule them during an entire week after school so that the job coaches can attend once the daily internships are finished. Every effort should be made to accommodate the parent's/family's schedule. Getting all the meetings on the calendar at the beginning of the school year will make it easier to have the meetings at the same time each month, which is one way to ensure attendance of all team members. The job search process should be determined before the beginning of the Project SEARCH program to ensure that the right people are at the meetings.

Students should begin leading the meeting as early in the school year as possible (with the goal of starting this practice by the second meeting). Many sites encourage students to utilize technology to share their information, e.g. with a PowerPoint or iPad presentation. There are many tools the interns can utilize to share the information at the monthly meetings:

- Internship evaluations
- Electronic and paper portfolio documents
- Training matrix forms that document progress in skill acquisition
- Low- and high-technology accommodations and adaptations
- Written career goals (possibly in the individual plan for employment)

Purpose/Agenda

- Review skill acquisition during the current internships.
- Plan for next internship.
- Address any barriers that may be affecting skill development.
- Discuss needed accommodations and adaptations at the internship.
- Plan for job development employment.

Frequency

Monthly Student Progress Meetings should be held every 4 to 6 weeks (at least twice during each internship).

(continued)

(continued)

Monthly Meeting Members

- Student intern*
- Project SEARCH instructor*
- Job coach (if possible)
- Family member*
- Vocational rehabilitation counselor*
- Job developer* (if different from the job coach—this person should be attending the meeting at least by January)
- If necessary, support personnel such as case managers, occupational therapists, physical therapists, or speech consultants
- Internship managers and business liaisons (these are always welcome but not necessary. The Project SEARCH instructor, job coach, or student can get the information from the internship manager to share at the monthly meeting)

*Denotes team member whose attendance is essential.

development can begin smoothly. The employment specialist from the supported employment agency takes the lead in the job search for a given student, but all the members of a student's team should be involved. Family members and other team members are excellent sources for information on possible job opportunities. Job development is based on the student's experiences, strengths, preferences, and skills. It is important that the job developer attends the student's monthly employment-planning meetings so that he or she can bring to bear all available information about the student, such as individual interests, skills, work behavior, adaptations, and preferences with regard to locale, as the job search progresses. The job developer's role and how it evolves throughout program planning and implementation, and throughout the program year, is depicted in Figure 3.7.

Project SEARCH programs are increasingly integrating technology the job search process. For example, students are creating PowerPoint presentations to document their internships, upload-

Role: Job Developer

▤ **Student recruitment:** organize school presentations, information sessions, tours, skills assessment days, student interviews, selection process and perform associated tasks such as application process selection rubric and eligibility determination

▨ **Internships:** identify and analyze potential internship locations, develop task designs for internship areas, provide job coaching, monitor and evaluate intern progress, provide education and communicate with internship site staff, and create job accommodations

▨ **Job development:** analyze employment climate, connect with community employers, build vocational profiles for interns, provide individual job search activities, and facilitate supports for competitive employment

▨ **Meetings and marketing:** develop and utilize marketing tools and facilitate Business Advisory Committee, intern employment-planning meetings, individualized education program (IEP) meetings, and other problem-solving team meetings

■ **Teaching and curriculum:** orientation to host business, individual, and group classroom instruction

▦ **Training and staff development:** participate in Project SEARCH®–sponsored training, prepare and deliver family involvement curriculum, and prepare and deliver program information to internal and external partners

▨ **Technical assistance:** work with the internal Project SEARCH team on program development and continuous improvement

▨ **Paperwork:** process licensing agreement, intern attendance sheets, Commission on Accreditation of Rehabilitation Facilities (CARF) reports, intern progress reports, billing to funders, grant-related reports; create materials for interns and businesses

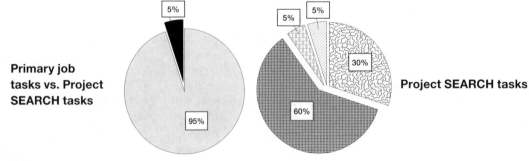

Primary job tasks vs. Project SEARCH tasks

Project SEARCH tasks

Program Phase: Planning Year, 1st Quarter through 4th Quarter

Assumption: A Project SEARCH® job developer may be from a community rehabilitation agency or the educational system. The roles for the job developer in the planning process may be to learn about the program, assist the planning team to identify a host business, and assist the staff to identify quality internships that can match jobs in the community.

Figure 3.7. Job developer responsibilities. Pie charts at left indicate time spent on primary job tasks (gray) versus Project SEARCH tasks (black); charts at right break down the Project SEARCH tasks (see key above).

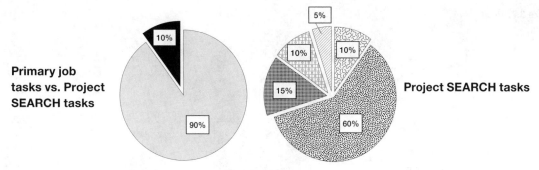

Primary job tasks vs. Project SEARCH tasks

Project SEARCH tasks

Program Phase: Year 1, 1st Quarter—September, October, and November

Assumption: A job developer is a valuable resource for the teacher and staff because he or she develops quality internships that build the skills necessary for jobs in the community. Although the job developer may not be directly involved in the program planning or the first half of the program year, the developer typically has knowledge and experience that may be useful for teacher and job coach training.

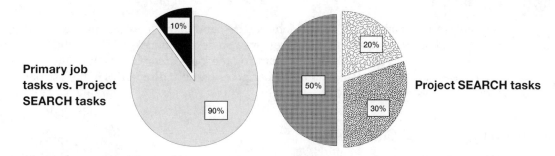

Primary job tasks vs. Project SEARCH tasks

Project SEARCH tasks

Program Phase: Year 1, 2nd Quarter—December, January, and February

Assumption: The job developer becomes more involved in the program activities during this quarter. He or she should attend monthly meetings and be part of the job planning process. Also, he or she continues to a consult for the staff in developing quality internships.

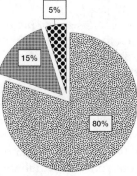

Program Phase: Year 1, 3rd Quarter—March, April, and May

Assumption: The job developer provides intense individualized job development during this quarter. The percentage of time for primary job versus Project SEARCH tasks depends upon how many consumers the job developer serves.

(continued)

Figure 3.7. *(continued)*

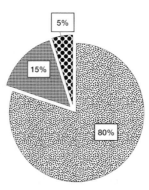

Program Phase: Year 1, 4th Quarter—June, July, and August

Assumption: The job developer continues intense individualized job development during this quarter. The percentage of time for primary job versus Project SEARCH tasks depends upon how many consumers the job developer serves.

ing their resumes and doing virtual job searches, and using iPads for picture task lists, social stories, and other accommodations. They are also developing ePortfolios, which will improve their overall technology skills while enhancing the job search process. It is important that our students are able to compete with any other peers without disabilities in the use of both mainstream and assistive technology.

Program Completion and Graduation

Upon satisfactory completion of the program (95% or better attendance, good attitude, successful skill acquisition at each job site), many students receive a "Career Passport." The contents of this packet will vary among Project SEARCH program sites but will usually include a resume, letters of recommendation, a competency profile, any awards or special recognition received while in the program, and a certificate from the education partner. The Career Passport gives a prospective employer a thorough and accurate picture of the capabilities and experience of the student and, as such, has proven to be very helpful in guiding hiring decisions.

Project SEARCH defines a successful outcome as competitive employment in the community with a work schedule of at least 20 hours per week and pay at the prevailing wage. The program lasts for a full school year, and the goal is to achieve competitive employment for each student within 3 months after the end of the school year. Sometimes, a situation arises in which a student excels in an internship and the host business wants to hire a Project SEARCH intern into an open position before the school year ends. This practice is encouraged if it is determined that the job is a good fit for the student and that it meets the Project SEARCH criteria for a successful employment outcome. If a student is hired during the school year, she or he can retain student status for school funding and insurance purposes. If having the diploma is a criterion for accepting the position, the student can accept the diploma at this point. When hired, the student should assume the schedule and persona of a young worker in that business with support and assistance from the Project SEARCH team.

At the end of the school year, each Project SEARCH site plans and implements a completion ceremony or graduation, which is usually held at the host business. This event is an important way to recognize the accomplishments of the student interns and to highlight employment outcomes. It is also an excellent opportunity to publicly thank the host business, internship managers, the families, and the Project SEARCH partner agencies. It's a good idea to involve all partners in the event as speakers, planners, or recognized guests. Giving students an active role in planning and implementing the event makes it especially rewarding for them and provides another opportunity for learning teamwork, organizational skills, and good communication.

Project SEARCH® Student Selection Rubric Guide
High School Transition Program

Student name _____ Date completed _____ Completed by _____

TOTAL SCORE (OUT OF A POSSIBLE 85): [ ]

Criteria	1	2	3	4	5
Age and school status	Under 18 or over 22 years of age.	Student has had 2 or more possible years of school eligibility, lacks maturity, and is working toward skills for employment.	Student needs one or two credit requirements for graduation and can be fulfilled through participation in the Project SEARCH High School Transition Program.	Student has had 2 possible years of school eligibility remaining but student agreed that this will be the last year and has the end goal of employment.	Student will be in last school year of eligibility and has all credits necessary for high school graduation.
Commitment to community employment	Student is unsure of interest in community employment.	Student is unsure of interest in community employment, but parent is supportive and encouraging.	Student demonstrates commitment to work but has significant restrictions such as inappropriate work goal, location, or type of work.	One member of the team—student or family member—may be noncommittal to the goal of community employment.	Student and family are committed, are appropriate, and will be flexible to meet the work goal.
Attendance	10+ unexcused absences.	10+ excused and unexcused absences or tardies within the past school year.	5–10 excused and unexcused absences or tardies within the past school year.	1–5 excused absences or tardies within the past school year.	Student has no absences or tardies within the past school year.
Independent daily living and self-care skills	Student has very poor or no independent daily living and self-care skills. She or he may rely on parents and staff for some basic needs to be met.	Student has not been exposed to any daily living skills training but displays some skills in these areas and in self-care. Team should begin planning for training/practice in these areas.	Student has participated in limited or informal training for daily living and self-care skills. She or he can demonstrate minimal skills in these areas. If toileting and feeding are still dependent, team could investigate accommodations.	Through training, the student demonstrates basic proficiency in daily living skills and self-care skills. Self-care skills include toileting, feeding, taking medication, and bathing.	Student practices and demonstrates daily living and self-care skills such as cooking, sleeping, budgeting, and handling money and is also able to take care of self-care needs independently.
Appearance and professional presentation	Student does not possess any personal hygiene skills and clothes are not neat and clean.	Student needs assistance in making sure clean clothes are worn daily. Personal appearance may vary each day.	Student wears neat and clean clothing and has appropriate grooming on most days.	Student is neat, clean, and well groomed but makes inappropriate clothing choices for work based on place of business, dress code, and weather.	Student possesses good personal hygiene skills and will always arrive to Project SEARCH and/or work neat and clean, according to the dress code and weather.

(continued)
page 1 of 3

High School Transition That Works: Lessons Learned from Project SEARCH® by Maryellen Daston, J. Erin Riehle, and Susan Rutkowski.

Criteria	1	2	3	4	5
Transportation	Student is not eligible, has not been trained in any independent method, and family does not have the resources to provide transportation.	Family is willing to provide ongoing transportation to the Project SEARCH and/or community worksite.	Student is eligible for transportation from outside resources like DD or other disability-related service.	Student can utilize public transportation including a door-to-door system with basic skills.	Student can utilize public transportation and/or a door-to-door system as well as other transportation options (e.g., calling a cab).
Appropriate social and behavior skills	Student frequently displays inappropriate social and behavior skills.	Student periodically displays inappropriate social and behavior skills.	Student is appropriate in the presence of adult supervision but is not independent.	Student displays appropriate social and behavior skills in most situations.	Student displays appropriate social and behavior skills in all (or nearly all) situations.
Interpersonal communication	Student has no grasp of interpersonal relationships.	Student uses appropriate body language (e.g., smiles, waves) but does not engage in appropriate conversation.	Student engages in some conversation when prompted.	Student engages in conversation independently but the topic is inappropriate.	Student uses appropriate tone of voice, body language, and conversation topics.
Verbal communication	Student has no way of clearly communicating with others.	Student is not fluent or easily understood even with assistive technology or support.	Student can be understood with one or two repetitions or when asked to speak more clearly.	Student uses a voice box or other assistive technology to communicate and is understood using these tools.	Student has the ability to communicate with all others and be understood easily.
Problem solving and conflict resolution	Student has no independent problem-solving and conflict resolution skills.	Student has difficulty in problem-solving and conflict resolution skills.	Student has demonstrated capacity to expand problem-solving and conflict resolution skills.	Student possesses good problem-solving skills.	Student possesses good problem-solving skills and initiates problem solving independently.
Physical ability • Mobility • Stamina	Student has limited physical abilities as well as limited capacity to take care of own personal needs.	Student has the mobility and stamina to perform some of the tasks including personal needs with limitations.	Student has low but improving mobility and the stamina and ability to take care of own personal self-care needs.	Student has the mobility and stamina to perform all tasks with accommodations (e.g., a cart to help transport mailings or a wheelchair/scooter for mobility). The student has developed strategies to take care of own personal needs with limited assistance.	Student has the ability, mobility, and stamina to perform all tasks including self-care independently and successfully.
Pace and work quality	Student seldom gets work finished in allotted time period or by deadline.	Student is methodical, which affects pace, productivity, and output.	Student can achieve appropriate work pace but quality suffers or work quality is sufficient but quantity is affected.	Pace and quality of work are mildly deficient but improving and work is neat.	Student is able to achieve both quality and quantity of work, maintains neatness/organization, and completes work according to deadlines.

High School Transition That Works: Lessons Learned from Project SEARCH® by Maryellen Daston, J. Erin Riehle, and Susan Rutkowski.
Copyright © 2012 Cincinnati Children's Hospital Medical Center. All rights reserved. Baltimore, MD: Paul H. Brookes Publishing Co., Inc.

Criteria	1	2	3	4	5
Employability skills	Student has not been exposed to any employability training.	Student has participated in limited or informal employability training.	Student has had 1 year or a consistent class devoted to employability skills.	Student has had more than 1 year of employability skills training.	Student demonstrates independent living skills and has 2 or more years of employability training.
Prior work experience	Student has no prior work experience.	Student has had one or more in-school work experiences.	Student has volunteer or paid enclave work experience.	Student has had 1 year or less of competitive work experience.	Student has had more than 1 year or multiple competitive work experiences.
Academic skills	Student cannot read nor do any simple math computations.	Student has some basic academic skills such as rote counting and can file using two to three digits with numbers or letters.	Student can read simple functional information and can perform simple math computations (with or without a calculator).	Student can read and comprehend material at or above a second-grade level, can tell time with a clock or analog watch to 5 minutes, and count money/make change.	All academic skills are above a fourth-grade level.
Computer skills	Student has no computer skills.	Student has basic knowledge of keyboard and keyboard functions.	Student can access Internet and can utilize search engines for information and for entertainment.	Student can utilize some Microsoft products at a beginner level.	Student can utilize Microsoft products; can save, edit, and retrieve documents with basic proficiency.
Timeline	Application is late and is lacking required documentation.	Application is received late with some of the required documentation.	Application is received according to the established timeline but missing some required documentation.	Application is complete with all documentation but is received after the timeline deadline.	Application is received according to the established timeline with all required documentation.
				TOTAL SCORE	85

Additional notes: _____

_____

_____

High School Transition That Works: Lessons Learned from Project SEARCH® by Maryellen Daston, J. Erin Riehle, and Susan Rutkowski.
Copyright © 2012 Cincinnati Children's Hospital Medical Center. All rights reserved. Baltimore, MD: Paul H. Brookes Publishing Co., Inc.

Project | SEARCH

Meet Matthew

Matthew (Matt) was a member of the Project SEARCH class of 2005–2006 at the Clinton Memorial Hospital Regional Health System in rural southwest Ohio. Matt chose to participate in the Project SEARCH program after completing his educational requirements at Lynchburg-Clay School District, a small district in a town of 1,300 people. Once in the program, Matt proved to be a remarkable intern. His excellent memory and attention to detail were well suited for internship sites such as the sterile processing area and materials supply. These traits were helpful in the classroom, too; each day, Matt would calculate the number of days of the school year the class had completed and the number they had yet to go. He was so dependable and precise, his teacher and job coaches came to rely on him much as one might rely on a calendar.

Matt was also a stickler for facts. After reading that a person is more likely to get injured if riding in the front seat of a car, Matt always chose to ride in the back seat. This made it highly unlikely that he would be willing to work toward getting a driver's license. And because there was very limited public transportation in the rural area where he lived, when it came time to find Matt a job, the only choice was his small home town.

Fortunately, small companies are everywhere and, often, they are looking for the perfect employee. Within walking distance of Matt's home is Mirac, Inc., a small but growing electronics assembly and fabrication company that has been in business since 1992. Matt's attention to detail was a skill that was highly valued by this company because of the necessity for precision in the work that they do. The president and CEO, Ralph Captain, reviewed Matt's application and offered him employment. Recently, Ralph stated that Matt "is an exceptional young man." According to Matt, the best part about his job is the being with his co-workers and ordering lunch in on Fridays.

As an activity in the Project SEARCH program, the interns identified their favorite quotes to live by. The Project SEARCH instructor for Matt's class, Linda Emery, still remembers Matt's favorite quote: "It is nice to be important, but more important to be nice." To this day, she is thankful to Matt for that important reminder!

4 Designing Effective Internships

Success is dependent on effort.

Sophocles

Real-life, hands-on, community-based learning in the workplace is the focal point of the Project SEARCH® High School Transition model. Like student teachers, student nurses, or medical students on rotations, Project SEARCH students work alongside experienced mentors in a series of unpaid worksite experiences (internships) in which the students have the opportunity to develop their competence, demonstrate their capacity to learn and grow, and gain the skills and qualifications that they need to become paid employees. While these internships bring about many positive effects—on the student and on the workplace as a whole—the foremost purpose of the internships is for the students to receive high-quality training in marketable job skills. To meet that purpose, it is critical for the student and for the host business to fully embrace the concept that the student interns are on a competitive learning mission. Accordingly, the internships must be carefully chosen to ensure that the students learn skills that match the qualifications that the business (and similar businesses in the community) require for entry-level employment and monitored to ensure that new tasks are added as skills are mastered. Strict adherence to this framework brings mutual benefits to the students and to the businesses: The students gain relevant job skills and an understanding of how to function in a real-world work environment while the

The Project SEARCH Philosophy on Paid versus Unpaid Internships

One of our favorite quotes is by Stephen Simon, who wrote in the Ohio *ADA Quarterly* in 1998, that "people with disabilities have the right to choose a path toward education and employment. However, while freedom of choice is given, the right to work is earned. Earning the right to work is dependent upon the student's preparation." At Project SEARCH, we believe with all our heart that people with significant disabilities are capable of working and must have a role in choosing that work. However, we believe just as strongly that people with disabilities must earn the right to work just as those without disabilities do, by seeking out appropriate education and training opportunities. True personal choice comes with an equally important obligation to prepare for that choice.

There are numerous examples of fields of work in which practitioners are expected to gain skills through unpaid work experiences. Across the country, student teachers work in classrooms as part of their training. Among health care fields, student nurses, child life therapists, nursing assistants, and medical assistants are trained in clinical settings. None of these students are paid during their training. Instead, it is understood

(continued)

(continued)

that earning the right to work obliges them to prepare for their chosen work. In fact, unlike Project SEARCH interns, most of these trainees actually pay for the internship in the form of college tuition and as part of their overall training program.

We believe that it is important to hold young people with intellectual and developmental disabilities to the same standard. If we fail to do so, this can foster a condescending atmosphere of low expectations and promote the status quo of learned helplessness.

High school students with disabilities who take part in Project SEARCH are given the opportunity to gain work experience and learn skills in internships that are structured to meet the following guidelines to ensure a meaningful training opportunity:

1. The interns may **contribute** to the business but may not do a complete job, fill an empty position, or cover for people on vacation. Internships are intended to help the young person learn meaningful skills, not to help the business meet the bottom line.
2. The young people take part in "internships" or "work experiences," not work itself.
3. Supervisors from the host business and the educational staff negotiate the tasks to be learned and skills to be acquired based on entry-level skills needed for competitive employment. The training is designated with a task list, work aids, and/or other accommodations.
4. At no time are the interns learning independently. There is always an instructor, job coach, and natural support available onsite.
5. The interns are identified on their badges as Project SEARCH student interns and not as employees.
6. Every Project SEARCH site must have an onsite classroom at the workplace.
7. The interns follow the school schedule.
8. The interns spend a portion of each day in the onsite classroom learning employability skills through a school district or state-approved curriculum and lesson plans.
9. The interns receive a grade and credits (if needed for their school district).

In order to create a learning situation that is similar to that experienced by other young adults, the internships in Project SEARCH are not paid. Instead, we provide them with the training necessary to go out into the world and work as capable, prepared adults.

business gains a continuous supply of skilled potential workers who are familiar with their culture and who are trained to the exact specifications of their business. As one of our Scottish business liaisons put it, "The purpose of the internships is to 'skill them up.'"

Although there is some controversy surrounding the concept of unpaid internships, both within and outside of the context of disability, our experience with Project SEARCH has shown that, if the educational goal is fully accepted by all parties and the internships are well planned, the interaction is highly effective and not exploitative. In fact, this practice actually strengthens the purpose of the internships. That is, when money is taken out of the equation, it avoids the patronizing and often self-defeating dynamic of allowing students to do subpar work for nominal pay and keeps the focus on maximizing performance. When Project SEARCH students gain employment and start receiving a paycheck, it comes with the satisfaction of knowing that they are fully qualified and that they are being paid to do their work to the same standards that apply to all employees.

INTERNSHIPS ARE CONSISTENT WITH THE TRAINING MISSION OF MOST LARGE BUSINESSES

Training and education are functions that are common to nearly all large employers, and Project SEARCH's program of internships is a direct fit with this aspect of business culture. This means that, in most business environments, infrastructure is in place to support learning and teaching as well as a philosophical precedent and a built-in familiarity that facilitates acceptance of the interns and the concept of the program. Moreover, the internships require that department staff become directly involved as teachers and mentors, and this leads to a sense of ownership of the program and a stake in its success, which is good for both the business and the Project SEARCH students.

The Fifth Third Bank is a Project SEARCH host business that has recognized and built on the relationship between Project SEARCH and the other training programs within its organization. Fifth Third has established a very productive linkage between the Project SEARCH student interns and the participants in a training program that they offer for future leaders in the company.

THE STRUCTURE OF PROJECT SEARCH INTERNSHIPS

Internships are integrated into the daily schedule of students during their year in the Project SEARCH program. Each day, students spend approximately 1 1/2 hours in an onsite classroom, learning employability and independent-living skills, and roughly 5 hours (including lunch) at their worksite internships (with an absolute minimum of 4 hours per day). This begins to approximate a 20-hour-a-week job to build physical and mental stamina in preparation for full-time employment. With a total of 6 1/2 hours a day at the business—in the classroom and at the worksite—students participate in approximately 1,040 hours of skill development over the course of a school year. As a result, students gain a level of exposure to the working world that is rarely available to students with disabilities but that is widely acknowledged as critical in enhancing a young person's likelihood of achieving postschool employment (Certo, Luecking, Murphy, Brown, Courey, & Belanger, 2008; Kohler & Field, 2003).

Typically, during the course of the Project SEARCH school year, students rotate through three internships, each lasting approximately 10 weeks. The 10-week rotation schedule can be modified under certain circumstances as long as students continue to add new skills to their repertoires and remain on course to gain all the necessary skills required to qualify for competitive employment and to meet their individual career goals. In the initial years of Project SEARCH we had four internships to mirror the traditional quarters of the high school. Although this schedule accommodated the school and was easier for families to follow, we found that it created too many changes for the business and for the students. On the other hand, two rotations did not offer enough opportunities to learn core skills or practice flexibility in the workplace. Moving through three internships seemed to be the optimal number to maximize time for skill acquisition in a variety of settings and expose students to different kinds of supervisors and co-workers. However, there are a few sites that have chosen, through a consensus of all the partner organizations, to include only two internships during the Project SEARCH year.

The actual duration of a particular worksite rotation will depend on factors such as the complexity of the specific tasks involved, the number of different tasks to be learned, and the potential benefit to the student (see Table 4.1). In addition, a student might do multiple internship rotations at a given worksite if the skills learned are a particularly good match for the student's career goals or if there is a strong possibility that the student will be hired in that department. However, two criteria must be met in order for this to happen: New skills must be added to the student's repertoire as soon as skills are mastered; and, whereas the wage and hour law permits the student to contribute to the business, he or she must not be doing an entire job or filling an empty position. It is also possible for a student to participate in more than one work experience in a single rotation cycle, depending on the scheduling parameters of the department and the student. For example, in a hospital setting, there are sometimes clinics that want to host an intern but they have limited hours and days of operation. In cases like this, the clinic rotation could be paired with a work experience at another site that will expand the range of skills to be learned.

At the worksite, students are supported by job coaches. As the student's competence increases and she or he begins to gain independence on particular tasks, the presence of the job coach may decrease and the role that the department staff play as natural supports becomes more prominent. The staff members reinforce skills that the students learned through working with the job coach. This relationship with the staff members is also critical for learning appropriate work behavior and what it means to function as part of a group. It is hard to overestimate the impact that it has on the students to go from being outsiders to being an integral

Project SEARCH and the Training Mission at Fifth Third Bank

The success of Project SEARCH at Fifth Third Bank is attributed to the fact that this program has the support of the most senior executives of the bank and is recognized as a key component of a comprehensive talent development strategy.

Project SEARCH interns participate in a year-long development program, which includes rotational assignments focused on developing business skills that will enhance the intern's competitiveness for jobs within the Fifth Third Bank, as well as in the external labor market. The goal of the program is the placement of interns in gainful and meaningful employment—whether that employment occurs within Fifth Third Bank or through partnerships with other companies within the communities in which Fifth Third Bank operates.

Fifth Third Bank leverages Project SEARCH in other development programs, including its college-graduate accelerated leadership programs. Leadership program participants are often paired with Project SEARCH interns to provide mentorship and assistance to interns to better understand the Fifth Third Bank's business environment, to answer questions, and to guide and coach. Specific guidance and coaching provided by leadership program participants to Project SEARCH interns include assistance with resume writing, interviewing skills, professional dress and grooming, and other aspects important to success in a professional business environment. Leadership program participants also assist with the development of interpersonal skills including an awareness of the types of workplace conversations that are appropriate and the importance of eye contact in social interactions. In exchange, leadership program participants gain experience in mentoring others and in building their own leadership capabilities.

Table 4.1. Week-by-week structure of worksite internships

In preparation for the internships, Project SEARCH® (PS) staff members spend time with managers at internship sites observing and analyzing the work of the department, negotiating a task list (task design), and often giving information about working with and supervising someone with a disability. During the internship, the job coach or instructor will be in regular communication with the manager or mentor/point person to gain feedback regarding progress and challenges of the intern. This table describes the activities of Project SEARCH staff and students and the host business personnel involved in Project SEARCH. It also shows the level of interaction and the content of communications among the job coach, Project SEARCH instructor, internship managers, mentors, and student interns. In this table the title "job coach" could represent the Project SEARCH instructor or the job coach, as both will have some job coaching duties during the internships.

Week and day	Activities and objectives
Prior to day 1: In preparation for the internship to begin	• With assistance from the business liaison, the Project SEARCH staff identify those departments that can provide high-quality training. • The Project SEARCH instructor and/or job coach meet with department manager and other staff to discuss work of the department and possible tasks to be done by the intern. • The manager identifies a mentor or "point-of-contact" person who will assist in training and be the conduit for information flow between the intern and PS staff for feedback and evaluation, and for identifying skills to be learned, skills to be added once student reaches satisfactory work levels, etc. • PS instructor and job coach observe the work of the department and develop task design/job description with the mentor. Concerns regarding skills, safety, environment, and productivity are discussed and addressed. The skill level for job satisfaction regarding productivity and quality should be determined by the manager, mentor, and PS staff. • The Project SEARCH staff create and confirm a task design (standard work) with the manager and mentor. The list includes the initial tasks as well as additional tasks to be added as the student masters the original tasks. Project SEARCH staff may design job accommodations if necessary for intern to perform work successfully. These could include created work aids, standard operating procedure lists, or mainstream technology such as a smart phone or iPad that could prompt and reinforce the intern. • The Project SEARCH staff can present information about the program, the goal of the internships (*to gain marketable, transferable skills in order for the students to secure a competitive job at the host business or in their community*), and any communication about the student's learning style, career goals, individual student needs, and optimum environments for the student and internship site to be successful. They will also discuss how the internship experience and skills can help in attaining the career goals and lead to employment. • PS staff share additional information about the internship experience and schedule (hours of time on the internship, school vacation days, lunch, expectation of support from the job coach, etc.) • The mentor orients the job coach and instructor to the internship site regarding dress, lunch protocol, staff meetings, supplies, use of equipment, code of conduct, etc. The mentor or manager identifies a work space for the intern. • The job coach and instructor adapt the Project SEARCH internship evaluation instrument to reflect the skills and culture of the individual internship sites. • The internship manager or mentor interview the student and confirm or decline his or her participation in the internship. (Because of the in-depth task analysis and communication prior to the interview, this activity typically functions as a learning experience rather than a selection tool.) • In the rare occasion that the student is not a good match for a given internship, the PS staff will repeat the process until a good student-internship match is found. • Additional departments within the host business may decide to be internship sites after learning about Project SEARCH.
Week 1, day 1	• The student arrives at the internship on time with the job coach. • The mentor or manager introduces student and job coach to co-workers and other important staff. • The mentor orients student and job coach to the department's physical space and protocol (e.g., appropriate dress, supplies and use, equipment usage, restroom, water fountain, microwave, safety process, policies, staff meetings, and procedures). • With possible supervision from the mentor, the job coach and student learn to operate appropriate office or department equipment using safety procedures. • The student discusses chain of command, protocol, unwritten rules, dress code, and other departmental issues with the mentor and job coach. • The job coach teaches and reinforces the skills to be learned. • The job coach teaches the initial tasks on the job description/task list (this is individualized for each student according to his or her abilities and skills). The coach checks for understanding with the student and evaluates progress. • The job coach facilitates the student's lunch and breaks. It is suggested that the intern eat lunch with the peer mentor and co-workers as early in the internship as possible. At the beginning of the internship the job coach may eat lunch with the student. • The job coach analyzes work process and flow and creates accommodations or work aids when needed. • The job coach fosters self-advocacy; for example, if the intern has a question about work procedures or tasks, the student is encouraged to ask the department staff directly (with coach support and check for understanding). • The job coach gives tools and techniques on supervising the interns to the mentor and co-workers to facilitate natural supports and independence as soon as possible.

(continued)

Week and day	Activities and objectives
Week 1, day 2	• The student arrives at the internship on time (with or without job coach, depending on student independence and department need). • The student continues orientation and learning the use of equipment within the department as needed. • The job coach continues teaching the tasks and skills as well as implementing work aids to foster productivity, quality, and mastery. • The job coach and student interact with peer mentor and other staff as appropriate to ask questions and accomplish tasks. • The intern (and coach at the beginning) attends staff meetings and department functions as appropriate to foster natural supports, work-based learning, and becoming part of the work culture. • The job coach assesses student using Project SEARCH internship evaluation with input from department mentor and student.
Week 1, days 3 and 4	• The student arrives on time (with or without job coach, depending on student independence and department need). • The student continues orientation and learning the use of equipment within department as needed. • The coach continues to teach tasks at the student's work station. • The student interacts with peer mentor and other staff more independently to accomplish tasks and become part of the work team. • The student continues to learn tasks at work station with support of job coach as needed. • The student may begin interacting directly with the mentor for direction and tasks. • The job coach develops a productivity log as a tool to help student work at an acceptable pace toward a standard quota of speed and quality.
Week 1, day 5	• The student learns to work directly off the task list with productivity log if necessary. • The student returns from lunch and any breaks on time independently. • The job coach completes the first weekly evaluation with student and peer mentor.
Week 2	• The student learns tasks with job coach support as necessary. (Some students will be independent by week 2; other students will continue to need job coaching support.) • The job coach creates or modifies additional work aids as necessary. • The job coach fades support as appropriate. If there are any issues related to skill performance, conduct, dress or behavior, the mentor can contact the job coach through a cell phone or internal e-mail. • Regular communication between the coach, student, and mentor facilitates maximum skills acquisition. • The job coach evaluates the student using Project SEARCH internship evaluation on a weekly basis with student and peer mentor. • Even if the job coach has faded from the internship site, the coach or teacher should have a daily check (which could be very quick) with the mentor regarding progress and challenges of the student.
Weeks 3 through 7	• The job coach teaches the student new skills as appropriate with input from the mentor and co-workers. The mentor may choose to teach and reinforce skills without job coach assistance. • The student works toward department standards and quality levels. • The job coach analyzes the work process and flow and creates accommodations or work aids as needed. • The Project SEARCH teacher prepares for and implements the monthly employment-planning meeting (information on skill acquisition, progress, and issues will be gathered and presented by the student, teacher, and job coach). The first meeting will be facilitated by the teacher and the student will be prepared to lead the second monthly meeting. The team can utilize the meeting to align work and employability skills gained during work experience with individual career plan goals. • The mentor and job coach work together to address any issues related to skill performance, conduct, dress or behavior. Communication between the coach, student, and mentor facilitates maximum skills acquisition. • The job coach evaluates student on a weekly basis using Project SEARCH internship evaluation tool with the student and peer mentor. The student also participates in self-evaluation.
Weeks 8 and 9	• The student gives his or her 2 weeks' notice. • The student continues to layer on additional skills and utilizes the job coach for training of new tasks as necessary. • The student works toward department standards and quality levels. • The team (including the student, job coach, mentor, and teacher) discusses possible open positions and facilitates application process. • The job coach evaluates the student using Project SEARCH internship evaluation with student, job coach, and peer mentor. The student also participates in self-evaluation.
Week 10	• The student can participate in an exit interview with the department manager or peer mentor. • The student can ask manager/peer mentor for letter of recommendation if appropriate. The letter becomes part of the student's portfolio and is utilized for the job search process.
Postinternship	• The Project SEARCH teacher and job coach conduct an internship survey with all the participating managers using a face-to-face meeting and/or electronic survey. The meetings can be both celebratory and evaluative. This information is used to improve the internship process and address any concerns in communication among the student, the coach, and internship staff.

Project SEARCH Employability Skills Curriculum Lesson Plan: Using Internship Evaluations and Explaining Rubrics

Purpose

Evaluating students' work performance in their worksites is basic to the program. Students will need to understand the rating system you are using so that they know what is expected.

Goal

Students will identify the attributes of rubric scores such as excellent, doing well, improving, and needs improvement.

Objectives

Students will

- Define rubric and evaluation
- List attributes of rubric classifications
- Demonstrate knowledge of evaluation areas

Materials

- Baggies containing four chocolate chip cookies–one that is slightly burnt, one that is small, one that only has one chocolate chip, and one that is "perfect"
- A plate of chocolate chip cookies

Activities

Before class time, prepare a batch of chocolate chip cookies. Make at least four cookies that are burnt, four that are small, four that have only one chocolate chip, and four that are "perfect."

1. Provide samples of work evaluations forms—preferably the one your host site uses.
2. Discuss the purpose of written work evaluations and how they are used.
3. Have the students read each statement on the sample work evaluation and, as a group, define the statements. It is important that the students know what each statement is evaluating.
4. Tell the students that we are going to be the owners of the "Perfect Chocolate Chip Cookie Company." It is our job to create an evaluation of our product so that we can be certain that our cookie is the best on the market.
5. Lead the group in preparing a simple evaluation document that has five or six statements for evaluating a cookie. List these statements on the board. For example, "There are a lot of chocolate chips"; "The cookie is properly baked"; "The cookie is the right size." Make sure the statements allow for subjective evaluation.

(continued)

part of a genuine team with shared goals and accountability. The student's integration into the department might include activities such as attending staff meetings, taking part in departmental training sessions, and attending staff luncheons and celebrations. In this way, students begin to live the Code of Conduct instead of just hearing about it and learn to respond to the same kinds of cues that help other workers to do their work correctly.

Many aspects of the internships help to prepare the student for the hiring process. First, before starting a rotation, the student sends a resume and cover letter to the manager at the job site. The student will then arrange and participate in an interview with the manager, after which, a representative from the department will contact the student with a follow-up call to confirm the details of the internship. Classroom time is used for preparation in which students learn how to create resumes and write letters and are given the opportunity to hone their interviewing skills through practice and role playing. Those students who don't read or write use multiple adaptations to perform these tasks. They might dictate their thoughts for a teacher or coach to write down, use pictures, or even iPad apps. In turn, the department heads are also given preparation in the form of a list of questions for the interview because they are often just as nervous as the students. To illustrate, a manager at a Project SEARCH program site was interviewing a young man for his first internship position. "Kevin" (the manager) had not been aware prior to the interview that the young man was deaf and that he used an interpreter and sign language to communicate. Kevin was very uncomfortable during the first few minutes of the interview and kept directing all of his comments to the interpreter. Finally, with some direction from the interpreter, Kevin began to talk directly to the student and found that they had many things in common and that he would be a great fit for the internship. As a result of this experience, Kevin, along with many co-workers, took a sign language class so that they could communicate with their new intern.

During the internship, while gaining valuable job skills, the students get ample practice in appropriate worksite interactions. They are expected to communicate with the departmental supervisor or mentor in the same way that a regular employee would if any issues or questions arise. They must notify the teacher *and* the department if they are going to be absent or late, attend staff meetings when appropriate, and participate in a 360° evaluation of the internship and of their own performance.

For internship evaluations, many of our sites use a versatile template (developed by Linda Emery, an experienced Project SEARCH instructor) that can be customized for each internship (see Appendix 4.1). If the students are required by their school to receive grades, this tool can also serve that purpose. For most of the sites, staff use a 1 to 4 scale to rate the students in several areas including social behavior, communication, appearance, and job performance. The tool also includes an "action plan" to address challenges to progress. The instructor, job coach, manager, and peer mentor (at the worksite) all use this tool on a daily or weekly basis. At the beginning of the internship, it could be used daily; but as the student progresses and needs less support, it could be filled out once or twice a week. The student should also have the responsibility to self-evaluate. Using this common form, the student gets feedback from all of his or her significant work support staff. The results can be shared at the monthly meetings with the team, with funders, human resources (HR) staff, and others. It can be used as an indicator of when it is time to layer on more tasks to challenge the learner or to increase support and training or concentrate on needed employability skills. To help students understand the concept of evaluation rubrics and how to rate themselves, Linda Emery designed an engaging and entertaining classroom exercise, which is included in the Project SEARCH curriculum, that uses chocolate chip cookies to teach the students how to rate themselves on a 4-point scale.

Toward the end of an internship, the student gives "2-weeks' notice" to the departmental supervisor, mentor, or both. The last step in each rotation is for the students to participate in exit interviews and final evaluations, write thank you letters to their site managers and mentors, and update their portfolios to include the skills and competencies learned during the internship.

(continued)

6. Next, divide the class into four groups and give each group a baggie of the four cookies.
7. Ask them to use the evaluation document and rate the cookies in the bag, keeping in mind they are the owners of the "Perfect Chocolate Chip Cookie Company."
8. After the group has evaluated the cookies, have them explain their evaluation process to the larger group.
9. You may have differences of opinions, but the perfect cookie will have the best score. Therefore, everyone should better understand the attributes of a "perfect cookie."
10. Discuss how this relates to their work evaluations. They can decide whether they want to be a "perfect cookie" as they go through the year.

Everyone gets to enjoy the rest of the cookies!

THE BENEFITS OF TOTAL WORKPLACE IMMERSION

The effectiveness of the worksite internships is in a large part due to the impact of total workplace immersion—a core component of the Project SEARCH model. Being located in the place of business instead of a school gives ready access to a wide variety of training opportunities. In addition, students learn in the context of the workplace, which allows for immediate real-life application of new skills as well as continuous improvement through feedback from the teacher, job coaches, managers, and co-workers.

Research has shown that work-based learning promotes problem-solving abilities, adult thinking processes, team work, and social relationships (see, e.g., Devlin, 2011). Indeed, we hear from Project SEARCH sites all over the country with reports of students who exhibit dramatic growth and maturation during the course of their participation in internships. All of these stories, the research-based evidence, and our own experiences with students have convinced us that the Project SEARCH internship experience is substantially different from the typical school-based mechanisms for providing workplace exposure, such as supervised site visits, career technical labs, job shadowing, or simulated worksites. Unlike these other arrangements, total workplace immersion dictates strict adherence to business norms and makes no allowance for the poor attitudes and inattention to grooming that are often tolerated in a high school setting. Instead, students respond to the high expectations and seriousness of purpose of the workplace in a positive way, and shifts in behavior and attitude happen naturally—without relying on an excessively rigid or punitive atmosphere.

Bill M., the father of Lena, a Project SEARCH student at the Ohio State University Medical Center site, saw first hand how the internship experience influenced his daughter. In high school, Lena spent 8 years in a very good special education classroom where she received individualized instruction, worked on self-esteem and social skills, and benefited from speech therapy and other services and activities that enriched her life. In the last 4 years, she stayed in the same classroom but was moved into a vocational track in which she would leave school for a couple of hours in the afternoons, accompanied by a job coach, to go to worksites in the community that had been arranged through the school. She worked at an athletic club and two different nursing facilities for the elderly and people with Alzheimer's disease. In each of these work experiences, the result was the same—everyone adored Lena, but she had a hard time staying on task, and her work performance was poor. As Bill put it, "Lena was there to develop job skills, but she had a hard time negotiating between hanging out and being social and doing her job." It was the same story when her vocational rehabilitation (VR) counselor arranged for her to try out summer jobs at a child care facility and at a family homeless shelter—Lena was popular and well liked on a personal level, and she loved and was loved by her co-workers and the clientele—but she never mastered the job skills. To her teachers and VR counselors, it was beginning to look as though Lena was not going to be employable, and she and Bill started getting used to the idea of placement in a day program. But in her final year of high school eligibility, Bill started hearing about a Project SEARCH program starting at the Ohio State University Medical Center. Lena applied and was accepted in the program, where she had the opportunity to try an internship at the Ohio State University Nisonger Center Dental Clinic, a facility that specializes in serving patients with disabilities. At first Bill thought, "Well, we've been here before," but then, things started looking up and Bill began getting "thumbs-up" reports every week. The job coach worked with Lena in the dental clinic on cleaning instruments, setting up trays for the next day's appointments, cleaning the examination rooms, and other tasks. Lena learned it all and, according to her father,

> After years of looking like she wasn't going to exhibit employable skills, she *was*. And when she tasted that success, oh my goodness, things just clicked. When she graduated, she was offered a job at a commensurate rates in the dental clinic....She just stepped up to the plate.

When asked what he thinks the difference was, Bill says he thinks it was a combination of things: Lena had matured over time, the job and work environment were a good fit for her, and the expectations in the Project SEARCH program were different. As Bill put it,

> In all the other jobs it was like, "Let's get a few kids with disabilities in here and give them something to do and we'll love 'em." It was almost patronizing. But the dental clinic—that was a real job. It was a small group too. The expectation was that Lena would perform certain functions. If Lena didn't do the work, her co-workers would have to pick up the slack and do those things because they needed to be done. She knew the difference. There was an expectation—these are your duties, if you don't do it, we have to. Her progress was measured—percent completion, and other measures. Each month, her stats went up and up to where she could do it in the same time as the hygienist who'd been doing it before Lena started—she matched the time. And she did it with 100% accuracy.

DESIGNING INTERNSHIPS STRATEGICALLY

When we refer to the strategic design of internships, we are talking about the procedures that Project SEARCH uses to ensure that internships will provide valuable work experience and teach marketable, transferable skills (see Table 4.2). In entering a new community or a new business sector, Project SEARCH starts with a broad perspective (the "5,000-foot view"), to understand the scope of jobs and job opportunities for program graduates, and then narrows the perspective down to a detailed analysis of specific tasks involved in each prospective job (the "5-foot view"). Sometimes, we need to go even further, to the 1-foot level, which refers to breaking down a task that includes very difficult steps for the student to master. In these cases, we break those tasks down even further, pinpointing the difficult steps and creating work aids or accommodations to build basic competence and eventually mastery. Once the student is performing the difficult task, we can reintroduce it to the chain of steps within the task, and the student moves forward incorporating the new knowledge level. At all stages, Project SEARCH internships are designed from an employer's perspective with input from the host business at the onset of planning and throughout the ongoing process of internship development.

Table 4.2. Assessing training and employment opportunities from 5,000' to ground level

Project SEARCH® encourages systematic development of program components. As the business community, education personnel, and supported employment staff work together, it is important to develop processes that are organized, shared, and sustainable. Project SEARCH suggests that the process of developing potential program host sites, employment opportunities, internships, job tasks, and individual instruction is most effective if it starts at the "5,000-foot" level and proceeds to the "1-foot" level. In other words, begin with the "bird's eye" view of your employment community, then drill down through the layers of individual businesses, specific departments, specific job tasks, and individualized task performance. By following a systematic approach, we are more likely to build training that meets employers' needs while giving interns the support they need to develop required skills that will result in competitive employment.

Program Level	Organizational level: What organizations are assessed and who is responsible for analysis at this level?	Analysis: What information is to be gathered?	Implications for internship and training: How will this information help us develop employment, training and internship sites?	Implications for employment: How will understanding this information help our interns gain/maintain employment?	Tools and methods to gain information: How can we complete this analysis?
5,000' level: What is the employment picture in your community from a bird's eye view? What type of employment exists? Who are the large employers and what industry segment do they represent? What is the future trend for jobs in this community?	This level includes analysis of the community (at the city or county level), including the nature of large and small employers within the community and future business trends. Job developers, teachers, job coaches, transition coordinators, and everyone whose job is to assist students in gaining and maintaining employment needs to be familiar with this information.	Analyze industry sectors, identify large and small organizations that employ large and small organizations that employ workers, understand future employment trends. For example, do you have a large number of health/medical facility employers? Do you have warehouses? Do you have manufacturers? Do you have a large number of small business owners? What is unique about your community's employment picture?	When we identify and understand the organizations that have a variety of entry-level work and have sufficient employee turnover, we can create internships that build skills for targeted jobs. We can also create training/internships for future jobs. For instance, if most of the jobs in our community are in health care, we should make sure we have internships that build skills for that industry.	We can make sure we are training our interns for jobs that exist in our community. We can locate employment opportunities outside of the host site, which can impact the long-term sustainability of the program. We can identify potential Business Advisory Committee members for program continuous improvement. We can identify logistical issues such as public transportation and availability of other services.	It is important to research your community and area. Connect with your local Chamber of Commerce, business-to-business networks, industrial parks, Rotary Club, and community business web sites. Search the Department of Labor web site for statistics related to your area. Invite local business representatives to your class as speakers and to serve on your advisory committee. Check with your school leadership to see if they are already part of local business initiatives.
500' level: What is the employment picture within the larger employers in your community?	Job developers, Project SEARCH staff and community-supported employment agencies should gather data and information regarding specific businesses or employers within the community.	Analysis of one or more specific businesses in the community for employment and training opportunities. Analyze the culture, employment needs, formal and informal employee support systems, transportation resources, etc. to determine the potential for employment of interns or the feasibility of hosting a Project SEARCH program.	When we analyze specific employers we can identify the general skills that employers desire as well as critical job-specific skills. It is important to identify skills that can be taught at the host site and transferred to other community employers. By learning about individual employers, we can arrange career-related field trips and/or job shadowing opportunities that contribute to reaching the employment goal.	Analyzing local employers lets us find employers with open positions consistent with intern competencies in proximity to the host business and/or students' homes. We can locate potential offsite sites for third internships that have potential to lead to employment. We can make connections to individuals within local businesses who can help our interns network with a variety of employers.	Use a consistent "Business Profile"/Employer Analysis form or process so that you gather the same information on a variety of businesses in your community. Gather information such as skill set needed, cultural and physical environment, turnover, employee support, business outlook and history, etc. Set up informational interviews with area businesses. Set up tours of businesses. Attend and participate in job fairs. Invite business leaders to visit your program and serve on your advisory committee.

(continued)

Table 4.2. *(continued)*

Program Level	Organizational level: What organizations are assessed and who is responsible for analysis at this level?	Analysis: What information is to be gathered?	Implications for internship and training: How will this information help us develop employment, training, and internship sites?	Implications for employment: How will understanding this information help our interns gain/maintain employment?	Tools and methods to gain information: How can we complete this analysis?
50' level: What are the required skills and employment culture in the specific departments in your host site or neighboring businesses? Also, what are the unmet needs of these departments?	Project SEARCH staff, job developers, job coaches, should analyze a variety of individual departments within the host site business and/or other employer organizations	Identify the entry-level and/or complex and systematic/routine jobs. Analyze the skills needed, environmental requirements, supervisory support, etc. that are specific to that department. Look specifically for unmet needs, waste, lack of productivity or timeliness in tasks, higher paid individuals completing routine tasks, and the misuse of other resources.	This analysis guides the process of matching interns to high-quality appropriate training so that interns build on previously acquired skills/interests. By identifying the skill set that is used in a specific department or by building job-specific skills that are relevant to that department or another department with similar skill requirements.	Analyzing departments can lead to employment for interns either by identifying and addressing the unmet needs of a department or by building job-specific skills that are relevant to that department or another department with similar skill requirements.	Use a consistent form such as a "department profile" to analyze the department skill set, culture, physical requirements etc. Also, and maybe more importantly, develop and use your observation skills such as "standing in the circle" (a Lean tool) to identify unmet needs, waste, misuse of resources, etc. Complete an environmental analysis and training matrix to track core skills that are available to learn.
5' level: What tasks will your interns do within a department? What support will they have? What are the steps the intern must follow to complete the job successfully?	The Project SEARCH staff or job developer will determine and record the jobs or components of jobs within each department.	Analyze the job description/procedures, determine core skills/essential functions and prepare a standard of work including the steps to teach those core skills.	Creating documents that detail and list the job tasks will guide the training process and promote consistent teaching strategies among onsite staff. It also documents the interns' skill acquisition, and identifies areas for continued training.	Specific job analysis allows interns to confirm or alter their employment goals. It also documents the interns' skill acquisition for portfolio development and the job placement process.	Use a consistent form to list the job tasks or steps. This form or process is often called a Task design or standard work. Create supports such as pictures, checklists, or videos. Use the task design document to audit progress, quality, productivity, and safety. Also, use the task design to identify problem areas for the intern that can be addressed.
1' level: What steps are problematic for the intern? How can he/she be taught to complete those steps?	Project SEARCH staff will identify specific steps within the task design that are problematic for an individual intern.	Analyze the problem area(s) and break down the task into very small steps that can be taught and/or practiced by the intern. For instance, if a student is having difficulty wrapping hospital supplies, the staff would list each specific step to identify the problem step and teach the specific skill needed.	Tasks that are not performed independently can be broken down for further training. Interns can be taught complex tasks with individualized task-specific training. The task analysis also identifies areas for error proofing (accommodations).	Interns will learn complex tasks needed for specific jobs. This process expands the intern's range of competencies and increases employment potential.	Use a consistent form to list the specific steps within a task. This process is often called a task analysis. Create individualized accommodations, adaptations, and targeted training specific to difficult skills.

66

Some examples of internship opportunities at different Project SEARCH sites around the country are included in Appendixes 4.2 through 4.4.

The first step in introducing Project SEARCH into any workplace is to assess the work of the business and to ask the question, "What do you do here?" The answer will clarify the general, broad categories of work. In a hospital, for example, these might include materials management, clerical work, transportation, infrastructure, patient care, and food service. This knowledge, combined with the recent history of job openings and hirings in health care facilities in the community, will help to identify the skills that are most likely to make program graduates attractive to potential employers. Another example comes from our Project SEARCH sites that are in banks or other financial institutions. As in a health care setting, our ultimate goal in designing internships at these sites is for the students to gain employment in entry-level jobs at the host bank or at other similar companies in the community. For most employers, a classification scheme is used in which jobs are categorized by "grade" or "band." By working with HR, we can identify the core skills needed for entry-level jobs, which tend to be in bands 2 through 4. These entry-level jobs tend to be numerous and, particularly in a bank or other office setting, all utilize a similar skill set. This important piece of knowledge helps us design internships that teach those core skills. We track the students' acquisition of those core skills as well as the additional skills that are gained at the various internships. This helps us to strategically design each student's sequence of internships to ensure she or he is exposed to the skills required for successful employment.

The strategic design of training experiences is somewhat of a balancing act between the future needs of the business and the training needs of the student. On the one hand, the hiring patterns of the business are an important consideration because there is no point in training for jobs that don't exist either at the host business or in the community. On the other hand, there is also the risk of focusing too much on a specific job and creating graduates who are too narrow in their skill sets. We address this need for balance by keeping the future hiring needs of the business in mind while developing the list of core skills. At the same time, we make sure to keep that list as broad as possible so that the students will have a wide range of job opportunities for which they will be eligible when they finish their year in Project SEARCH. Only about 20% of Project SEARCH interns gain jobs at the host business. All other students use the skills they learn to find jobs in the community. This emphasizes the need to have a broad skill set that can be used at a company in the same industry sector as the host business or in the general community.

Defining Core Skills

The next step is to take a closer look at the work in individual departments and determine the specific skills that must be mastered to meet the qualifications for employment. This exercise leads to the development of lists of the core skills necessary for the different job categories. At Project SEARCH sites with an active Business Advisory Council, this question should be addressed to the group as a whole to obtain the most comprehensive and relevant lists possible that reflect skills needed in the larger community. Moreover, the core skills should be revisited on a regular basis to make sure that they keep up with technological advances and shifts in business priorities. For example, in training for office work, the phasing out of paper records and the emergence of electronic record storage means that alphanumeric and Jeter filing is becoming less important and skills associated with document scanning and imaging are gaining increasing importance.

For certain businesses, the core skills will vary considerably from department to department. For example, in a hospital, clinical sterilization requires very different skills from those of patient transport or materials management. In these cases, the work of establishing a list of core skills will be somewhat harder than in an insurance company or bank where there is more uniformity across departments in the type of tasks performed. It may require the development of multiple lists or other modifications. Appendix 4.5 includes an example of a core skills matrix for a hospital, in which the different skills are separated into categories including administrative, patient services, and general employability skills.

The Training Matrix

Once the core skills for an industry are established, the next step is to find departments in which students can learn those skills. This is one of the areas in which Project SEARCH makes use of Lean tools. In this case, the training matrix comes into play. It is a simple grid where, in this use, the X axis lists all the core skills of a business and the available internships are listed on the Y axis. With the training matrix in place, it is easy to show which internships provide which core skills, and this makes it easier to ensure that, over the school year, each student is exposed to all the skills relevant to his or her employment goal. The training matrix also makes it easier to say no when a department wants to host an intern to do work that needs to be done but which doesn't teach core skills. For example, in a children's hospital, there is always a need to wash dirty toys, and busy staff rarely have time to do it. In this situation, it might be tempting for the department to propose a "toy washing" internship and give this work to a student. In a case like this, the Project SEARCH teacher can refer to the matrix and ask, "Is this a skill that your organization requires for an entry-level position?" If the answer is no, then it is easy to reach agreement that this is not an appropriate internship unless it is coupled with activities that are on the matrix.

The training matrix has an additional purpose of reinforcing high expectations for students. A matrix can be created, again with the core skills on the X axis and with the individual students making up the Y axis. This helps in tracking the core skills to which each student has been exposed and to show the degree to which she or he has mastered those skills. This is a good way to chart progress and to set up the clear expectation that all students will reach their highest possible score for each skill. It is also an effective tool in communicating the message that it is the collective responsibility of the teacher, the job coaches, the manager, and the student to see that each student reaches that goal.

MATCHING STUDENTS WITH INTERNSHIPS

An important axiom at Project SEARCH is that a large business can be considered a microcosm of the working world. In a sense, the workplace resembles a small city in which a variety of services are delivered and a correspondingly large variety of job training opportunities are available. This means that a student who attends a Project SEARCH program in a hospital won't necessarily be limited to work in a health care facility after graduation. In fact, by creating a customized training matrix and carefully choosing a student's internships, almost any career goal can be accommodated. For example, one young woman entered a hospital-based program with the dream of working in a Hallmark store. She had become enchanted by one in a mall near her home and, before she entered Project SEARCH, had been unsuccessful in her effort to be hired there because she wasn't qualified. Her teacher used her creativity in helping the student plan her internships to reach her goal. She worked on the loading dock and learned to unpack merchandise; in the pharmacy, she learned about stocking shelves; and in the gift shop she learned about creating seasonal displays. Based on the core skills she gained, the instructor was able to negotiate a job with the Hallmark store, and the young woman was able to realize her employment goal.

Students play an important role in choosing their own internships. The Project SEARCH curriculum includes an exercise that instructors can use to help guide students in this process. The lesson plan describing this exercise, as well as a sample list of internships, is included in Appendix 4.6.

Environmental Considerations

When choosing internships for students, it is important to look at the environment in which the internship will take place. This helps in finding a good match and in preparing the student for potential challenges. Performing the environmental analysis involves another Lean tool known as "standing in the circle." This is a format for job coaches and teachers to develop good observational skills. The idea is to observe the work without judgment and ask questions that will help in understanding the work process and flow—that is, why things are done in a certain way or in a certain order. The observer will also look at things like the pace of work, the noise level, whether a student will be working alone or in a group, whether the air temperature is hot or cold, whether the work is indoors or outdoors, whether it involves working with machinery or with paper and pencil, and how much the intern will be expected to interface with other people—co-workers or customers.

A thorough environmental analysis will help guide the job coach or teacher in identifying the questions he or she will ask when he or she visits the department and will set the stage so that potential problems can be addressed in advance. For example, if a student has autism and it is known that she or he doesn't relate well in large groups, the internship team might decide that a given internship isn't going to work at all. Alternately, they might decide to add additional steps to prepare the student for the rotation, prior to its start and early in the rotation. This might involve role playing interactions with co-workers, using social stories to give cues about expected behaviors, or introducing the work experience in shorter time increments. Giving information to the manager and co-workers at the internship worksite about the student's learning style will also help the student be successful in the internship. We have found that the departments are eager to interact in a positive way, and this knowledge allows them to be an important part of the teaching and learning process.

THE INTERNSHIP FROM THE STUDENTS' PERSPECTIVE

Project SEARCH internships are carefully designed to give students with developmental disabilities the

Divine Intervention: With the Right Training, All Things Are Possible

Sarah M. was a young woman with a calling. Deeply committed to her Catholic faith, Sarah's dream was to become a nun. Because of her difficulties with reading and writing, Sarah wasn't sure that her dream was realistic. But that didn't keep her from trying. For two summers prior to attending Project SEARCH, Sarah worked at a summer camp associated with a Catholic mission on a reservation in North Dakota, and every summer she hoped that she would be chosen to stay on to work toward becoming a resident nun. She tried several years in a row but, each time, was told that she was too sensitive, too easily stressed, and too dependent on others to be successful at the mission.

When she finished high school, Sarah joined the Project SEARCH High School Transition Program at Xavier University in Cincinnati, Ohio. It was clear to her teacher, Trish Heim, and to others involved in the program that she had the caring, patient, and nurturing personality of a nun, but that she did, indeed, need to work on her self-confidence. Trish Heim assessed the opportunities at Xavier and put together a series of internships that would help her to acquire the strength and skills she needed to realize her dream. She worked in the university's Montessori laboratory school, where she impressed her mentors with her natural rapport with children and with how quickly she understood and embraced the Montessori method. She had to walk half a mile across the Xavier campus from the Project SEARCH classroom to the school, which contributed to her growing sense of independence. Another internship was in the office of Interfaith Community Engagement. She worked with the Rabbi there to help him assemble "Breakfast and Blessings" packets, which contained breakfast treats accompanied by written blessings. Sarah also took part in distributing the packets to students as they left the dormitories and headed out to morning classes. In this role, doing something she cared about and truly believed in, she strengthened her ability to initiate interactions and to assert herself.

Sarah received more than one job offer during her time as a Project SEARCH student, but she turned them down so she could return to the North Dakota mission in the summer. When she got there, it was clear to the directors of the camp that Sarah had grown and matured and that she was a better fit than she had been before. That year, Sarah was invited to stay as a year-round resident at the mission. By the end of the summer, she had taken the first step toward achieving her dream.

opportunity to show what they can do. However, no amount of analysis and planning on the part of teachers, job coaches, and managers will have any effect on actual outcomes without the dedication and hard work of the student interns. For this reason, we felt that it was important to include the students' perspective on the internship experience and to let them tell their stories in their own words.

The following eloquent and articulate comments were excerpted from essays created by students in the 2010–2011 Project SEARCH class at Medtronic in Minneapolis as a response to an inspired assignment from their teacher, Pat Bergstrom, in which they were asked to reflect upon their internship experiences to answer a series of questions.

From Matthew P.:

Working independently was my favorite part of being an intern. I could always ask my job coach for help when I didn't understand something.

Being an intern was different than being a student in several ways. The most obvious difference is that an intern dresses in business clothes….It made me feel like a part of all the workers at Medtronic. When I was a student in high school, I was learning things that would just benefit me…. As an intern, I learned new things that made me a better employee for Medtronic. That helped both of us. And, people at Medtronic are friendly and nice. At school, not all of the kids are nice. It made me feel good to go to work every day and know there wouldn't be any problems.

Seminar class is like a classroom, but we learned life skills….Everything we learned in seminar class will help us be more independent in the future.

The ultimate goal of Project SEARCH is to get a good job. I am proud to say that I was offered a job at the University of Minnesota Physicians in Minneapolis. I know that the skills I gained at Medtronic made me a good candidate for the position. I will continue to gain new skills so that I stay a good candidate in the workforce. I owe it all to Project SEARCH.

From Jared L.:

There is no recess at Medtronic like there is at school, and you dress up a lot more at work than you do at school….The things I have learned by being an intern at Medtronic are balancing checkbooks, doing interviews, learning how to do a resume and reference list, and I loved learning about all of the Medtronic products when speakers would come in to talk about them.

The intern experience helped me grow as a person because it made me more responsible. I learned that I am a hard worker and very organized. I also learned that the work I do is very important and it helps save people's lives.

The advice I would give to an intern coming to Medtronic next fall is to work hard, pay attention, and enjoy the change in the work environment.

From Ken H.:

While an intern at Medtronic, I learned many new and important things, such as how to index records in the document solutions department. Completing a project for a senior design technician in the computer science and engineering lab was what I enjoyed most about being an intern.

I grew as a person from all the new experiences, and my mom said that I have more manners now.

The advice I would give an intern coming to Medtronic next fall would be to always go to your job coach for support. They are there to help you learn and grow.

From Tony J.:

I think the primary difference in being an intern is gaining professional experience in an actual work environment as opposed to a school environment.

I believe I have learned many things while I have been at Medtronic. I know how to enter a conversation with strangers and how to dress for the corporate world. I am learning how important doing tasks on a timely basis is.

I believe I am a much more mature person because I have had this opportunity.

From Shane M.:

I feel like, since I became an intern at Medtronic, I gained a list of hard and soft skills too long to mention.

I really enjoyed going to work after seminar and working in Digital Print Solutions, the record center, accounts payable, and expense express. I will miss coming to Medtronic after today because to me I felt like I was at home. The intern experience here at Medtronic helped me regain my inner confidence in the kind of work that I can do.

Some advice I would give to the new interns is to leave the bad attitude at home and bring a good attitude to work every day.

From Micah R.:

I am currently working at the Moundsview Medtronic and am working in the print shop. Medtronic is different than going to school because I am in a work environment rather than a classroom. I like hands-on activities.

The things I am learning in seminar class are that when people come into class to speak about Medtronic, it helps me to understand what I am handling in the workplace. Things that I am learning in seminar class that will help me be more independent in my future are learning how to dress and act appropriately for the workplace and learning about punctuality and how it can affect me in the workplace.

From Jim D.:

I currently work at the University of Minnesota Physicians in Minneapolis, working in the human resources department. As an intern in Project SEARCH, I was able to practice all the things I learned in school and in seminar class, in a real work setting.

The interns learn their work skills in three rotations and have a chance to practice job skills, interviewing skills, and writing thank you letters as well as 2-week notice letters. These are things you can learn about in a classroom, but Project SEARCH allows you to learn them in seminar class and practice them in a way that helps the information all make sense.

With each rotation, your performance is evaluated so that you can do a little better each time. You also have midrotation meetings that let you know how you are doing and where you need to improve. I always did my best to improve, and I found the feedback to be very helpful. My score climbed higher with each evaluation, and I am very proud of my work at Medtronic....Being a Project SEARCH intern helped me to become more confident in what I can do and be sure of myself.

I would tell them (new interns) to learn as much as they can from the other employees and supervisors in their rotations so they can be more confident and successful in the future when they leave Project SEARCH. I would also tell them to enjoy the time they have in Project SEARCH, because it will really go fast!

Project SEARCH Internship Evaluation

Project | SEARCH

NAME OF STUDENT _____ DATE _____

EVALUATOR _____ INTERNSHIP_____

Number the appropriate column indicating student skill level for related behaviors.

4—Excellent   **3—Doing well**   **2—Improving**   **1—Needs improvement**

Work-related behaviors

SOCIAL BEHAVIOR	M	T	W	TH	F	AVG
Handles stress						
Makes eye contact						
Refrains from unnecessary social interaction (talking)						
Admits mistakes						
Accepts praise						
Cooperative and courteous						
Comments:	TOTAL					

COMMUNICATION	M	T	W	TH	F	AVG
Listens and pays attention						
Expresses personal needs (restroom breaks, doctor visits)						
Respects the rights and privacy of others						
Asks for help and clarification when needed						
Communicates adequately (initiates conversation, does not interrupt)						
Comments:	TOTAL					

APPEARANCE	M	T	W	TH	F	AVG
Maintains clean appearance						
Dresses appropriately for the job						
Body hygiene						
Comments:	TOTAL					

JOB PERFORMANCE	M	T	W	TH	F	AVG
Follows directions						
Accepts constructive criticism/feedback						
Follows rules and regulations						
Maintains good attendance						
Arrives on time for work and leaves on time						
Attends to job tasks consistently						
Completes tasks accurately						
Works at an appropriate rate						
Initiates new tasks						
Works well with co-workers						
Follows the proper "chain of command"						
Comments:	TOTAL					

Total for all columns

100–90=A 90–80=B 80–70=C 70–60=D Below 60=F

Address areas that were rated 1 and/or 2

Concerns:	Plan of action:	Results:

Signatures and comments

INSTRUCTOR	DATE

STUDENT	DATE

JOB COACH	DATE

SUPERVISOR/CO-WORKER	DATE

PARENT	DATE:

Baptist Hospital Project SEARCH internship sites

Department	Tasks
Cardiovascular services *Notes:* Small office environment Very supportive Lots of work to do	• Alumni club • Update database. • Send out meeting reminders. • Send out newsletters. • Screenings/surveys • Scan screenings into computer. • Call customers who may not have completed any questions. • Several screenings per month • Phone menu tree • Take reservations and calls from customers. • Create messages for staff. • Calls are separated into several areas. • Respond to routine calls. • Prepare various kinds of patient packets daily. • Clerical backup to inpatient flow • Fax chart information to nursing homes. • Print out a patient census each day. • Enter log of patients into computer. • General office work • Copy work • Put away inventory. • Order supplies. • Complete supply expense log. • Pre- or postwork for "quality registry" • Look for opportunities to help with this process.
Cardiac rehabilitation *Notes:* Small exercise area Most patients age 40–95 Student needs to be able to handle lots of stimulation. Customer contact	• Straighten and stock supplies in the locker room. • Clean exercise equipment daily. • Send mail outs to doctor offices. • Send letters to patients. • Make copies. • General office/clerical work • Fax reports and run copies for patients to take to their doctor. • Take patient's blood pressure (if they can learn it). • Print out daily reports and file them in the patient charts. • Each day's filing can be saved and performed the next day. • Assemble new patient charts. • Stock and organize shelves in conference room. • Prepare for education classes (e.g., assemble packets, staple information). • Sign people in for education classes. • Attend education classes.
Respiratory *Notes:* More of a technical area, work here gives therapists more patient care time.	• Deliver and locate oxygen tanks throughout hospital. • Change oxygen cylinders and put regulator tags on. • Take empty cylinders to specific areas. • Stock and check par levels in storage closets. • Bring oxygen tanks to code blue areas. • Be present for oxygen tank deliveries; verify readings and deliveries. • Reprocess ventilator equipment (very marketable skill) • Clean bottles. • Assemble new circuits on ventilators. • Collect oxymetry probes throughout hospital for recycling. • Assist respiratory therapists with transports. • Process bronchosopy scopes; check for leaks. • Order and put away supplies in department.

(continued)

High School Transition That Works: Lessons Learned from Project SEARCH® by Maryellen Daston, J. Erin Riehle, and Susan Rutkowski.
Copyright © 2012 Cincinnati Children's Hospital Medical Center. All rights reserved. Baltimore, MD: Paul H. Brookes Publishing Co., Inc.

Department	Tasks

Care management
 	
Notes: Two case managers and one social worker for each unit. Approximately 36 beds per unit.
Five units in area: 2E (orthopedics/neurology), 2W (postsurgical), 4E (chronically ill), 4W (cardiology), and 3W (oncology)
	• Copy information such as physician orders, progress notes, 24-hour medicine orders, physical and occupational therapy notes, and handwritten information from patient chart for discharge and nursing home.
	• Prepare information for emergency medical service; face sheet, medical record, history and physical examination.
	• IM letters (Important Message from Medicare)
	  • Each Medicare patient gets IM letter upon intake and discharge.
	  • Deliver IM letters to rooms.
	  • Verify that IM letter is in each patient's chart.
	  • Patients have to sign letter and copy goes in patient's file.
	• Utilize a document system—notes are printed out and then filed in patient's charts.
	• Assist receptionist (Sheila) based on office needs.
	• Student can wear a pager when staff need them as soon as possible.
	• Could use two students and split work in units between students.

Patient access/registration *Notes:* Scanning system to be implemented in October throughout hospital.	• Data entry of reports • Preregistration filing by dates • Take phone messages. • Patient transport • Take paperwork to nurses stations throughout hospital. • Greet patients. • Send face sheet to doctors from admitting from night before. • Scan orders.
Radiology *Notes:* Three departments of radiology—inpatient, out-patient, and interventional	• One student for three radiology areas • Escort patients and take them back and forth to towers and other parts of hospital. • Transport patient and maneuver bed, oxygen tanks, and/or pumps to assist technicians. • General errands: delivery within departments • Scanning—possible opportunity when new system is implemented • Minimal filing • Stock in interventional radiology. • Assist radiology technicians with tasks.
Infusion center *Notes:* 22 patients a day (approximately)	• Filing (more at beginning of month) • Work with patient care technician (learn vital signs). • Stock supplies. • Get lunches for patients from cafeteria. • Assist patients with feeding, personal care. • Run errands for departments, such as pharmacy for intravenous equipment. • Change linens on chairs after patient visits.
Postsurgical (nursing) *Notes:* Students will need to deal with sick patients and difficult personalities. A census can be printed for the students each day. Digital picture adaptations will assist training.	Student 1 • Pick up breakfast trays from patients. • Deliver to and pick up lunch trays from patients. • Load trays in carts and return to kitchen. • Take refrigerator temperatures and document. Student 2 • Make "welcome packets" for patients (60 daily, approximately eight items). • Deliver packets to all units. • Print stickers and place in patient charts. • Fill safety boxes with three items: gown, mask, and booties. • Remove any additional items from box. • Stock gloves in all patient rooms (delivered on Wednesday and Friday). • Stuff charts with blank order sheets and doctor notes pages. • Break down charts.

(continued)

Department	Tasks
Finance *Notes:* Needs to be someone good with numbers	• Data entry • Patient billing • Business office functions
Risk management	• File contracts.
Human resources	• Mailings • Put "new hire" packets together. • Pick up mail from mailroom and deliver to department staff. • File new hire paperwork. • Payroll—employment information • Box up previous year's information, data entry of previous year's information.

Materials management (MM)/central supply	• Break out—dispense items/unpack supplies.
	• Place stickers on items.
	• Pull product and deliver supplies.
	• Retrieve and locate pumps and poles.
	• Clean pumps and poles and other equipment.
	• Work with technician to count equipment: cycling count (mini-inventories).
	• Take isolation carts to certain areas.
	• Utilize handheld device and synchronize information into computer.
	• Assemble and wrap chest tube trays, take to sterile processing.
	• Wrap equipment.
	• Restock a variety of crash carts: infant, pediatric, adult, trauma (five must be set up at all times).
	• Deliver other equipment such as wound vacuums.
	• Future possibilities
	  • Data entry of chargeable items for patients
	  • Answer phones/take and deliver messages regarding equipment needs.

MM/mailroom *Notes:* Owing to Health Information Portability and Privacy Act (HIPPA, PL 104-191), computers can't be left alone when they are running a job	• Sort and deliver interoffice mail to towers. • Drop patient bills (computerized); could possibly assist manually with machine (such as loading paper). • Run mail meter (weigh, seal, and stamp).
MM/warehouse *Notes:* One team picks and one team delivers. Currently updating shelves.	• Unload delivery trucks (4 days a week). • Check in new inventory (bigger, bulkier products than central supply). • Stock shelves. • Pick, fill, and deliver department orders. • Assist with outbound shipping (FedEx, DHL).
MM/print shop	• Retrieve print jobs as they come off the printer and stack in boxes. • Binding • Clerical assistance • Get information about orders from customers over the phone.
Other possible departments for student internships	• Endoscopy laboratory • Sterile processing • Linens • Grounds keeping • Cafeteria • Marketing

City of Miami–Dade County internship sites

Project | SEARCH

Department(s)	Tasks
Agenda office	• Filing • Scanning • Copying • Assisting in setting commission agenda calendar/performing data entry through Legistar • Administering 311 program • Assisting with the preparation of consents, public hearings, personnel applications, and resolutions
Budget	• Sorting and alphabetizing invoices, requests for direct payment, and expense reports/filling • Sorting and distributing personnel action documents • Making double-sided copies • Scanning documents into hard drives • Delivering documents to departments/picking up mail • Shredding • Delivering invoices to finance department
Building	• Scanning documents • Preparing lead sheets • Reviewing scans to ensure quality • Preparing blueprints for shipping
Code enforcement	• Identifying easements • Posting violation notices • Preparing task logging sheets • E-mailing and/or mailing tax card notices
Community development	• Assisting with checklist for grant processing, preparing and taking paperwork to storage, and paperwork for Section 8 housing
Communications	• Sorting and alphabetizing videotapes • Archiving videos into network • Assisting with creating PSAs (public service announcements) • Assisting in storing and setting up equipment/minimizing event on tapes • Creating library tapes
Employee relations	• Labeling boxes of documents for storage • Answering phone calls/transferring phone calls • Performing data entry • Scanning documents • Screening applications • Greeting applicants
Finance	• Shredding documents • Making copies • Assisting with mail returns • Finding documents • Assisting with preparing documents for auditing • Maintaining packages for storage • Performing clerical duties • Performing data entry • Managing records

(continued)

Department(s)	Tasks
Grants	• Maintaining hard copy files • Maintaining backup files • Routing documents • Performing and maintaining data entry • Assisting with event planning • Assisting with MSI (Miami Sustainable Initiatives)
Fire safety	• Entering inspection forms into data system • Finding locations on a map and region identification • Answering phone calls • Filing
Human resources	• Assisting with preparing testing packets • Performing data entry • Scheduling examinations • Shredding confidential documents • Handing receipts to applicants • Mailing and label preparation
Information technology	• Managing inventory • Processing work orders • Assisting technician with dismantling CPU (central processing unit) • Transporting equipment/clearing hard drives • Processing kill disks (clearing memories from CPU) • Archiving data
Mailroom	• Sorting incoming mail • Placing postage on outgoing mail per departmental budget and code • Delivering mail to departments with administrative building • Maintaining mailroom.
Parks and recreations	• Organizing documents • Assisting with form request forms • Distributing internal mail • Faxing • Copying • Filing • Performing data entry • Transporting equipment • Assisting with summer surveys for all parks
Public facilities	• Updating market values • Updating acreage for properties • Sorting and sending property taxes • Maintaining insurance files • Maintaining legal files • Maintaining correspondence files • Finding easements in archives • Filing lien notices • Scanning status monitoring
Operations	• Managing inventory • Performing data entry into MP2 system • Performing clerical duties

(continued)

Department(s)	Tasks
Public works	• Answering phone calls • Assisting with permit reviews • Processing and retrieving logging • Scheduling inspections • Retrieving permits
Purchasing	• Revising supplier contact registration information • Assisting with the revision of the catalog • Answering and routing phone calls • Reviewing contracts • Copying • Filing • Scanning • Reviewing renewal dates
Planning	• Assisting with certificates of appropriateness • Indexing historical resolutions and ordinances • Logging property addresses • Answering and routing calls • Performing general clerical duties
Risk management	• Assisting with order forms • Preparing open enrollment packets • Creating mail list for employees • Assisting with special events (e.g., cancer awareness) • Assisting with presentation preparation • Answering and routing calls • Working with Excel spreadsheets • Assisting with walk-in clients
Zoning	• Assisting with certificate of use processing • Copying • Filing • Answering and routing calls • Scanning documents • Archiving microfiche and microfilm

Project SEARCH Xavier University internship sites

Project | SEARCH

Department	Tasks
Cintas Center Gallagher Center	• Work according to meeting setup plan. • Break down previous function. • Move chairs, tables, and other equipment as necessary. • Set up audiovisual equipment.
Physical plant	• Perform basic janitorial duties. • Change light bulbs. • Clean and monitor air ducts.
Dean's offices and admissions department offices	• Sort mail. • Deliver interoffice mail to other departments. • File by alphabetical and/or numerical. • Set up files. • Do copy work. • Perform data entry. • Perform basic computer work. • Collate packets of information. • Shred documents. • Perform document imaging.
Library	• Shelve books according to correct system. • Perform office filing. • Do copy work. • Perform data entry. • Perform basic computer work. • Collate packets of information. • Shred documents. • Perform document imaging.
Post office	• Sort postal service and interoffice mail for delivery to appropriate mail location. • Deliver mail to correct location. • Pick up outgoing mail. • Operate postage machines and scales. Identify and use the appropriate class of mail. Adhere to postal requirements. Complete postal service mailing forms. • Presort mail according to postal service requirements. • Identify insufficiently addressed mail. Use ZIP code directory to assign ZIP code. • Process mail and packages being shipped by special mail services (e.g., overnight mail, FedEx).
Landscape	• Perform basic grounds maintenance. • Plant flowers and bulbs. • Trim bushes and trees.
Various dining rooms	• Perform basic food preparation. • Stock food items. • Stock soda and vending machines. • Operate dishwasher, wash pots and pans. • Set tables. • Bus tables. • Stock other food items. • Set up salad bars.

(continued)

Department	Tasks
Bookstore	• Stock books and other items on shelves. • Serve as cashier (if able). • Unpack books. • Take inventory.
Recreation center	• Give out towels, locker keys to students and staff. • Perform basic maintenance of equipment, locker rooms. • Perform basic office work.
Health center	• Perform basic office work. • Register students. • Set up files.
Computer laboratory	• Perform basic computer maintenance. • Perform routine computer imaging and setup. • Perform basic office work.

Project SEARCH CORE Skills

Project|SEARCH

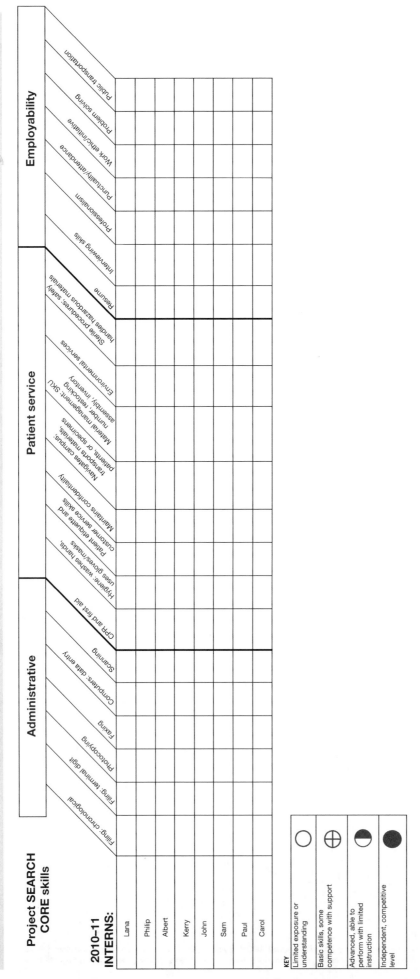

Project SEARCH CORE skills	Administrative						Patient service									Employability						
2010–11 INTERNS:	Filing: chronological	Filing: terminal digit	Photocopying	Faxing	Computers: data entry	Scanning	CPR and first aid	Hygiene: washes hands, uses gloves/masks	Patient etiquette and customer service skills	Maintains confidentiality	Navigates campus; transports materials, patients, or specimens	Material management: SKU number, restocking, assembly, inventory	Environmental services	Sterile procedures; safely handles hazardous materials	Resume	Interviewing skills	Professionalism	Punctuality/attendance	Work ethic/initiative	Problem solving	Public transportation
Lana																					
Philip																					
Albert																					
Kerry																					
John																					
Sam																					
Paul																					
Carol																					

KEY

○ Limited exposure or understanding

⊕ Basic skills, some competence with support

◐ Advanced, able to perform with limited instruction

● Independent, competitive level

Lesson Plan for Choosing Internships

Project | SEARCH

PURPOSE

When students start the process of choosing the internships that they want to do, it can be a challenging task. Using a chart like the one attached can help make the process more organized.

GOAL

Students will be involved in the internship selection process.

MATERIALS

A worksheet similar to the one provided but formatted for your host site

ACTIVITIES

1. Create a table with each student's name and a space for the student's first, second, third, and fourth choices for internships.
2. Create a list of the possible worksites, skills needed, skills learned, and related jobs.
3. At the beginning of the year, distribute the worksheet and list of worksites to the students.
4. Use this for discussion of the worksites and then have each student list their choices.
5. At the beginning of each internship rotation, distribute the worksheets again and make any necessary changes.

NOTES

- Most students will choose appropriate worksites with your guidance. If a student insists on an inappropriate worksite, address this individually in a meeting with the parents, student, and vocational rehabilitation counselor.
- Job shadowing in the internship sites prior to choosing internships can also help with this process.
- A jobsite analysis form is also provided to assist you with analyzing internship sites.

PROJECT SEARCH WORK ROTATIONS OPTIONS

Please look at the attached internship list and write your name and four internship sites where you would like to work. Not all students will get their first choice each time. All efforts will be made to give you your first and second choices before the year is over. You should consider internships in areas that match your skills, interests, and values and that would help you gain employment. If there is an area that you want to try, but it is not listed, please see the instructor. You will have an opportunity to change your choices near the end of each internship. Once you begin an internship, you are expected to stay in that area for the entire internship period.

Student name	1st choice	2nd choice	3rd choice	4th choice

(continued)

Project SEARCH internship rotations, 2008–2009

Project | SEARCH

Rotation name and department	Skills needed	Specific job skills gained	Related to what specific competitive job skill?	Soft skills/notes
Distribution/materials	Able to lift boxes, walk, reach, bend, stoop, match numbers, use a box cutter, and count	Using a number system to locate items in an inventory storage system. Using a box cutter, operating a trash compacter, lifting, bending, counting, and banding supplies. Learning medical terminology.	Order selector—PC connections, and so on. Warehouse inventory, packing/picking, or stocking	Teamwork, show initiative, work independently, prioritize work.
Linen/laundry	Stand or sit in one place for a long time, reach, and bend.	Folding with accuracy, route delivery, operating commercial washer and dryer, operating the heat stamp machine.	Commercial laundries, nursing home laundries, or hotel laundries. There are many in the local area.	Teamwork, the ability to work fast to meet deadlines, do more than one job
Sterile processing	Stand or sit in one place for a long time, match numbers and letters, and attention to detail.	Processing instruments for medical settings. Using lint roller, medical terminology, labeling and locating supplies, and working in a sterile environment.	Dentist offices, commercial laboratory processing centers such as Labcorp	Teamwork, working in a variety of temperatures, ability to do repetitive work without showing boredom
Office assistant	Alphabetize, type, ability to talk on the phone, write. Some knowledge of computers, Microsoft Word and Excel.	Filing, copying, faxing, computer keyboarding, Microsoft Word and Excel, oversight of projects, stuffing and mailing, answering phone, taking messages, and customer service.	Medical offices, insurance offices, banking centers. Entry-level clerical	Problem solving, teamwork, customer service
Financial services	Match numbers, sit for a long period of time	Matching invoices, purchase orders, filing, and copying.	Banking processing centers. Entry-level clerical	Same as above
Cancer center	Accurate alphabetizing	Filing, copying, preparing patient files.	Entry-level clerical	Same as above
CMH foundation office	Sit for a long period of time, type, use a computer, save files, detail oriented.	Enter data from newspapers into database program.	R & L Trucking company and global logistics. Data entry, using database programs	Checking all work, attention to detail.
Unit clerk assistant in patient areas	Ability to walk a lot, be polite, follow safety procedures, remain quiet, and keep information confidential.	Interaction with patients, stocking, record keeping, following safety procedures, medical terminology	Resident assistant in assisted living centers; preparation for state-tested nursing assistant (STNA) course; activity assistants in nursing homes; unit clerk in hospital	Career exploration for health care/nursing field, customer service, teamwork, confidentiality

(continued)

Rotation name and department	Skills needed	Specific job skills gained	Related to what specific competitive job skill?	Soft skills/ notes
Environmental services	Walk, bend, stoop, use chemicals, and work outside or in.	Cleaning windows, sweeping entrances, emptying trash, and light grounds keeping	CMH environmental services assistant. Entry-level cleaning/ housekeeping in area hotels and cleaning companies.	Work independently, attention to detail, follow safety procedures, teamwork.
Cafeteria	Stand, bend, walk, and use kitchen utensils.	Work in dish room, assist with salad preparation, assist with baking and assembly of meals on wheels	Most phases of food service except cooking	Teamwork, ability to work quickly, maintain stamina.
Mailroom	Attention to detail	Retrieve, stamp and sort patient and insurance checks	Entry-level clerical jobs, combined with other internships	Attention to detail, speed, meeting a deadline
Performance improvement	Walking, getting around in the building independently, using keys to open boxes, matching numbers, and counting	Going to all areas of the hospital to gather, count, and record service award cards. Keep track of keys for lock boxes. Use record-keeping system to record numbers.	Combined with other internships, entry-level clerical and a wide variety of jobs	Sense of responsibility, working independently, appearance
Community education	Answering the phone, problem solving	Assisting the manager of community education with daily activities (e.g., taking messages, preparing consumer packets, scheduling appointments)	Working in doctor's or hospital offices	Problem solving, customer service, strong communication skills
Family health center	Talking on the phone, computer skills, alphabetizing	Filing, copying, preparing patient charts, answering the phone	Doctor's offices or clinics	Teamwork, problem solving, communication, customer service
Maintenance	Lifting, walking, bending, and stooping	Repairing furniture, safely moving items, room setup, grounds keeping	Moving companies, storage companies, warehouses	Teamwork, safety procedures
Security	Walking, ability to handle a fast-paced environment, safety conscious	Using walkie-talkie, clear communications, quick response, problem solving	Security companies, loss prevention	Teamwork, responsible actions, safety procedures
Information technology	Extensive computer knowledge	Varies depending upon student's starting point.	Employment in this area typically requires advanced training.	Problem solving, career exploration in computer field
Other				

Project | SEARCH

Meet Perla

Perla is a 2009 graduate of the Project SEARCH program at Northeast Georgia Medical Center in Gainesville, Georgia. Now, Perla is successfully employed at a job she loves, but her journey to Project SEARCH was not without hurdles. In her senior year in high school, she began to lose confidence and nearly dropped out of school before graduating. But with vital encouragement from her parents and her own considerable determination, she gathered the courage to ask for the help she needed to graduate and become eligible for Project SEARCH. This opportunity for job training in a hospital setting was a dream come true for Perla, who had always wanted to work in the field of medicine.

Perla thrived as a student intern, and when she completed her year in the Project SEARCH program, she was hired in the emergency department as a patient care technician. At work, she is responsible for stocking examination rooms, taking vital signs, and transporting patients—her favorite part of the job. Perla is a real people person and loves to talk with patients and reassure them as she takes them where they need to be. Janet Fletcher, her mentor on the job, says, "Perla has been an asset to our department. She takes pride in her job and is willing to learn" (Sharee, 2009, p. 20).

One recent afternoon, Perla had the chance to put her training to the test in a dramatic way. That day, while relaxing at a park with her family, Perla came upon another family whose 2-year-old daughter had just been pulled from the lake after being submerged for nearly 2 minutes. The little girl was blue and unresponsive. Perla knew exactly what to do because of the required cardiopulmonary resuscitation (CPR) training she had taken at work. To the joy of the child's family, Perla performed CPR and revived the little girl, who because of Perla's quick thinking, survived the ordeal with no injuries. Clearly, with her compassion, commitment, and excellent training, Perla is an asset to her community on and off the job.

5 Project SEARCH Is a Collaborative Model

> *Coming together is a beginning. Keeping together is progress.*
> *Working together is success.*
>
> Henry Ford

Many organizations share the common goal of increasing employment opportunities for people with disabilities. But too often, the channels of communication among the critical players—businesses, education providers, vocational rehabilitation (VR), and other service agencies—are inefficient or nonexistent. With all of these organizations working separately and arriving at parallel procedures to reach the same goals, redundancy and inefficiency are introduced into the system—not to mention confusion and less-than-optimal outcomes for the users of their services.

All of these groups do excellent work, and they all possess considerable expertise and valuable resources. However, difficulties arise because of structural elements in the system that promote competition and provide little incentive for cooperation. As a presidential task force put it, barriers to employment are "ours as a nation, embedded in policies, practices, and attitudes that have evolved over decades" (President's Commission on Employment of People with Disabilities, 1998).

Competition for funding is a major barrier to collaboration. This competition arises at the federal level because the Department of Education oversees both the nation's school systems and the VR system. As a result, these organizations with overlapping missions are funded from a single pot of money, which fosters an atmosphere of competition and works against cooperation. At the local level, VR contracts with community rehabilitation partners (CRPs) to deliver services, thus setting up a system of competition among CRPs that compete for limited local funding. With this system in place, at the national, state, and local levels, organizations are reluctant to pay for services that they consider the responsibility of another organization, and procedures are carefully designed to avoid such overlap. Over time, the result is agencies that operate in silos with different priorities and completely separate procedures. One example of this is the concept of eligibility for services within the school systems as opposed to that of VR. Schools operate under the strictures of the Individuals with Disabilities Education Act (IDEA, PL 108-446), wherein the successful "placement" of a young person with a disability can include further education, a day program, military service, or a job. Thus, the schools use a much broader definition of disability than VR, for which competitive employment is the sole focus. For example, in many states, mental illness is considered a disability by the schools but not by VR or DD.

Although the missions of federal agencies are defined by federal mandates, these mandates are broadly written so that agencies have sufficient latitude in designing day-to-day operations. But these broad definitions also mean that, when money is tight, the agencies can retrench and more narrowly define their missions. A recent example is the "Order of Selection" implemented by VR in many states in the 2010–2011 fiscal year in response to funding shortages. Under this order, the VR can serve only those individuals determined to be the "most severely disabled" (MSD). This means that young people with disabilities may fall through the cracks if they do not qualify as MSD with VR while, at the same time, they are not well served by the vocational training programs offered through their schools.

In many ways, the Project SEARCH® model was conceived and shaped in response to frustration with the normal operating and funding procedures for rehabilitation and training. Although other employment initiatives may have been similarly inspired, what makes Project SEARCH unique is that, rather than being an additional program that operates outside of or is layered on top of the existing bureaucracy, it instead brings these organizations together in a strategic way. That is, the model requires that a network of business leaders, special education teachers, job coaches, VR case managers, and other employment specialists perform carefully crafted, integrated roles that allow for the most efficient and effective use of the available expertise and funding streams. As a result, the program can be a catalyst for the real systemic change that is needed to facilitate competitive employment for individuals with disabilities.

THE ESSENTIAL PARTNERS: THEIR ROLES AND RESPONSIBILITIES

Overview

Project SEARCH is a partnership between business, education, VR, long-term supported employment agencies (e.g., DD), and CRPs. Together, these organizations—with vital input from people with disabilities, their families, and the Social Security Administration (SSA)—implement a program model that is self-sustainable as long as the partners fulfill their respective roles and responsibilities. The host business provides a variety of internships that teach core skills of the business, as well as a liaison, who coordinates the program within the business. The educational organization (e.g., a school district, a career and technical district, or an educational service center [ESC] or other local education agency [LEA]) provides an instructor and recruits appropriate participants from its student body. State VR agencies provide individualized career counseling and services for eligible student participants, which often include funding for job coaching and placement. CRPs provide direct assistance to the student interns by providing the job coaches and assistance with the competitive job search and placement in the community. DD agencies provide long-term retention and follow-along for eligible individuals who receive a competitive job at the host business or in the community. Additional partners may include, but are not limited to, state departments of education, Social Security offices, and workforce development boards.

The Host Business

Project SEARCH is a business-driven program, so it is essential that the host business participates as an active partner and not just as a passive sponsor. To effectively establish this active participation, it is important that the business representatives involved in the initiation of a new Project SEARCH program include policy makers, policy enforcers, and the people who do the day-to-day work of the business.

A manifestation of business's critical role is a focus on training for competitive employment as the only acceptable outcome. That employment could be at the host business or with another business in the community. The important factor is that participants leave the program with the necessary competitive skills to be employed. A critical program element that is designed to help meet this goal is the concept of total immersion in the workplace. This means that the business's physical location is where all of the activities of Project SEARCH take place, which requires full commitment on the part of the business. First, the business must provide onsite space for a classroom to accommodate the High School Transition Program. In addition, the business provides access to a variety of high-quality internships that teach the core skills that are important to the industry sector and that are required to gain entry-level employment. The third essential contribution that the business makes to the partnership is a business liaison—an employee who will spend a portion of his or her effort coordinating the business's role in the program. The business should expect the liaison to devote about 5% to 10% of his or her time to Project SEARCH. The amount of time spent on the specific responsibilities that make up the liaison's role will shift as a program moves from the planning stage to the implementation stage. Once the program is in operation, there are regular annual cycles of events and priorities and responsibilities and the business liaison's role changes accordingly. This progression is shown schematically in Figure 5.1.

Role: Business Liaison

Student recruitment: organize school presentations, information sessions, tours, skills assessment days, student interviews, selection process; perform associated tasks such as application process selection rubric and eligibility determination

Internships: identify and analyze potential internship locations, develop task designs for internship areas, provide job coaching, monitor and evaluate intern progress, provide education and communicate with internship site staff, and create job accommodations

Job development: analyze employment climate, connect with community employers, build vocational profiles for interns, provide individual job search activities, and facilitate supports for competitive employment

Meetings and marketing: develop and utilize marketing tools and facilitate Business Advisory Committee, intern employment-planning meetings, individualized education program (IEP) meetings, and other problem-solving team meetings

Teaching and curriculum: orientation to host business, individual, and group classroom instruction

Training and staff development: participate in Project SEARCH®–sponsored training, prepare and deliver family involvement curriculum, and prepare and deliver program information to internal and external partners

Technical assistance: work with the internal Project SEARCH team on program development and continuous improvement

Paperwork: process licensing agreement, intern attendance sheets, Commission on Accreditation of Rehabilitation Facilities (CARF) reports, intern progress reports, billing to funders, grant-related reports; create materials for interns and businesses

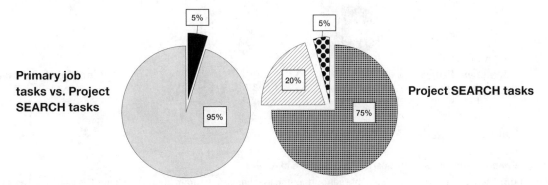

Program Phase: Planning Year, 1st Quarter—September, October, and November

Assumption: The business liaison may or may not be identified during the first quarter of the planning year. There should be minimal involvement from a selected host business until other details, such as service providers and funding, are determined. Once the original planning team identifies a host business and a liaison, that person(s) would become an active team participant.

Figure 5.1. Business liaison responsibilities. Pie charts at left indicate time spent on primary job tasks (gray) versus Project SEARCH tasks (black); charts at right break down the Project SEARCH tasks (see key above).

(continued)

Figure 5.1. *(continued)*

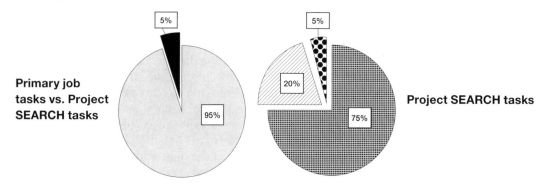

Program Phase: Planning Year, 2nd Quarter—December, January, and February

Assumption: The business liaison is involved with the planning team to determine specific logistics for the program (classroom, equipment, intern orientation requirements) and work with the partners on general program setup.

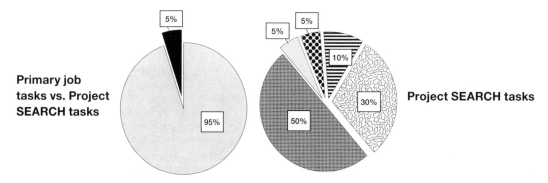

Program Phase: Planning Year, 3rd Quarter—March, April, and May

Assumption: The role of the business liaison will increase somewhat. The liaison's activities include identifying potential internship sites within the organization, serving on the intern selection committee, and identifying the specific intern orientation process. The liaison continues to work with team in planning general program setup.

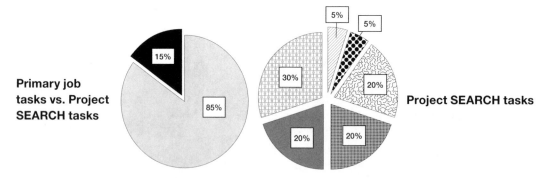

Program Phase: Planning Year, 4th Quarter—June, July, and August

Assumption: The business liaison is a valuable support for the teacher and program during this time. The liaison will assist with the teacher's orientation to the business, guide the orientation process for interns, provide teacher/job coach access to managers and internship sites, and introduce Project SEARCH® information to the entire host site staff.

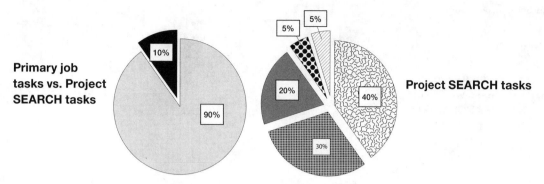

Program Phase: Year 1, 1st Quarter—September, October, and November

Assumption: The business liaison is the primary person to help interns and the program staff become immersed into the business culture. Activities include connecting the teacher and job coaches to managers and mentors, supporting introductory activities for the program, and monitoring the intern orientation process.

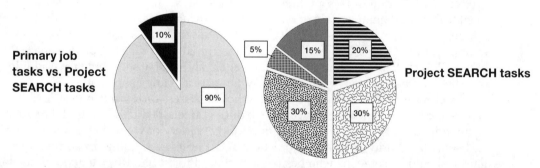

Program Phase: Year 1, 2nd Quarter—December, January, and February

Assumption: The business liaison continues to assist the teacher and job coaches in meeting with managers and mentors for internship development. The liaison also helps interns understand the transition from student to intern to potential employee. In addition, the liaison may assist managers or human resources staff to identify hiring situations within the host site and serve on the program recruitment selection committee.

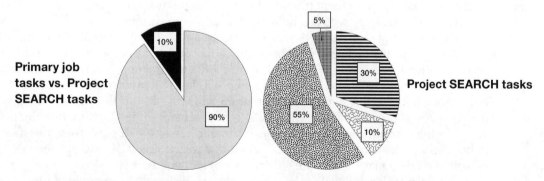

Program Phase: Year 1, 3rd Quarter—March, April, and May

Assumption: The focus of the business liaison moves to job placement for interns and assisting in the selection of students for the following year. The liaison may reach out to other similar businesses in the community or to human resource consortiums to market the program and interns' portfolios. The liaison is also vital to the evaluation of the program's first year.

(continued)

Figure 5.1. *(continued)*

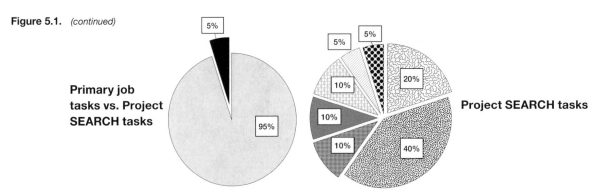

Primary job tasks vs. Project SEARCH tasks

Project SEARCH tasks

Program Phase: Year 1, 4th Quarter—June, July, and August

Assumption: The liaison is vital to the evaluation of the program's first year and for the transition from intern to employee for interns hired at the host site. The liaison also continues to be involved in job development for current year students and building new internships for the new program year.

In some cases, a business liaison may initially spend more than the usual amount of time on Project SEARCH duties. This might happen if the host business chooses to make a bigger investment to start a program quickly or on a larger-than-usual scale. In such cases, the business might ask the liaison to make Project SEARCH nearly a full-time job, at least in the start-up phase. For example, at The Denver Children's Hospital, they hired a full-time liaison to manage the start-up of their Project SEARCH program, with the understanding that she would have additional duties once the program had moved from its early stages to a maintenance status.

To be most effective, a business liaison should possess certain attributes. First of all, the liaison should be someone whose primary job duties dovetail with the goals of the program—that is, an individual who has an appreciation for the variety of work that is done in the business and some familiarity with hiring practices and employee training. In addition, the business liaison should be someone who has passion about Project SEARCH, a good understanding of how the program fits into the mission of the company, and detailed knowledge about the work being performed. The liaison will be most effective if she or he is an employee with history and clout in the organization. The best choice is usually someone at the level of a middle manager or higher who knows how to navigate up and down the hierarchy—that is, someone who feels comfortable contacting the chief executive officer (CEO) but who also knows the right person to call in the maintenance department when the classroom needs to be painted or the information technology (IT) guy who can hook up the classroom computers.

All of the program partners will need to be involved in internal marketing of Project SEARCH within the business, but the business liaison has a special role in coordinating this activity. Internal marketing is essential to promote buy-in among as many managers as possible, and the business liaison is the one who will know the most efficient channels of communication to make this happen. The program will work best if there is broad knowledge in the company about what Project SEARCH is and general understanding that the program is active in the company and that every department has a role to play in making it a success. A heightened awareness and understanding of Project SEARCH leads to the very tangible benefit of more managers who are willing to host student interns.

The business liaison's role in planning internships is a good example of how the collaborative aspect of the Project SEARCH model can work to everyone's advantage. This is an area in which the business liaison and the teacher work closely together. These are two individuals who, outside of the context of Project SEARCH, would not ordinarily ever encounter each other. But because the classroom is at the business, the teacher and the liaison can be in contact on a daily basis, and important information can be exchanged efficiently—through regular debriefings as well as through the occasional quick chat during chance hallway meetings. By working together, the teacher and the liaison can balance the long-term workforce needs of the industry with the immediate needs of the student by thinking strategically about how internships will foster the development of skills that will lead to real jobs. Although it is ultimately the teacher and job coach who solidify the details of an internship, the business liaison acts as a planter of seeds. That is, the liaison capitalizes on the natural contacts that he or she has with people throughout the company and uses those contacts to learn about emerging labor needs that can drive internship opportunities in a strategic way so that students are being trained for jobs that are most likely to be available. This is an ongoing activity that can be carried out through formal Project SEARCH internal marketing events and other gatherings of the business leadership, as well as through the casual conversations that happen naturally on a daily basis. In this way, the liaison gets people thinking about what skills could be learned in their departments and can report back to the teacher with ideas for new training opportunities. The teacher then has a solid footing when approaching managers and is never put in the awkward position of making cold calls. Instead, she or he is able to build off the positive relationship of the business liaison.

Another function of the business liaison is to recruit members to form a Project SEARCH Business Advisory Council (BAC). The BAC is a group of local executives who represent other businesses in the same industry sector as the Project SEARCH host business. The role of the BAC is to create employment opportunities in the community in similar businesses where students can utilize the core skills they gain through their internships.

The Local Education Agency

Under the provisions of IDEA, public schools are required to prepare children with disabilities for "further education, employment, and independent living." The High School Transition Program at the heart of the Project SEARCH model is an effective way for schools to meet this mandate. Accordingly, the LEA plays a central role in planning and carrying out the program. Moreover, it is the education partner who provides the instructor—a certified special education teacher—and who has the primary responsibility for recruiting and assessing potential student participants. However, other partners, such as the business and the VR counselor, play important roles in the process of interviewing and selecting from among the prospective recruits.

The Project SEARCH Business Advisory Council

The Business Advisory Council (BAC) concept, as it pertains to Project SEARCH, was adapted and formalized by LinkAbilities, a nonprofit disability employment resource that coordinates Project SEARCH programs in New Hampshire. A Project SEARCH BAC is a group of industry representatives that provides the expertise necessary for Project SEARCH program sites to stay connected to local employers and to understand workforce development needs in their business sector. An active, sector-based BAC can create competitive employment opportunities for Project SEARCH graduates. In fact, St. Joseph Hospital in Nashua, New Hampshire, credits their BAC with helping that site achieve 100% employment among the 2009 graduates. A Project SEARCH BAC can also be an effective advocate for diversity policies that include people with disabilities as well as hiring practices that target candidates with disabilities. The BAC can also be a resource for creating networking opportunities for businesses to share best practices in disability employment.

The first step that a Project SEARCH program site should take in forming a BAC is to find champions within local businesses who are interested in participating. BAC members should be industry representatives who can provide guidance on relevant skill development and who can open doors and connect the Project SEARCH program with the right people. The ideal BAC members will have these characteristics:

- Powerful enough to influence hiring practices within their organization
- Committed to Project SEARCH and the goal of 100% employment for program participants
- Connected within the community
- Willing to reach out to other employers and colleagues to discuss and promote Project SEARCH

Managing the curriculum is another important function of the LEA. Project SEARCH provides a standard curriculum (which is described in more detail in Chapter 3) that the school adapts to meet the particular needs of the students and the business and to accommodate any circumstances unique to the particular locale. Travel training is an important part of the curriculum for which the school shares responsibility with VR. The school also provides standard supplies, such as paper and pens, although in some cases, the business will allow the classroom to be supplied with these items from the in-house stockroom. A Project SEARCH classroom doesn't require a lot of supplies, but a certain level of technology is important. The truly essential items are a few computers, a digital camera, a laminator, and a color printer.

As in any school program, the LEA is responsible for providing individual students with any necessary educational therapies, such as speech therapy or occupational therapy. In the Project SEARCH model, it is important that this therapy be tailored to the work environment. For example, if a student receives regular speech therapy, the school could coordinate a visit from a speech therapist at the beginning of each internship to determine optimal communication strategies among the student, the Project SEARCH staff, and the department staff and to figure out what support is needed for the student to perform the specific job functions in that particular setting. This assistance is essential so that the students can actively participate in the internships, learning core competitive skills with supervision from the teacher, job coach, and co-workers. The school is also responsible for providing liability insurance.

Because the teacher is located in the business, one hazard of the job is a tendency to feel isolated from the school environment and the camaraderie and support that it provides. For this reason, it is very important that the LEA create a system that ensures administrative support for the teacher. For example, the teacher should be in regular contact with the special education department to ensure individualized education program (IEP) compliance and, in general, to keep the lines of communication flowing in both directions. The teacher should also have a means to receive help in reinforcing discipline if a student is not following the code of conduct of the school or the business.

Vocational Rehabilitation

VR is the general term for the various state-level agencies that administer Title I funding from the U.S. Department of Education's Office of Special Education and Rehabilitation Services. The purpose of these funds is to provide employment-related services to people with disabilities. In the context of Project SEARCH, VR's primary role is to cover the cost of job coaching for eligible students while they are in the High School Transition Program. VR also provides individualized career counseling and guidance for eligible student participants, which may include assistance in finding employment, job coaching at the worksite during the training period, or both. VR counselors have a budget to provide these services for their entire caseload, and they are given considerable leeway in terms of how they allocate that funding. In this way, vocational planning and support can be tailored to the needs of the individual. Some additional services that VR can purchase include travel training and driver evaluation and lessons, and VR can also secure funds to cover uniforms, specialized equipment, or assistive technologies.

The role of VR in Project SEARCH is carried out most effectively if each program site is served by a single VR counselor. Like the business liaison, that counselor's specific Project SEARCH–related duties will shift over time as the program moves from the planning stage to implementation and with the annual calendar of activities (see Figure 5.2).

VR services are time-limited—that is, eligibility extends until 90 days past independence on the final competitive job. If an individual is still employed at that time, VR closes the case successfully. However, in keeping with the flexibility given to VR counselors, they can make exceptions to the 90-day limit in special cases in which a convincing argument can be made for additional coaching or other support.

All of the services and funding that come from VR are provided on the basis of the eligibility of individual students. Thus, it is important that VR counselors are part of the selection

Role: VR Counselor

▤ **Student recruitment:** organize school presentations, information sessions, tours, skills assessment days, student interviews, selection process; perform associated tasks such as application process selection rubric and eligibility determination

▨ **Internships:** identify and analyze potential internship locations, develop task designs for internship areas, provide job coaching, monitor and evaluate intern progress, provide education and communicate with internship site staff, and create job accommodations

▦ **Job development:** analyze employment climate, connect with community employers, build vocational profiles for interns, provide individual job search activities, and facilitate supports for competitive employment

▤ **Meetings and marketing:** develop and utilize marketing tools and facilitate Business Advisory Committee, intern employment-planning meetings, individualized education program (IEP) meetings, and other problem-solving team meetings

▨ **Teaching and curriculum:** orientation to host business, individual, and group classroom instruction

▦ **Training and staff development:** participate in Project SEARCH®–sponsored training, prepare and deliver family involvement curriculum, and prepare and deliver program information to internal and external partners

▨ **Technical assistance:** work with the internal Project SEARCH team on program development and continuous improvement

▨ **Paperwork:** process licensing agreement, intern attendance sheets, Commission on Accreditation of Rehabilitation Facilities (CARF) reports, intern progress reports, billing to funders, grant-related reports; create materials for interns and businesses

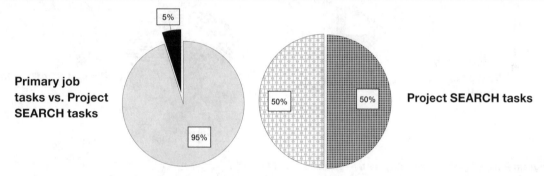

Primary job tasks vs. Project SEARCH tasks

Project SEARCH tasks

Program Phase: Planning Year, 1st Quarter – September, October, and November

Assumption: During the initial planning time, individual VR counselors may have limited involvement. Activities for the VR counselors may include meeting or training with VR supervisory staff to learn about the program.

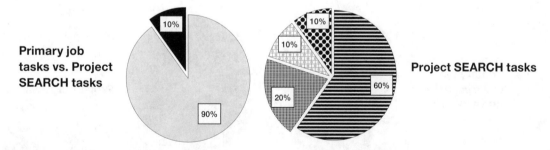

Primary job tasks vs. Project SEARCH tasks

Project SEARCH tasks

Program Phase: Planning Year, 2nd Quarter—December, January, and February

Assumption: The VR counselor is vital as the program begins recruitment of new interns.

Figure 5.2. Vocational rehabilitation (VR) counselor responsibilities. Pie charts at left indicate time spent on primary job tasks (gray) versus Project SEARCH tasks (black); charts at right break down the Project SEARCH tasks (see key above).

(continued)

Figure 5.2. *(continued)*

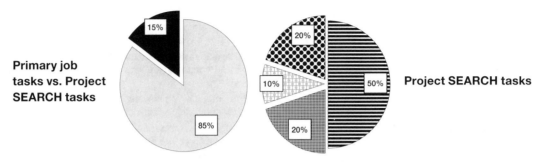

Program Phase: Planning Year, 3rd Quarter—March, April, and May

Assumption: The VR counselor is vital as the program continues recruitment of new interns and eligibility for VR services is determined. The program may utilize one or two counselors for all students.

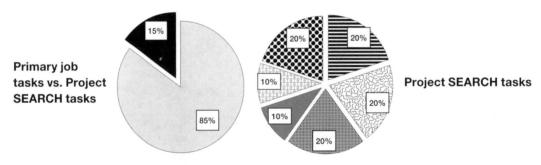

Program Phase: Planning Year, 4th Quarter—June, July, and August

Assumption: The VR counselor(s) will be involved in developing individual plans for the interns and will be a valuable resource for the program staff in planning quality internships and addressing individual job goals for the intern.

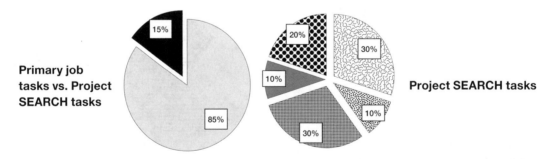

Program Phase: Year 1, 1st Quarter—September, October, and November

Assumption: The VR counselor(s) will participate in monthly meetings and is an important team member supporting the individual intern and the general program activities.

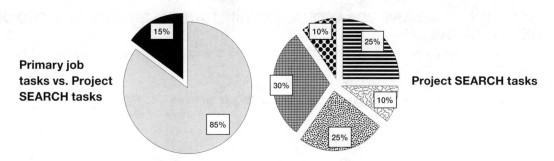

Program Phase: Year 1, 2nd Quarter—December, January, and February

Assumption: The VR counselor(s) will participate in monthly meetings and is an important team member supporting the individual intern and the general program activities. Monthly meetings focus on job placement planning. The VR counselor also participates in the intern recruitment and selection process.

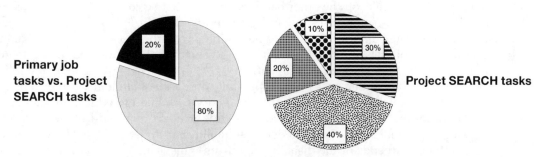

Program Phase: Year 1, 3rd Quarter—March, April, and May

Assumption: The VR counselor is vital to job placement activities—planning, benefits analysis, job coaching support, and so on. The counselor also is involved in recruitment and selection of the incoming student group.

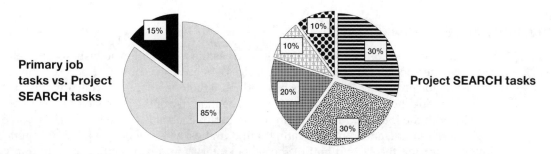

Program Phase: Year 1, 4th Quarter—June, July, and August

Assumption: The VR counselor(s) follows job placement through 90 days post–job coaching for completing interns and completes the intake process and initial planning for new interns.

ELIGIBILITY TO RECEIVE VOCATIONAL REHABILITATION SERVICES IS BASED ON THREE FACTORS

- "You have a physical or mental impairment that constitutes or results in a substantial impediment to employment.
- You can benefit from services in terms of an employment outcome.
- You require vocational rehabilitation services to retain or gain employment."

Source: Ohio Rehabilitation Services Commission, n.d.

---

committee to make sure all students are eligible before they enter the program. To decide that a given young person is eligible, the VR counselor must believe that—with the appropriate training and support—he or she is capable of becoming an independent competitive worker and that the individual will benefit from VR services. This definition leaves a lot of room for interpretation and creates a situation in which meeting eligibility is somewhat of a balancing act. On the one hand, it is necessary that the individual have a significant disability that is a barrier to employment while, on the other hand, he or she must be considered capable of successful employment. Also, some states are under "order of selection," which means that, in times of funding shortages, priority is given to individuals with the most significant disabilities. VR uses a variety of tools, including vocational assessments, interviews, and disability documentation, to make these difficult determinations.

Because of the differences in their missions, this issue of eligibility can be a point of contention in the collaboration between the LEA and VR. Unlike VR, education is an entitlement, which means that the school is required to provide an appropriate education to every child. As a result, the school is motivated to define suitability for Project SEARCH more broadly than does VR, on both ends of the disability spectrum. This is an area in which Project SEARCH partners may need to compromise on a decision, and it could be necessary for one partner to be in a position in which they have to come to a consensus that is very difficult. However, it is also an opportunity for the partners to learn from each other and gain new insights through firsthand exposure to the perspectives of the different organizations. This is one of the points that illustrates both the benefits and the challenges of partnership.

Community Rehabilitation Provider

CRPs are the community-based agencies, such as the Goodwill or Jewish Vocational Services, that provide specialized rehabilitation services. As a Project SEARCH partner, the CRP is responsible for providing the job coaches and job developers. The job coach works at the business alongside the students and the teacher. The majority of the job coach's time is spent at the job site with the interns, training them in competitive job skills. The job coaches also do some internal marketing and communicating with families, as needed. The job developers become involved during the second half of the school year to find competitive jobs. In many Project SEARCH programs, the instructor and job coach take major responsibility for the job search process because they are the ones who have the most knowledge about the skills and abilities of the interns. In addition, the families are very involved in locating employment using their connections in the community to assist with job development.

County Board of Developmental Disabilities

These agencies provide long-term job retention services and follow-along for eligible individuals who receive a competitive job at the host business or in the community. The DD case managers are involved in helping people with disabilities navigate difficulties at work or in their home lives that can interfere with their ability to continue working. For example, DD can

ON USING THE TITLE "JOB COACH" TO DESCRIBE TRAINERS

In Chapter 1 and Appendix 1.1, we discussed the negative impact of using specialized, rehabilitation industry jargon instead of standard business terminology. The use of "job coaching" to describe what is usually called "on-the-job training" was one example we gave. Nonetheless, you will notice that we have chosen to use the term "job coach" to describe the individuals who provide training in the Project SEARCH model. Currently, we see no good way of getting around this inconsistency between philosophy and practice because "job coach" is the universally accepted title among the agencies that collaborate with Project SEARCH. If we were to uni-laterally decide on a new term, it would cause logistical and communication difficulties. So, for now, we will call our job trainers "job coaches" and, in the meantime, continue working to influence the use of language in the rehabilitation field.

intervene if there is a major life change, such as the death of a parent, or a disruptive worksite change, such as a new manager or the introduction of new technology. To be consistent with the Project SEARCH model, the DD agency must agree to place an employment specialist onsite to handle follow-along at the host business when the population of employees with significant disabilities reaches critical mass (i.e., 15 to 20 people).

Social Security Administration

The SSA has a status different from that of the other Project SEARCH partners. It is not criti-cal that this agency take part in planning the program, and they do not participate directly in the day-to-day operations. However, it is vital for every Project SEARCH site to have access to information on SSA programs. Representatives from the SSA can play an important role in ad-vising Project SEARCH staff on SSA programs and work incentives through which individuals can receive funding for resources that Project SEARCH partners can't otherwise pay for. One of these mechanisms is the PASS (Program to Achieve Self-Support) plan, which allows an in-dividual with a disability who is employed to shelter some of her or his Supplemental Security Income (SSI) for items or services that are required to sustain employment. For example, if the individual requires a car to transport to the employment site, she or he can continue to receive a portion of the SSI check sufficient to cover car payments until the car is paid off. Or, if an individual is not DD eligible, provisions of the PASS plan can be used to pay for follow-along. Another important function of the SSA involvement is to assure parents and other guardians that, financially, competitive employment will be a net gain and not a loss for the family. This is an important educational piece that should be presented to parents as early as possible—ideally, before the program begins so that the family can get individualized information and have the opportunity to form a relationship with the local SSA office. This allows the family to be an active participant in writing plans, sheltering resources, and making a successful transi-tion from relying on public benefits to working competitively.

Families

The families of people with disabilities are integral to every aspect of Project SEARCH—so much so that it is difficult to define a distinct role for this group. And, of course, because dis-ability touches the lives of so many people, many of the professionals involved in establishing and maintaining a Project SEARCH program are individuals who play a dual role—as an ad-ministrator and as a parent of a child with a disability.

Research demonstrates that, when families are involved in the transition process, it increas-es the chances that their young adult children will achieve satisfactory employment outcomes (Hanley-Maxwell, Pogoloff, & Whitney-Thomas, 1995; NCWD for Youth, 2011; Timmons, Hall, Bose, Wolfe, & Winsor, 2011). The family plays a rich and complex role throughout the Project

THE CHANGING DEFINITION OF "FAMILY"

"A young person may live in any number of family constructs, including ones in which couples are married, cohabitating, or the same sex, or in single-parent, blended, grandparent-led, foster care, or a group home. A youth's 'family' may not always include a mother and a father. Rather, a sibling, aunt/uncle, grandparent, neighbor, teacher, peer, or other influential adult may play a guiding role for a young person. The National Collaborative on Workforce and Disability for Youth defines family this way in its Family Guideposts: 'Family is defined broadly as adults and children related biologically, emotionally, or legally, including single parents, blended families, unrelated individuals living cooperatively, and partnered couples who live with biological, adopted, and foster children.' It is important that professionals working to help youth prepare for and find employment acknowledge the many forms 'family' can take and allow input and participation from a wider variety of adults who have a positive influence on a youth."

(From Roy, C. [2011, April]. Tapping into the power of families: How families of youth with disabilities can assist in job search and retention. NWCD for Youth Brief. Retrieved from http://www.ncwd-youth.info/sites/default/files/infobrief_issue27.pdf. This document was developed by the National Collaborative on Workforce and Disability for Youth, funded by a grant/contract/cooperative agreement from the U.S. Department of Labor, Office of Disability Employment [Number #OD-16519-07-75-4-11].)

Project SEARCH adheres to this inclusive definition of "family" that was so eloquently expressed by NCWD for Youth.

SEARCH experience; however, the initial requirements are that the family learn about Project SEARCH and arrange the IEP meeting to change the child's placement from his or her current educational setting to the Project SEARCH program. Throughout the year that their student is attending the Project SEARCH High School Transition Program, the minimal requirement of the family is that a representative attends monthly employment-planning meetings. These meetings are attended by the teacher, the parents (or other guardians), the student intern, the job coach (if possible), and the student's VR counselor. The purpose of the meetings is to take stock of the student's career goal, what he or she is doing to attain that goal, and the challenges he or she is encountering along the way. As such, each meeting includes a short recap of the skills the student is working on in his or her current internship and a look ahead to form a plan for building on those skills. At the beginning of the school year, the teacher leads the meeting, but later, the student takes over this role as he or she gains confidence.

In recognition of the critical role of families, Project SEARCH has developed a formalized Family Involvement component of the program (see Chapter 3). This program consists of training sessions and activities, led by parent volunteers, to help families learn what they can do to prepare their children for competitive employment, network to create employment opportunities, and learn how they can provide the best possible support systems for their children as they move into good jobs and grow in their chosen careers.

TRUE COLLABORATION IS TRANSFORMATIONAL

Collaboration is at the heart of the successful implementation of Project SEARCH practices. The partner organizations must go beyond simple cooperation, in which partners work toward common goals, but do so without making any major changes in their basic services, policies, or administrative regulations. In contrast, the Project SEARCH model requires a "transformational" collaboration in which each partner organization is fundamentally changed. Most importantly, the partners must focus on outcomes for the whole community rather than defending traditional "territory." Along these lines, they must be flexible with regard to where and how their employees do their work. That is, the partners are expected to assign personnel to the Project SEARCH program while still handling the salary, benefits, performance evaluations, and so on. For example, the rehabilitation and education partners must allow their job coaches, follow-along staff, and teachers to be housed in the Project SEARCH host business, outside of the usual agency structure. In turn, the host business must accommodate the onsite teaching, training, and follow-along personnel. Moreover, supervisors, managers, and HR per-

NECESSARY CONDITIONS FOR TRUE COLLABORATION

- Visionary leadership—willing to take risks and facilitate change
- Shared leadership—willing to cultivate a new style of leadership
- Atmosphere of mutual respect, tolerance, and trust
- Involvement of all key players for shared decision making and support and recognition for their efforts
- Ownership at all levels
- Pooling of resources
- Acceptance of public responsibility for what the collaborative does or does not accomplish
- Mission or unifying theme that conveys the group's message to potential partners
- Shared space with equal access and opportunity for interaction
- Opportunities for exploration and experimentation
- Goals that are shared, understood, and significant
- Competence of collaborating members
- Creation of value
- Continuity to the interactions
- Inclusion of consumers in planning and assessment of satisfaction

sonnel within the host business must accept and interact with the onsite Project SEARCH staff while still allowing them to do their jobs of teaching and coaching.

Project SEARCH Was Formed in an Era When Collaboration Was Rare

When Project SEARCH started in 1996, the formation of corporate alliances was not common practice. The resistance to collaboration in the business world was natural because, any time groups with differing philosophies, practices, and motivations try to work together, difficulties are bound to arise. If the need for forming alliances isn't there, businesses will tend to avoid it, and in 1996, the business landscape didn't often present the need to join forces. Competition was simpler, and companies didn't have to excel in a broad range of expertise to be successful (Harbison & Pekar, 1998). Ironically, the very organizations that make up Project SEARCH— schools, hospitals, and public agencies—are among those that tend to be most resistant to collaboration (Pekar, 2001).

But around the time that Project SEARCH was forming, the environment began to change. Since that time, the landscape has become progressively more conducive to collaboration; competition is no longer simple, and companies are now required to excel in a wide range of areas to be competitive. Now, alliances in the business world are necessary and common, and they often occur between former competitors. The same trend holds true in the not-for-profit world where, likewise, money is scarce and the environment is more complex. Whether it's in the for-profit or not-for-profit sector, the reasons for collaborating are the same: to remain competitive, to leverage needed resources, to provide growth opportunities, to share risks, and to achieve greater efficiency and productivity.

The Different Forms of Partnership

There are important differences between "cooperation" and "collaboration" that are not always appreciated. Cooperation is more commonly practiced than true collaboration because it is much easier to achieve. In a cooperative relationship, each organization uses its own set of knowledge and abilities rather than joining together to create a new set of knowledge and abilities. The organizations attempt to solve problems on their own, and they may or may not assist one another. The result is separate paths to the same outcome. For example, schools are charged with delivering education, but under IDEA, they are also required to ensure that students with disabilities are prepared for employment. So, VR and the school systems share a common goal, but they tend to create separate programs to meet that goal. As a result, the federally mandated resources that they manage are delivered serially and in an uncoordinated fashion as individuals with disabilities leave the education system and enter the VR or DD systems. But, by bringing these organizations together, it becomes possible to coordinate the delivery of services in a way that makes sense for the individual. As a result, the young person with a disability experiences a smoother transition from school to adult services, and the different agencies end up spending less.

How Do Organizations Achieve True Collaboration?

It takes considerable effort and careful planning to establish and maintain a productive collaboration. To increase the chances that a collaborative effort will enhance the productivity of all the partners, it is important that the group spend the time and energy up front on all the necessary steps in the process:

- Assessment: This is where partners determine whether collaboration is a reasonable goal and whether the right partners are at the table.

- Planning: In this phase, the partner responsibilities are clearly defined, the financial details are worked out, and the group agrees on ground rules for interacting, decision making, and conflict resolution.

- Implementation: Contracts, agreements, and procedures for day-to-day operations are put into place.

- Evaluation: This is an ongoing process in which the partners continually assess the value and functionality of the collaboration.

Assessment

This is the initial stage when hard questions need to be asked: Will the benefits of collaboration outweigh the costs for our organization? Is there a history of communication, cooperation, and trust among the partners? Are the appropriate partners at the table? In initial meetings, weaknesses in communication are often exposed. It often becomes clear that the different agencies—even those that think they understand one another and work together regularly—don't know the language or goals of the other potential partners. This is the time to look closely at those areas where there is limited communication, cooperation, and trust and to address them head on.

The next step is to assess the individual partners. For each partner, the group needs to determine what the partner offers and whether those resources are complementary to those offered by the other partners. It is important to determine whether each organization fits in strategically, operationally, and culturally and whether each partner can assist in achieving the goal of the partnership. The group also needs to ask whether each partner organization is stable enough to withstand the change that integrating services would introduce. Schools, VR, and the host business are usually stable enough. However, the CRP is often too small to provide the necessary resources. In this case, the partners can decide to issue an RFP (Request for Proposals) to identify an appropriate CRP in the region (see Appendix 5.1). The school district might also be too small to supply a cohort of 10 to 12 eligible transition-age students and may decide to partner with other local schools. This adds to the complexity of the collaboration and can have an impact on timing.

HOW TO AVOID POTENTIAL LANDMINES

- Do not waste time! Capitalize on the enthusiasm of a wisely selected and excited core group.
- Try to make allies out of adversaries.
- Don't allow one partner organization to assume control of the group. Establish the expectation of shared leadership.
- Don't allow political pressure to control the agenda.
- Take time periodically to reflect on milestones and landmines.
- Establish clear ground rules.
- Include all important partners from the beginning.

In addition to assessing the partner agencies, it is also critical to take a close look at the individuals representing the partner organizations. It is critical that these are people with sufficient clout in their respective agencies. This can be a sticking point because it is often the case that the people who have the time and energy to put toward the process are not the people who have the necessary decision-making authority. Conversely, people with the appropriate level of authority often don't have the time that it takes to establish the collaboration. But these problems can be overcome if the partner organizations are fully committed and are willing to be flexible.

Planning

The planning process is the stage in which the partners work out the details of the specific responsibilities of the different partners, the flow of information, the flow of funds, and the timetable for implementation. In setting the ground rules for collaboration, it is critical that these rules lead to a structure in which everyone in the group contributes, that everyone develops a stake in the process, that everyone's time is used wisely, and that communication among partners is maintained at all times.

Implementation

Once the partners are chosen, and the broad structure of the program has been agreed upon, it is time for implementation. In this phase, the planning comes down to the detailed procedural level. The partners should develop and sign an agreement spelling out roles and responsibilities of the different partner organizations, or a "memo of understanding" (a template agreement is included in Appendix 5.2). Once this agreement is in place, student eligibility guidelines must be revised, application procedures adapted from the template (from the start-up materials provided to licensed Project SEARCH program sites) and put into place, the curriculum finalized, the yearly timeline of program activities determined, and the procedures for accessing job coaching and follow-along established.

It is important to note that additional issues often arise once the program starts and new issues rise to the surface, such as a need for additional job coaching hours. If there is a solid base of trust and cooperation to start with, these difficulties are much easier to solve.

Evaluation

Once it is established, if a Project SEARCH program is going to continue to run smoothly, it is necessary that the collaboration be evaluated on a regular basis. In the evaluation, the partners should ask the following questions:

- Do members share collective accountability for improving training and employment outcomes?

- Does the collaboration have broad short- and long-range outcomes?

- Do the partners agree upon the definition of the data to be collected?

- Are data collected and outcomes tracked on a regular basis?

- Are successes well publicized and used to sustain commitment to the effort?

- Is the collaboration organized and structured in a way that facilitates decision making and conflict resolution?

- Are members supported in implementing their recommendations?

- Are evaluations truly interactive and designed to help collaborators continue to improve their efforts?

THE CRITICAL CONCEPT OF BRAIDED FUNDING

A cornerstone of the Project SEARCH model is "braided funding," which means that dollars and other resources for different aspects of the program come from all of the partners. When it is structured appropriately, each partner contributes an amount similar to, and often less than, what they would spend if they were each investing in training programs separately. For example, education funds follow the students as they move from their schools to the Project SEARCH High School Transition Program. These funds are used to pay for the teacher's salary. VR partners cover part of the cost of the job coaches for students while they are in the High School Transition Program, rather than waiting until they graduate and incurring the total cost of job placement. The funding for job coaches moves from VR to the CRP, and then enters the Project SEARCH program in the form of the job coaching services provided by the CRP. Most program sites have a per-student "fee-for-service" that they have negotiated with VR, and this sum is reexamined with the CRP and VR as part of the planning process. The payments from VR are made at six outcome points: one at intake to the program, one at the conclusion of each of the three internships, one at job placement, and one after 90 days of successful employment (known as a "90-day closure" or "26").

TOOLS FOR COMMUNICATING, BRAINSTORMING, AND CONSENSUS BUILDING

Because Project SEARCH relies on close collaboration among multiple partner organizations, communication and consensus building are critical. As such, there are many continuous quality improvement tools and communication strategies that Project SEARCH routinely uses to successfully interact with all of the players and build consensus around critical issues. Many of these are described in the book, *The Memory Jogger 2* (Brassard & Ritter, 2010), and others are standard organizational tools primarily from the field of education. These tools can be adapted for the audience, the issue, or the time. The following are some fun and productive activities that we use with Project SEARCH implementation teams, along with examples of situations in which they can be used.

The Plus/Delta Chart

The plus/delta chart (Figure 5.3) is a tool that can be used to capture information about an event, activity, or process that has already occurred or is in place. It can be done in a very short

+ What went well	Δ What could be changed	Goals (This column is optional—you could develop goals from the delta column)
Eight out of 12 students were hired.	Four students were not hired.	Set a higher expectation for employment with all partners.
Students were hired at prevailing wage.	We waited too late in the year to begin the job placement process.	Find way to pay the job placement specialist to attend all monthly employment-planning meetings from the beginning of the year.
Most are able to take public transportation.	Some of our families are unwilling to explore employment owing to Social Security benefits.	Work with vocational rehabilitation to fund a benefits analysis for each student as soon as she or he is selected for the Project SEARCH® program.
Host business hired two students.	Work with other local hospitals.	Build Business Advisory Council and invite representatives from other local hospitals, as well as other identified businesses whose needed entry-level skills match those of our interns.

Figure 5.3. The plus/delta chart.

amount of time (depending on the number in the group). You can use a white board or flipchart paper to capture the group responses. The exercise allows the group to assess the activity in a manner that is positive and action oriented. The facilitator begins the exercise by asking the participants, "What went well?" Those responses go in the *plus* column. The next question is "What would you change?" Those responses go under the *delta* symbol. It is best to have an equal number of plus/delta responses. Depending on time, you can follow with a discussion about the responses or choose some of the items in the "delta" column to turn into goals to improve the activity. It's best to use "low-hanging fruit" or some items that are easy to change for the initial goals so that the group will be encouraged by seeing some immediate results. Some Project SEARCH situations in which this tool could be useful include the following:

- Reviewing the internship process with students, onsite Project SEARCH staff, or department managers

- Evaluating student recruitment events (such as open houses)

- Discussing the job placement process

Affinity Diagram

The affinity diagram is a consensus-building and brainstorming tool that is used to help organizations strategize around important issues. It is a great method for helping partners see the value of Project SEARCH processes and goals. This interactive activity takes about 1 hour, or a little more if time is included for the development of goal-setting strategies. The facilitator should begin by asking a focus question or posing a dilemma such as "How can we all work together to reach our goal of 100% employment?" The groups then follow the steps outlined herein:

- Each individual comes up with at least 10 answers or strategies to address the focus questions in 5 to 10 minutes.

- The participants are grouped in pairs to compare their lists. The object is for each pair to consolidate their two original lists into a new list of 5 strategies that address the focus question (paring down each original list of 10 to a combined list of 5 agreed-upon responses). Give each pair five half sheets of paper and ask them to write each individual response in bold lettering on a separate sheet. This step should take 10 to 15 minutes.

- Once the pairs have decided on their 5 responses, the facilitator asks questions of the large group. In response, the pairs choose from among their list of 5 responses the strategy that best answers the question (the questions should be adapted to the specific situations). The facilitator captures all of these responses and posts them for the whole group to see. The following are examples of questions that can be asked:

  - Which strategy will have the biggest impact on our common goal?

  - Which strategy will be the hardest to implement?

  - Which strategy will be the easiest to implement?

  - Which strategy can be implemented immediately?

  - Which strategy can we achieve without spending any financial resources?

- The questions are simply a way to elicit and post the responses as well as facilitate consensus building within the small groups. As more and more responses are posted, similarities start to emerge. The facilitator, with permission from the participants, should begin grouping the responses into categories that make sense to the entire group. When all the answers are on the board and grouped together, there could be anywhere from 5 to 10 categories of responses. It is okay for some responses to stand alone, because these responses could be as important as others that fit into natural groups. This part of the exercise takes between 15 and 25 minutes.

- One possible variation is to have each small group come up to the front, put up their sticky notes, move the notes around, and create the common categories on their own. However, the first process allows for more discussion among the small groups and can create new team building with some members who don't typically work together.

- The facilitator leads a discussion to name each category and create a common goal based on the responses.

- Once the goals are identified, they can be prioritized and put into an action plan (possibly in another group meeting, or as a project that is completed by an individual and then distributed to the group for comment). Participants can volunteer to work on one or more of the goals. The groups could also decide not to pursue all of the goals (depending on time and resources), but instead to prioritize the goals and address those that the group agrees will yield the greatest results with regard to the original focus question (Table 5.1).

Brain Writing 6-3-5 for Brainstorming and Building

Brain writing 6-3-5 for brainstorming and building (Figure 5.4) provides time and structure for a team to generate a large number of ideas and to find helpful connections among those ideas. It allows for creativity and synergy among team members. An ideal number of team members for this exercise is six, but other group sizes can also work. The first step is to identify and clarify a problem statement. Once that is done, each person begins with a blank 6-3-5 worksheet and writes the problem statement exactly as the group has defined it. Each participant then works individually to write down three ideas in the top row of the worksheet within 5 minutes. The ideas should be written in concise but complete sentences. When everyone is finished, each participant passes the worksheets to the person on her or his right. With each turn, the participants should read all the ideas on the worksheet to stimulate further thinking and do the following:

- Expand on the ideas of others.

- Write a variation of a previous idea.

Table 5.1. Example of results from an affinity diagram exercise

Focus question: How can the onsite Project SEARCH® team work together to increase job placement results?				
Internships	Business Advisory Committee	Monthly employment-planning meetings	Internal communication	Community marketing
Ensure that the internships teach competitive skills.	Ask department managers to sit on the Business Advisory Committee.	Ask all team members at the monthly employment-planning meetings to say how they will be involved with job placement.	Job coach, teacher, and business liaison should meet weekly in second semester to brainstorm job search ideas.	Ask host business leadership for an invitation to attend Rotary and present about Project SEARCH.
Internships should reflect the "real" job of the department.	Ask the business liaison to use his or her internal and external contacts to create a Business Advisory Committee.	Ask parents to bring in one local job opening to each monthly meeting that could be appropriate for their child or another Project SEARCH intern.	Plan a "lunch and learn" for staff at host business who don't know about Project SEARCH.	Speak to the leadership of similar businesses in the community that may have job openings that relate to students' skill set.
Create last internship opportunity in the community to expand the pool of possible businesses that consider students for hire.	Ask department hosts for contacts at similar businesses if they have openings and would interview/consider students.	Work with the intern to lead the monthly employment-planning meetings and review her or his specific job skills and continually clarify her or his job goal.	Meet with HR to identify the process for a student intern who wants to apply for an internal opening at the host site. Determine whether the students have any special internal status when applying for jobs such as "preferred candidates" or "Project SEARCH intern preferred." Ensure that students can execute this process successfully.	Create a reverse job fair and invite similar businesses to meet and interview the students for the purpose of considering them for hire at their organization.

Key: HR, human resources.

- Generate a completely new idea.

- If there are fewer than six people, circulate the worksheets until they are complete.

- Once the group gets to line 5 and 6, participants may need more time to read through all the ideas and generate the next line of responses.

The final step is to review all the ideas and clarify the responses that may be confusing, eliminate any duplicates but keep variations or extensions of a single idea, and come to consensus around one to three ideas to pursue further.

Sample problem statement: How can family members be involved in the Project SEARCH® program and contribute to the goal of employment?		
1	**2**	**3**
1 Family members can bring job openings to the monthly employment-planning meetings.	Families can look at their own place of employment for possible job openings and communicate the process for applications to the teacher.	Ask all of the families if they belong to Rotary, Kiwanis, or other community agencies and ask if we can give presentations to these about Project SEARCH.
2 Family members should bring job descriptions that could relate to any of the students (and not just their own student).	Schedule meeting with the specific HR person at the parent's place of employment to discuss Project SEARCH, ask about needed entry-level skills, and determine whether there is a match. Discuss building the new skills needed into existing internships.	Brainstorm other community agencies that could help create employment opportunities such as a local chapter of the Society for Human Resource Management.
3 Families that are interested and willing to share student information could meet and discuss all the students' career goals and internship plans to help them target employment opportunities and increase overall awareness and buy in.	If there is interest from the families' company and good receptivity from the HR staff, discuss possibility of doing a third internship for a student who might be a good match with that company.	Create a "marketing kit" so that any parent or anyone else on the team can make a presentation with the same information and message. The kit could contain a PPP, flyer about the program, CD, and so on. Families need some kinds of ID or business card when they give these presentations.
4 Ask one family member who has a strong interest and time to take a role of "family liaison." This person would help roll out the family involvement curriculum.	Ask that company to be part of the Project SEARCH Business Advisory Committee.	Poll the family members to see if there is media/PR/graphic design expertise in this group. Ask if that person could help with the development of a media kit.
5 Create a "family employment group" for all the current parents/family members. The group could choose to host a variety of activities including learning about all the students to help with employment ideas, becoming familiar with the Project SEARCH model, learning about how Social Security affects employment, and so on.	Ask the family to help brainstorm other similar businesses that might want to work with Project SEARCH and follow up with them to give general information and hopefully create employment opportunities.	Work with the business liaison and determine the feasibility of beginning a family support group at the host business. This group would be for any family members who work at the host business. Those family members may not have anything to do with Project SEARCH. This group would support one another in gaining independence for their own child with a disability.
6 Add prior parents to the "Project SEARCH family employment group," especially those whose youth may not have employment.	Organize a group presentation to all companies where the student's families work. Possible name: "Friends and Family of Project SEARCH." The goal would be general awareness and possible employment opportunities.	The host business support group could merge with the Project SEARCH family employment group for certain educational programs and other support services.

Key: HR, human resources; ID, identification; PPP, PowerPoint presentation; PR, public relations.

Figure 5.4. Example of a completed brain writing 6-3-5 worksheet.

Request for Proposals to Provide Job Coaching and Development Services for the Project SEARCH® Program

Project | SEARCH

Request for Proposals to Provide
Job Coaching and Development Services for
the _____ Project SEARCH Program

INTRODUCTION

_____ Schools is requesting proposals from Commission on Accreditation of Rehabilitation Facilities (CARF)–accredited agencies to provide Job Coaching and Job Development Services for students with disabilities enrolled in the _____ Project SEARCH program. The selected provider agency will provide services through Vocational Rehabilitation and work with _____ Schools for these services for the 20__–20__ program year. Proposals must be submitted to _____ (name) at _____ (location).

PROGRAM DESCRIPTIONS

The _____ Project SEARCH is a combined education and work experience program for students with developmental disabilities who have completed their high school academic requirements, but who have not yet officially graduated. This 1-year program prepares these students for competitive employment in the community. _____ Project SEARCH is modeled after Project SEARCH, a nationally recognized program initiated by Cincinnati Children's Hospital Medical Center. _____ Project SEARCH is currently located at one site, _____ (name of host site). In the Project SEARCH model, student "interns" spend their entire "school" day at a business site, which provides onsite space for a classroom as well as job rotation internships.

The students work on employability skills in the classroom for the first hour and last half hour of the day. The bulk of the day is spent on an internship for which they applied and were interviewed and selected. These work assignments are unpaid and rotate three times during the program year. They are designed to teach competitive, marketable skills. Students receive job coaching services in these job assignments, which are to fade over the course of each rotation.

The goal of the Project SEARCH program is for each student intern to be placed in a competitive job no later than 3 months after the end of the Project SEARCH program year. Job development placement services are to begin by the start of the second semester of the Project SEARCH program year.

Students may apply to be "permanently" employed in an open position within the host business site during the course of the school year. Students not employed or not anticipated to be employed by the host business by the end of the Project SEARCH program year will be actively assisted in finding employment with other community businesses using the skills they learn in Project SEARCH.

SCOPE OF SERVICES

Job Coaching Services Description

Job coaches are responsible for training and problem-solving issues related to the student and meeting the employer's expectation. Key elements of job coaching involve linking the student with onsite supports so that, eventually, the coach is able to fade from the internship, thus enabling the student to learn to work independently on the job.

The Provider Agency's responsibilities in Project SEARCH include

- Providing Job Coaches (for a maximum of four students to one staff ratio), one of which will act as the Lead Job Coach.

- Assisting in the development of the Project SEARCH internship rotations

- Assisting in the development of grant proposals for funding to support the job coaching services of the Project SEARCH program

(continued)

Project | SEARCH

- Fulfilling the requirements of the Vocational Rehabilitation Services Agency for their fees for services

- Participateing in relevant Project SEARCH team and individual student intern review meetings

The Provider Agency will be paid for Job Coaching Services rendered in accordance with an approved Vocational Rehabilitation Services fee schedule developed for this program.

Job Placement Services Description

Job Placement services include all activities related to a search for a job in the community, placement, and identification of training needs. Job Placement services are a required component of the Project SEARCH program. Activities include, but are not limited to

- Identifying job opportunities that match interests and abilities of the Project SEARCH interns

- Identifying job accommodations and support needs

- Performing follow-up on job leads

- Marketing the individuals to prospective employers

- Identifying and arranging on-the-job training needs

Job Placement services will be paid by the Vocational Rehabilitation Services Agency to the Provider Agency in accordance with their service agreement and approved fee schedule.

PROVIDER AGENCY/REQUEST FOR PROPOSAL REQUIREMENTS

Provider agencies responding to this Request for Proposals must be responsive to the following requirements and must submit the accompanying documentation with a cover letter as their proposal. Additional relevant documentation may be provided by applicant agency.

- The Provider shall provide evidence of and maintain CARF accreditation for Job Coaching and Development Services and must fulfill any other relevant requirements of the Vocational Rehabilitation Services Agency to qualify for their fees for services.

- Provide copies of relevant CARF accreditation certificates and related documents

- Provide documentation of current approved Rehabilitation Services Agency service fee schedules for agency

- Provide any other relevant documentation regarding agency's services to Vocational Rehabilitation–funded (sponsored) clients

The Provider shall demonstrate prior successful experience in job coaching and job development services for individuals with disabilities and, in particular, those with developmental disabilities.

- Provide a list of relevant past experience including the businesses where jobs have been developed and job coaching provided. Include letters of reference and/or support.

- Provide a list of the range of individuals served through job coaching and development services. Include examples of particularly challenging success stories and letters of support.

The Provider shall illustrate that it has the administrative infrastructure to support the provision and supervision of job coaching and job development services.

- Provide agency's table of organization including personnel involved with job coaching and development services and supervision.

- Provide a list of the qualifications, credentials, and experience of key agency personnel involved in the provision and supervision of these services.

- Provide job descriptions for the personnel that will provide and/or supervise the job training and job development services.

(continued)

The Provider shall demonstrate effective working relationships and collaboration with organizations that have contracted for their agency's job coaching and job development services.

- Provide a listing of these contract agencies and include letters of endorsement and support.

- Provide a listing of experience working with programs operated by _____ School and any relevant documentation of the performance of those services.

- Demonstrate experience with transition-aged students, if possible.

The Provider shall demonstrate compliance with state and federal statutes and regulations regarding nondiscrimination against any other employee, applicant for employment, or student on the basis of age, race, color, sex, national origin, religion, disability, or in any manner prohibited by law.

PROVIDER AGENCY/REQUEST FOR PROPOSAL REQUIREMENTS

The Provider shall provide evidence of and maintain CARF accreditation for Job Coaching and Development Services and fulfill any other relevant requirements of the Vocational Rehabilitation Services agency to qualify for their fees for services.

- Provide copies of relevant CARF accreditation certificates and related documents.

- Provide documentation of current approved Rehabilitation Services Agency service fee schedules for agency.

- Provide any other relevant documentation regarding agency's services to Vocational Rehabilitation–funded (sponsored) clients.

Rating:

_____ Provided responsive proposal

_____ Meets basic requirements

Comments: _____
_____
_____
_____

The Provider shall demonstrate prior successful experience in job coaching and job development services for individuals with disabilities and, in particular, those with developmental disabilities.

- Provide a list of relevant past experience and the businesses where jobs have been developed and job coaching provided. Include letters of reference and/or support.

- Provide a list of the range of individuals served through job coaching and development services. Include examples of particularly challenging success stories and letters of support.

Rating:

_____ Provided responsive proposal

_____ Meets basic requirements

_____ Has relevant service experience with target population

_____ Has excellent service experience with target population in _____ County

(continued)

Project | SEARCH

Comments: _____

_____

_____

_____

The Provider shall illustrate that it has the administrative infrastructure to support the provision and supervision of job coaching and job development services.

- Provide agency's table of organization including personnel involved with job coaching and development services and supervision.

- Provide a listing of the qualifications, credentials, and experience of key agency personnel involved in the provision and supervision of these services.

- Provide job descriptions for the personnel that will provide and/or supervise the job training and job development services.

Rating:

_____ Provided responsive proposal

_____ Meets basic requirements

_____ Has depth in administrative structure to support requested services

_____ Has evidence of highly qualified personnel to provide and supervise services

Comments: _____

_____

_____

_____

The Provider shall demonstrate effective working relationships and collaboration with organizations that have contracted for their agency's job coaching and job development services.

- Provide a listing of these contract agencies and include letters of endorsement and support

- Provide a listing of experience working with programs operated by _____ School and any relevant documentation of the performance of those services.

Rating:

_____ Provided responsive proposal

_____ Meets basic requirements

_____ Has relevant service experience with target population

_____ Has excellent service experience with target population in this geographic area

_____ Has prior working relationship with _____ School programs

_____ Has excellent service relationship with _____ School programs

_____ Has excellent service relationship with _____ School serving target population

Comments: _____

_____

_____

_____

(continued)

The Provider shall demonstrate compliance with state and federal statutes and regulations regarding nondiscrimination against any other employee, applicant for employment, or student on the basis of age, race, color, sex, national origin, religion, disability, or in any manner prohibited by law.

- Provide relevant agency policies and training.

Rating:

- Provided responsive proposal
- Meets basic requirements

Comments: _____
_____
_____
_____

Overall rating:

Comments: _____
_____
_____
_____

Agreement of roles and responsibilities for Project SEARCH®

The Parties to this Agreement are X agency, the X host business, the X Public School District, and the Division of Vocational Rehabilitation Services.

I. PURPOSE

The parties to this agreement will collaborate and cooperate to create a High School Project SEARCH Transition Program at the X host business for students with developmental disabilities and to foster and facilitate the acquisition of jobs by people with disabilities when possible. This agreement specifies the roles and responsibilities of the parties as they work in partnership to increase opportunities for persons with disabilities. The program will be titled "X—Project SEARCH." It is modeled after Project SEARCH at the Children's Hospital Medical Center in Cincinnati, Ohio.

II. ROLES AND RESPONSIBILITIES

The parties agree to the following roles and responsibilities.

A. The X Host Business will

- Provide classroom space (with white board or chalkboard, small tables to be used as student work areas, chairs, locked cabinet for student files, and computer connections), and separate instructor space, if possible (with telephone, fax, photocopy equipment, supplies, computer, and e-mail access)

- Provide workspace, telephone, fax, photocopy equipment, supplies, computer, and e-mail access to Project SEARCH Director

- Provide a business liaison that is available on a frequent basis to assist with jobsite development, introduce Project SEARCH staff to the business staff, market the program internally, attend periodic meetings to discuss and evaluate program progress, and work with the instructor to reinforce workplace rules

- Develop a minimum of X intern worksites and a point of contact at each site for the purpose of teaching competitive, marketable skills to the program participants. Facilitate job analysis of those sites for the Project SEARCH staff

- Provide access to hiring opportunities if a Project SEARCH participant is appropriate for an internal job opening

- Provide badges and parking access for Project SEARCH staff

- Provide managers of departments that are being used as worksites to give direction, feedback, and evaluation to students during their worksite rotations

- Provide access to conference space for open houses

- Provide assistance to the Project SEARCH staff through the marketing department, including marketing materials and public relations expertise

- Establish student eligibility guidelines and select students for program as a participating partner of the Advisory Committee.

B. The School System will

- Provide a special education instructor with transition experience to coordinate/teach the program

- Develop and provide curriculum and instructional materials that encompass employability skills, functional academics, transition, job development, and job readiness. Project SEARCH Curriculum already approved by the Ohio Department of Education can be used (and adapted for use if necessary).

- Assist the agency on development of intern worksites and coordinate and monitor intern activities

(continued)

- Facilitate student recruitment activities

- Establish student eligibility guidelines and select students for program as a participating partner of the Advisory Committee

- Provide travel training for students as necessary before program begins

- Provide expertise in adaptations and accommodations and implement as necessary

- Provide student liability insurance

- Provide travel reimbursement to teachers for home visits, job development, and so on

- Secure relationship with vocational rehabilitation for each student to allow for partial funding of job coaches and job development

- Provide additional support for students if necessary, such as interpreter service, speech or occupational therapy, transportation, and so on

- Coordinate regular meetings to discuss and evaluate program progress

- Collect data on student outcomes and report to all partners

- Liaison with Cincinnati Project SEARCH for technical assistance, data collection, and other issues related to model integrity

- Assist with public relations activities to promote Project SEARCH

- Liaison with Cincinnati Project SEARCH for technical assistance, data collection, and other issues related to model integrity

C. The X Supported Employment Agency will

- Provide job coaches to work with students on worksites throughout the host business

- Work with participating departments to identify intern worksite opportunities for individuals with disabilities and perform job analyses

- Examine existing open positions and determine their applicability for people with disabilities, predetermine high-turnover, entry-level support positions, or other applicable positions for proactive job analysis, and recommend prescreened applicants to the university

- Assist with classroom setup, curriculum development, and worksite rotation planning

- Assist with student recruitment activities

- Establish student eligibility guidelines and select students for the program as a participating partner of the Advisory Committee

- Provide travel training for students as necessary before program begins

- Provide expertise in adaptations and accommodations and implement as necessary

- Work with vocational rehabilitation to assist with obtaining adaptations and accommodations as necessary and to help secure funding for job coaching and job development

- Provide education and training to X host business employees regarding supporting people with disabilities in the workplace as necessary

- Attend regular meetings with team members from the parties to this agreement to discuss and evaluate program progress

(continued)

- Assist with public relations activities to promote the Project SEARCH program
- Liaison with Cincinnati Project SEARCH for technical assistance, data collection, and other issues related to model integrity

D. Vocational Rehabilitation will

- Provide funding support for eligible individuals to obtain job coaching and job development during the Project SEARCH program at the X business
- Provide expertise and assistance in adaptations and job accommodations
- Establish student eligibility guidelines and select students for program as a participating partner of the Advisory Committee
- Attend regular meetings to discuss and evaluate program progress
- Assist with public relations activities to promote Project SEARCH

E. Local/County Board of Developmental Disabilities Services will

- Coordinate education and training to the host organization employees regarding disability employment information
- Provide consistent job-retention staff once student interns are in successful employment at the host business or in the community
- Assist with program organization, planning, internship site development, and travel training for community employment
- Establish student eligibility guidelines and select students for the program as a participating partner of the Advisory Committee
- Provide expertise in designing individual adaptations and accommodations, and work with your local Vocational Rehabilitation agency to provide funding when necessary
- Attend regular meetings with team members from the parties to this agreement to discuss and evaluate program progress
- Assist with public relations activities to promote the Project SEARCH program
- Liaison with Cincinnati Project SEARCH for technical assistance, data collection, and other issues related to model integrity

III. MEASURABLE OBJECTIVES

All parties will work collaboratively to

- Provide intern opportunities for a minimum of 10 to 12 student participants (per school year) with developmental disabilities for the 20__–20__ school year and to provide employment opportunities when available to people with disabilities whenever possible, also during that time period
- Provide support necessary to maximize training and employment success of the program participants
- Develop a minimum of 10 to 15 intern worksites during the first school year of the program and continue to develop worksites as the program progresses.
- Publicize the collaboration and program activities with a minimum of two written materials and two public presentations

(continued)

IV. PERIOD OF AGREEMENT

The effective date of this agreement will be _____ to _____.

V. LIMITATION OF AGREEMENT

It is understood among the parties that this agreement is not a contract and is not binding.

VI. RELATIONSHIP OF PARTIES

No agent or employee of either party shall be deemed an agent or employee of the other party. Each party will be solely and entirely responsible for the acts of its agents, subcontractors, or employees.

This agreement is executed for the benefit of the parties and the public generally. It is not intended nor may it be construed to create any third-party beneficiaries.

SIGNATURES

_____   _____

Project | SEARCH

Meet Daniel

Daniel is a graduate of the inaugural Project SEARCH class at Seton Medical Center in Austin—the first Project SEARCH site in Texas. Daniel rotated through three different areas of the hospital: supply processing and distribution, sterile processing, and food services. The manager of the sterile processing department enjoyed having Daniel as an intern and noticed that his strengths aligned well with some of their complex, systematic work, such as assembling surgical sets, processing peel-packs, and making deliveries. Not long after he graduated in May 2008, Daniel was offered a part-time position in that department at Seton Medical Center. He accepted the position and came aboard as an associate in July 2008.

When Daniel entered the Project SEARCH program, he was living at Marbridge, a residential community of adults with cognitive challenges. Daniel had moved to Marbridge—a partner with Seton in the implementation of Project SEARCH—earlier that year from Krum, Texas. He and his family considered the residential community as a college-like experience where he could learn additional social, vocational, and living skills to help prepare him for independent living. After he transitioned into competitive employment, Daniel continued to work toward his goal of living more independently. He participated in training sessions offered at Marbridge on subjects such as cooking and budgeting while prospering in his new job at Seton.

Daniel continues to advance in his career at Seton. Since he came aboard in 2008, he has been steadily increasing his hours; he went from working 25 hours a week to a full-time, 40-hour schedule. He has had pay increases each year and, most years, has received a bonus, which was over $500 in 2011. Another important skill that Daniel has learned throughout his employment is to be flexible. This was evidenced by the ease with which he adjusted to three turnovers in his department's management team during the course of his employment there. As of now, Daniel is among the employees in his area with the longest tenure. Moreover, he missed only 1 day of work throughout his first 3 years on the job.

Two years after his graduation from Project SEARCH, Daniel, along with his parents and his training team at Marbridge, decided he was ready to make the transition to independent living. With assistance from the Seton Project SEARCH program coordinator, Jenny Hawkins, Daniel found an efficiency apartment about three blocks away from the hospital, and as of October 2010, he moved out on his own. Since then, he has learned to independently grocery shop, cook, and pay bills. Although his regular commute to work is a quick walk through Central Austin, Daniel has learned to use public

(continued)

transportation for errands and leisure activities. Daniel does all of these things with minimal support, and he has become an integral part of the neighborhood in which he lives. In his free time outside of his full-time job, Daniel enjoys frequenting the local bookstore. He also likes going to the neighborhood park and watching the dogs play, and occasionally, he joins some of his old friends from Marbridge for movies or outings.

Daniel's future goals are to plan and execute his own vacation. He also wants to continue learning how to drive and, someday, to have his own car. And—possibly the thing that excites him the most—he is saving up to get his own dog!

6 Expanding Horizons: Early Life Experiences that Promote Employability

The best preparation for good work tomorrow is to do good work today.

Elbert Hubbard

I t goes without saying that all parents want their children to grow up to be happy, successful adults. Traditionally, that success is defined as a good education leading to a fulfilling job, independent living arrangements, a steady romantic relationship, hobbies and other leisure activities, and an active social life. Of all these factors, employment is the pivotal factor on which all the others depend to some extent: A job supplies an income, which facilitates independent housing arrangements and leisure pursuits, and the community involvement that comes from being part of a workplace promotes social interaction. Given the disparities in employment for people with disabilities, it's not surprising that young people with disabilities are consistently failing to attain the same degree of life satisfaction as their peers without disabilities. The 2010 Kessler Foundation/NOD survey of Americans with disabilities confirmed the employment gap between people with and without disabilities and also showed that there are significant gaps with regard to other quality-of-life measures including household income, access to transportation and health care, socializing, going to restaurants, and general satisfaction with life (see also Liptak, 2008). For some of the measures, including overall life satisfaction and access to health care and transportation, the gaps between people with and without disabilities has gotten larger since 1986—the first year this survey was carried out. Moreover, a 2001 study found that life satisfaction for young people with disabilities dropped dramatically right around the time of transition from high school to adult life (Chamalian, 2001). That is, 50% of the 300 teenagers in the study between the ages of 11 and 16 reported being very happy. But among the older group, ages 19 through 36, 75% said their lives were lonely and that they lacked close friendships.

Despite the formidable barriers and what can seem like daunting odds, it is entirely possible for a young person with developmental disabilities to have a great quality of life. And a good transition experience at the end of the high school career is critical to achieving that quality of life. However, it has long been recognized that a successful transition is much more likely if preparation for adult life starts in early childhood. For example, nearly 30 years ago, Coughran and Daniels (1983) wrote the following:

Many of the skills developed during early childhood are crucial to later life/career success. In most children, the key skills of assuming responsibility for self, dealing with others, and physically dealing with the environment are well under development by the age of six. Thus, development of career skills begins at or shortly after birth and is a continual process.

With all of the young people that Project SEARCH® has assisted, we have witnessed first hand the profound impact of early life experiences—both negative and positive. As a result, the Project SEARCH team has gathered and synthesized advice from the experts and from our own experiences, which we share with parents, educators, doctors, and rehabilitation workers as we meet with groups around the country. That advice is summarized in the remainder of this chapter.

THE MESSAGES WE RECEIVE IN CHILDHOOD AND HOW THEY AFFECT US

Erin Riehle can tell you exactly where she was when it happened. As a teenager, Erin loved to play her guitar and sing, and it's something she did often. Until one summer day when she was sitting on her porch, strumming and singing, with her mother sitting nearby snapping green beans. At one point, her mother looked up from her beans and said, "You know, you should never sing because you have a really nasally voice." Well, if you need any convincing about the power of negative messages, consider this: from that day, Erin didn't sing around other people until age 50, when she finally decided that it was time to include more music in her life. On a conscious level, she knew her anxiety didn't make sense. Although she had no illusions of being a great singer, she knew she was good enough to hold her own around a campfire or at a sing-along. But still, she couldn't help but be influenced by her mother's words, and to this day, she has to actively fight that influence.

Sometimes, it's not someone else's negative opinion that gets in the way. Sometimes, it's our own childhood idiosyncrasies that shape our self-image and put limits on the choices we make. Another author of this book has her own experiences along these lines. Maryellen Daston was famously squeamish in her youth. In high school biology, her laboratory partner had to do the entire fetal pig dissection while Maryellen watched at a distance, peeking from behind her fingers. Later, she became notorious as the one who ran from the room and fainted in the hall during 10th-grade health class on the day the natural childbirth film was shown. Ironically, despite her weak stomach, biology was the subject that fascinated her the most. But when registering for classes before her first quarter of college, she gave into her fears and chose the course schedule of an entering art major. But then, right before classes began, she thought hard about her motivations in choosing art as her major and realized that, by giving in to her fears, she was denying herself the education she really wanted. At that point, she gathered up her courage and switched her major, which involved completely changing her course schedule in a last-minute frenzy. Much to the amazement of those who knew her in high school, she stuck with her decision, although she continued to struggle with squeamishness. She was ultimately able to overcome it and do what she needed to do, including dissections, small-animal surgeries, and even a lesson in taxidermy, to get her degrees in biological sciences.

It's a challenge for any young person to overcome his or her challenges and to resist the negative messages and low expectations that they inspire. But for children with disabilities, those messages tend to be more pervasive—coming not just from parents and the people close to them but from everyone they encounter. Strangers

Britney's Story—The Power of Perseverance and a Positive Attitude

At a very young age, Britney W. was diagnosed with mild developmental disability, attention-deficit/hyperactivity disorder (ADHD), and dyslexia. Not surprisingly, throughout her childhood and adolescence, she heard a lot about what she *couldn't* do. But—thanks to her strong spirit and parents who knew instinctively what they needed to do to help her reach her goals—Britney never let those negative messages get in her way.

As a child, Britney had trouble learning to tie her shoes because of her limited fine-motor skills. Her mother, Debbie B., didn't give up and buy her Velcro shoes. Instead, she came up with an ingenious tool to help her learn. Debbie turned a shoe box and some very long, thick shoelaces into a giant "shoe" that Britney could use to practice on until she mastered the task. Likewise, instead of shrugging it off as part of her disability when Britney had trouble coloring in the lines, Debbie created a system to help her learn. She used glue to turn the coloring lines into "walls" that functioned as guides for Britney's crayon. Debbie gradually made the walls lower and lower

(continued)

in the grocery store are more likely to just look away instead of smiling or making small talk. Moreover, children with disabilities are less likely than most children to be asked by their teachers and doctors what they want to be when they grow up. This is a reflection of the low expectations that plague young people with disabilities. A study of young people with cerebral palsy revealed that the teachers, care assistants, and other adults in the lives of these young people considered their prospects for employment to be poor (Stevenson, Pharoah, & Stevenson, 1997). In contrast, when the young people themselves were queried, those who were still in school ranked getting a job as a top priority.

Not only are children with developmental disabilities more likely to receive discouraging messages, they are also more vulnerable to the effects of those messages. They don't necessarily have the analytical capacity to evaluate the validity of the messages they receive, and because they tend to have less experience with decision making and self-determination, they may not have the volition to go against expectations. In recognition of this, Murphy, Molnar, and Lankasky (2000) published advice for youths with cerebral palsy (but it applies to all young people with disabilities) to help them overcome the low expectations of their peers and the adults around them as they enter high school. They instructed them to set their own goals, to reject unnecessary school restrictions imposed because of their disability, to seek out successful adult role models with a similar disability, and to understand that feelings of identity crisis are common to all adolescents.

This is good advice for children with disabilities and also for their parents. Just as they influence children, negative messages can also affect parents' beliefs about their children's potential and undermine their willingness to partner in meeting their children's educational needs. Indeed, it has been shown that families of children with disabilities are less likely to attend school functions or join school-related parent organizations (Westat, 1998). In addition, there is evidence suggesting that the behavior of teachers, counselors, and other school personnel fosters that alienation. In one study, parents complained of school personnel who did not seem to listen to them, who missed scheduled meetings or left meetings early, who failed to ask for input from parents, or who confused parents with impenetrable technical jargon (Salembier & Furney, 1997). And those discouraging messages to the parents can come back in a vicious circle to undermine the self-confidence of the child.

Ironically, good intentions are at the heart of many of the negative messages that children receive. After all, it is understandable that parents of children with developmental

(continued)

until Britney no longer needed them to help her stay in the lines, and pretty soon, she was coloring independently.

When Britney got older, she was told that she would never be able to drive. Again, Britney's parents refused to accept this verdict. Starting at age 11, they let her drive a golf cart on private property so that she would get the feel for steering, braking, and controlling speed with a gas pedal. When she came of age to take the written examination for her temporary permit, she memorized the shapes and colors of signs because of her limited reading ability and was allowed to take the test orally. It took her four tries, but she ultimately passed the behind-the-wheel portion of her driver's license examination as well. Once she was fully licensed, her father spent many hours helping her learn the routes that she would need to take in her daily travels as well as those that she might need to know in an emergency. First, he rode in the car with her, and then, he stepped up the challenge by letting Brittany drive the route on her own while he followed in another car.

When Britney was 10 years old, she had to cope with the illness and death of her beloved grandmother. Throughout this difficult time, Britney was actively involved in her grandmother's care, and Debbie noticed that, for someone so young, she had unusual compassion for people in need. This experience—as well as her own time spent in the hospital because of a gastrointestinal disorder—sparked Britney's interest in a career in health care. Like so many other things she wanted to do, Britney and her family were told by teachers and caseworkers that this was not a realistic goal. But toward the end of her high school career, Britney's family learned about a Project SEARCH program at a nearby hospital, and finally, Britney and her family felt as though they had found a place where the expectations for Britney were as high as their own. Britney excelled in the Project SEARCH program and was even a mentor and cheerleader for the other students. At the end of her year in Project SEARCH, Britney achieved her dream of a career in health care. She was hired as an endoscopy technician; in that job, she helps to clean and maintain equipment. She also has the opportunity to put her extraordinarily compassionate nature to use taking care of patients as they come out of anesthesia.

As Britney's mother, put it, "Project SEARCH allows us to see what the students are good at—what makes them shine—what they love to do."

Photo 6.1. Kristi enjoys the outdoors with her parents, Karen and Terry, and her companion dog.

disabilities might be wary of fostering false hopes or unrealistic expectations. For example, in the interest of protecting themselves and their children from disappointment or humiliation, parents may be reluctant to encourage their children to engage in work-related play. Consequently, they may be less likely to buy their children a toy doctor's bag or a firefighter's hat. As a result, children with disabilities don't experience the pretend play that such toys encourage, and they might miss the chance to build those critical early images of themselves as competent workers and participants in adult life.

Much of the time, parents don't get any advance warning or opportunity to prepare before they are faced with the challenge of raising a child with a developmental disability. They learn as they go along, and because the conventional wisdom that parents typically share may not apply to their children, and their concerns are different, they can become isolated from other parents. As a result, they tend to be even more dependent on the advice of experts. In that vulnerable position, it can be particularly difficult for parents to follow their instincts and defy the prevailing opinions. Consider the experience of Karen and Terry Q., whose daughter, Kristi, was born without a disability, but whose cognitive and physical function became impaired after a nearly fatal bout of viral encephalitis at the age of 2 years and 9 months. When Kristi reached school age, Karen and Terry got to know the special education teachers and counselors at the school and leaned on them heavily for advice and support. As a kindergartner, Kristi was evaluated by the school system with a series of educational assessment tools. Karen and Terry were bewildered when they were told that Kristi was functioning at the level of an 18-month-old child. It didn't make sense to them because they knew that Kristi was able to do many things that an 18-month-old infant could not do: She dressed herself, fed herself, and brushed her own teeth, like most 5 year olds. In addition to these ordinary abilities, she had some extraordinary visual-spatial skills. Karen and Terry routinely observed her assembling 100-piece puzzles in a matter of minutes. She had a system in which she would scan the pile of pieces, pick one up, turn it in her hands three times, and then put it in place. She had an uncanny ability to recognize the piece that fit in next in line, adjacent to the ones that were already in place. Certainly, this was a skill beyond the capability of any toddler. For that matter, it was beyond the abilities of most kindergarteners. But still, that assessment—18 months—weighed heavily on Kristi's parents. At face value, it precluded all hope for an independent adulthood for their daughter. And the idea of competitive employment for someone functioning at the level of an 18 month old seemed downright absurd. But Karen and Terry learned important lessons from that experience. First, they learned that, although they would find allies among the professionals, they themselves would have to be the primary advocates for Kristi. Second, they learned that evaluation tools must be interpreted carefully. In Kristi's case, it seems that her results reflected her unwillingness to take part in the testing more than it spoke to her actual capabilities. But regardless of how accurate the assessment, it is important to remember that a poor performance on a test shouldn't be interpreted too broadly. That is, low scores on a given evaluation shouldn't be assumed to reflect the test taker's abilities in another area. Moreover, a static test result doesn't speak to the test taker's potential to improve with proper training and the right motivation.

WHAT PARENTS CAN DO TO INCREASE THE LIKELIHOOD OF EMPLOYMENT FOR THEIR CHILD

Patience White, M.D., is a pediatric rheumatologist and a pioneer in recognizing the critical role of medical practitioners in assisting young people with chronic illnesses and disabilities in their transition to adult health care and independent adult life. She recognized employment

NINE STEPS TOWARD SUCCESSFUL EMPLOYMENT

What parents can do to help their children be ready for work:

1. Begin early talking about expectations.
2. Teach children about their disability.
3. Ask their opinions and involve them in decision making.
4. Give them chores.
5. Develop patterns of good attendance.
6. Maintain health in order to stay active.
7. Involve children in social and leisure activities without the family.
8. Talk about work with children, early and often.
9. Think about the transition plan in 1- to 2-year segments.

Source: White, 1997.

as an important element of fulfilled adulthood but noticed that the children she saw in her practice were not developing the basic skills or the appropriate mind-set in childhood that would get them ready to succeed in the workplace. In response, she defined nine steps toward successful employment as a guide for parents, teachers, and doctors to help them in preparing children with developmental disabilities for employment, starting in early childhood.

The first step is to **begin talking early about expectations.** It is critical that children with disabilities grow up knowing that their parents believe that, as adults, they will live as independently as possible. The parents can show this on a day-to-day level by having the same expectations of them with regard to helpfulness and responsibility as they do for their siblings without disabilities.

The second step is the recommendation that parents **teach children about their disability.** By understanding their disability, children can discuss it in a realistic way, without shame or euphemism. Straightforward language and explanations help children own their deficiencies and more readily identify their strengths. One young woman with Down syndrome who was in a Project SEARCH program, when asked about her disability would say, "I have hearing loss." This is what she had been taught by her family to say, and although it was true, it was not a helpful description for her or for the people she worked with. Although the intent was to make her feel better about herself, it instead made her feel as though her primary disability was something that shouldn't be discussed in public and something that she should be ashamed of.

The third step is to **ask children with disabilities their opinions and involve them in decision making.** Being involved in small decisions—such as what to wear, what to eat, what activities to participate in, or what color to paint a bedroom—is good practice for the bigger decisions that will come later. If a young person feels that her or his opinions matter, this goes a long way in establishing a pattern of self-determination that is critical for independent adult life.

The fourth step is to **give children with disabilities chores** around the house. Giving children the opportunity to successfully complete chores is a way to foster feelings of pride and accomplishment. More importantly, it helps to establish a self-image as a contributing member of the community and an appreciation for the value of meaningful work.

Another critical step is for parents to help their children **develop patterns of good attendance.** Often, for children with developmental disabilities, schools take a lax attitude toward tardiness and absences. Attendance records that would be considered unacceptable for a child without disabilities are often overlooked or excused. In fact, a Project SEARCH transition coordinator has seen cases in which a student has failed to attend school for most of a school year with no repercussions or follow-up from the school. This practice may be viewed as a way to relieve the pressure on families that might be coping with frequent doctor visits or behavioral challenges. But, although it may solve immediate problems for the parents, it sends the message to the student that her or his schooling is not important and that there are few consequences for not following rules. Moreover, in the long term, it deprives the student of the opportunity to learn that most critical of job skills—the commitment to showing up reliably and on time, regardless of the inevitable difficulties and complications.

The sixth step on the list is a reminder that **it is especially important for young people with disabilities to maintain their health so that they can remain active.** Healthy habits and regular medical attention are important in minimizing the disruptive effects that chronic illness and disability can have on education, transition, and successful employment.

The seventh suggestion on the list is that **children with disabilities should be involved in social activities that do not include their families.** Following this advice requires a degree of letting go that may be difficult for a parent who is used to interpreting his or her child's behavior for the world, managing the child's needs, and shielding the child from disapproval or disappointment. But it is imperative that children with disabilities learn to manage social situations independently, not only for the enhanced quality of life that a social life brings but also because the ability to interact with others is a critical job skill. In fact, inadequate social function is one of the main reasons that adults, with or without a disability, fail to get a job, or fail to keep a job once they are hired.

The eighth bit of advice for parents is to **talk about work with their children, early and often.** In fact, one of the most powerful predictors of successful employment in adult life is parental attitude in the early years of life (Murphy et al., 2000). When children are asked what they want to be when they grow up, it helps them to visualize themselves in a position of responsibility and to connect their actions today to their life as adults. As we discussed earlier, the exploration of adult life that occurs in early childhood is critical to laying the foundation for developing the necessary skills and attitudes for successful employment in adult life.

This list ends with the suggestion that parents **think about transition in 1- to 2-year segments**. Whereas preparation for transition needs to start in early childhood, it can be overwhelming to consider all at once the many steps that will need to be taken throughout the 15 or so years from preschool to high school graduation. Moreover, there are shifting priorities and different needs to consider at the various stages of development. Thus, it is much more practical and productive for families to focus their detailed planning on the present and the near future. With this in mind, we have compiled a list of suggestions for parents and caregivers and organized them according to the relevant developmental stages (Table 6.1).

PREPARING YOUNG PEOPLE FOR ENTRY INTO THE PROJECT SEARCH HIGH SCHOOL TRANSITION PROGRAM

Good preparation in childhood makes a big difference in a young person's likelihood of success in transition programs such as Project SEARCH. This is reflected in the approach that Project SEARCH uses to assess the readiness of young people with disabilities who are interested in entering the High School Transition Program. As one of several tools used for evaluating applicants, Project SEARCH has developed an eligibility rubric (described in detail in Chapter 3 and included in its entirety in Appendix 3.1) that focuses on several areas including school status, school attendance records, self-care skills, appearance and grooming, degree of independence in travel, social skills, verbal communication, physical limitations, prior work experience, and most importantly, commitment to employment.

The students themselves, and their parents (or other caregivers), are also asked to fill out a checklist that corresponds to the areas of focus on the eligibility rubric (see Appendix 6.1). We try to make this checklist available to students and families as soon as they express

Table 6.1. Preparation for transition from preschool through high school

	Developmental stage			
Preparation for transition from preschool to high school	Stage I: preschool	Stage II: elementary school	Stage III: secondary school	Stage IV: postsecondary school
Landmarks	Orientation to work, basic self-concept, basic skills development	Developing self-concept as a student/worker and gaining prevocational skills	Learn personal/social coping and time for vocational exploration and tryout.	Choices crystallized and implemented, subsequent choice modification, dealing with issues of being a worker with disability
Steps for parents	• Encourage the child to do things for herself or himself. • Have the child participate in family activities. • Help the child get to know people outside the immediate family circle. • Create the expectation that everything does not need to be special; life can go on. • Get information from parent groups, newsletters, the Internet.	• Teach the child basic knowledge about her or his special health care needs and disability. • Teach self-care and basic grooming. • Teach personal safety. • Talk about dreams and aspirations. • Promote leisure activities. • Encourage and support friendships and social opportunities. • Help decision making by giving structured choices. • Help the child learn to solve problems. • Let the child learn the consequences of her or his behavior. • Assign chores appropriate for the ability level. • Ask, "What will you want to do when you grow up?"	• Continue development of typical self-help skills as well as skills related to special health care needs. • Help develop a vision for the future. • Continue to encourage hobbies, leisure/social activities. • Continue to assign family chores. • Identify strengths and weaknesses. • Explore job opportunities. • Encourage work and/or volunteer activities in the community. • Provide opportunities to manage money. • Create work aid books to teach tasks. • Set productivity expectations and time work activities. • Begin teaching about time management by creating a schedule. • Teach basic counting skills and start early with adaptations as needed. • Learn what accommodations and adaptations work best and pass on to others. • Encourage participation with peers separate from family. • Explore adult service options. • Place child's name on agencies' waiting lists. • Begin to plan for living independently.	• Support the young adult to develop self-determination skills • Explore adult education opportunities and training. • Learn about eligibility for services. • Set up a personal bank account. • Plan for living independently. • Join community clubs, interest groups, support groups. • Learn to cook, clean, wash clothes. • Learn to develop healthy sexual relationships.

Sources: Hershenson (1981); Szymanski et al. (1988); and Paving the Road to a Brighter Future (pamphlet published by Lighthouse Youth Services, Cincinnati, OH).

interest in the Project SEARCH program—for example, when they attend an open house or other information-gathering event—because it is a useful tool to guide preparation for the Project SEARCH application process. It is also helpful as a more general guide for preparing young people for employment because of the close correspondence between Project SEARCH criteria and the priorities of employers.

Project SEARCH Preparation
Teacher/Parent Assessment

Project SEARCH® Preparation: Teacher/Parent Assessment

Student name:	**School district:**
Name of person filling out form:	**Relationship to student:**
Your phone:	**Your e-mail:**
Your address:	

Please be honest when filling out this information to help us appropriately place the student.

School status
☐ Student has all needed credits for graduation.
☐ School district allows deferred graduation.
☐ Student still needs the following classes in order to graduate (please fill out the classes still needed for graduation):

    ○ _____

    ○ _____

    ○ _____

☐ Student has one or more years of school eligibility.
☐ Student's school eligibility continues through:
    ○ The day s/he turns 22
    ○ The school year in which s/he turns 22

Commitment to community employment
☐ Student wants to get a job.
☐ Family supports the goal of competitive community employment.
☐ Student has a Social Security card.
☐ Student has a state ID and/or driver's license in addition to a school ID.
☐ Student can pass a preemployment drug screen.
☐ Student can pass a criminal background check.
☐ Student can be contacted through an answering machine or voice mail which has a business like greeting.
☐ Student has a professional working e-mail address. Please list: _____
☐ Student receives SSI and/or SSDI or other forms of public assistance.
☐ Student has had a benefits analysis and/or understands the impact of earned income on the benefits.

Attendance
☐ Student has had no absences or tardies within the past school year.
☐ Student has had 1–5 absences or tardies within the past school year.
☐ Student has had 5–10 absences or tardies within the past school year.
☐ Student has had 10 or more absences or tardies within the past school year.
☐ Student has had a medical condition that requires frequent hospital stays/excessive doctor/clinic visits (more than 20 days).
☐ If yes to 10 or more days:
    ○ Why has the student missed so much school? _____

_____

(continued)

Independent daily living and self-care skills

I am independent in daily living and self-care skills. On a scale of 1–5 (1 being not very good/competent and 5 being very good/competent), how competent are you in each of these areas?

	Not Very Good/Not Competent			Very Good/Competent	
Cooking and nutrition	1	2	3	4	5
Budgeting	1	2	3	4	5
Handling money/making change	1	2	3	4	5
Taking medication	1	2	3	4	5
Toileting	1	2	3	4	5
Daily shower/bath	1	2	3	4	5
Appropriate amount of sleep for school and work schedule	1	2	3	4	5

I need help with the following (from a parent/teacher/guardian/care taker):

	I need a lot of help			I don't need much help	
Cooking and nutrition	1	2	3	4	5
Budgeting	1	2	3	4	5
Handling money/making change	1	2	3	4	5
Taking medication	1	2	3	4	5
Toileting	1	2	3	4	5
Daily shower/bath	1	2	3	4	5
Appropriate amount of sleep for school and work schedule	1	2	3	4	5

Appearance and professional presentation

- ☐ Student arrives at school and/or work daily with:
    - ☐ Clean and combed hair
    - ☐ Clean clothing and underwear
    - ☐ Brushed teeth/oral hygiene
    - ☐ Clean clothes
- ☐ Student wears appropriate clothing for the weather.
- ☐ Student follows the school dress code.
- ☐ Student willingly follows the designated dress code of my employer including rules on:
    - ☐ Appropriate clothing
    - ☐ Shoes
    - ☐ Facial hair
    - ☐ Facial and body piercings
    - ☐ Tattoos
    - ☐ Jewelry
    - ☐ Fingernail polish and length

Transportation

- ☐ Student has his/her own car, driver's license, and insurance.
- ☐ Student knows how to use public transportation.
- ☐ Student is willing to learn to use public transportation.
- ☐ Student uses a door-to-door or paratransit system independently
    - ○ Parent or other guardian makes appointment for student.
    - ○ Student makes own appointments.

(continued)

Project | SEARCH

☐ Student is eligible for developmental disablity (or other disability-related) transportation assistance.
☐ Student has a family member/other who is willing to provide on-going transportation.
☐ Other transportation options _____

Appropriate social and behavior skills
☐ Student does not engage in flirting, inappropriate touching, or public displays of affection such as holding hands, hugging, or kissing.
☐ Student does not swear or use profanity in a school or work setting.
☐ Student shows respect to peers and adults.
☐ Student works cooperatively with others.
☐ Student accepts correction and criticism without a negative reaction.
☐ Student has appropriate behavior with adult supervision but may not be appropriate in all independent situations (or needs some adult prompts on an on-going basis).
☐ Student has lost temper in a school or work environment.
☐ Student has acted aggressively in a school or work setting:
    ☐ Screaming or yelling
    ☐ Hitting/punching
    ☐ Spitting
    ☐ Kicking
    ☐ Fighting

Interpersonal communication
☐ Student responds when someone speaks or asks questions.
☐ Student makes eye contact.
☐ Student uses an appropriate tone of voice.
☐ Student engages in appropriate conversation in a school or work environment.
☐ Student uses appropriate body language in the school or work environment:
    ☐ No inappropriate hand gestures
    ☐ Sitting appropriately in a chair/posture
    ☐ Respecting personal space
☐ Student uses a cell phone and electronic equipment (e.g., iPod, Walkman, Bluetooth) appropriately according to the school or business policy, including refraining from talking and answering the phone, texting, and listening to music during scheduled classtime or activities.

Verbal communication
☐ Student is easily understood by others.
☐ Student sometimes has trouble getting message across to others.
☐ Student uses adaptive equipment to communicate.
☐ Student is willing to learn to use adaptive equipment to communicate if appropriate.
☐ Student uses an interpreter and/or sign language to communicate.
☐ Student talks about the same topics over and over again.

Recreational activities
Student participates in organized group activities:
☐ Sports (please list) _____
☐ Band
☐ Choir
☐ Theater
☐ Scouts

(continued)

Project | SEARCH

- ☐ Church youth group
- ☐ Community recreation and/or Special Olympics
- ☐ Computer or electronic games
- ☐ Other

Student likes to exercise on own (e.g., walking, running, biking)
   Exercises _____ each week for at least 30 minutes each time.

Student enjoys sit-down activities such as:
- ☐ Computer or electronic games
- ☐ Watching television
- ☐ Reading
- ☐ Scrap booking
- ☐ Other

Student has the following hobbies: _____

Physical limitations
- ☐ Student has difficulty walking.

Student uses the following to walk/navigate:
- ☐ Cane
- ☐ Walker
- ☐ Wheelchair
- ☐ Scooter
- ☐ Other
- ☐ Student has limited use of arms and/or hands.
- ☐ Student has other physical limitations that may affect employment. Please list:

_____

_____

Production rate and work quality
- ☐ At work or school, student completes all tasks by due date.
- ☐ At work or school, student turns in assignments by deadline or due date.
- ☐ At work or school, it is difficult for the student to get all tasks finished or turned in on time.
- ☐ Please list strategies that have assisted the student to complete and turn in work on time

_____

_____

- ☐ At school or work, the student gets most of the tasks correct.
- ☐ If no, please explain: _____
- ☐ At school, with home chores or on the job, the student's work is organized and neat.
- ☐ Other comments: _____

Employability skills
- ☐ Student gets to school, work, or other appointments on time and independently.
- ☐ After lunch or a break, the student gets back to class or work on time.
- ☐ Student knows how to tell and keep track of time.
- ☐ Student is able to count money and make change accurately.
- ☐ Student stays on a task until it is finished.

(continued)

Project | SEARCH

☐ If interrupted, the student can return to the task and finish it.
☐ Student can access personal information to complete a paper application.
☐ Student has had experience with completing on-line applications.
☐ Student knows how to answer common interview questions.
☐ Student can tell his/her boss or co-workers what help is needed on their job.
☐ Please list strategies that have been successful and leads to success and independence:

   ○ _____

   ○ _____

   ○ _____

Prior work experience
☐ Student has had a paying job(s) in the community. Places he/she has worked are:

   ○ _____

   ○ _____

   ○ _____

☐ Student has worked at his/her school doing: _____
☐ Student has volunteered at: _____
☐ Student does the following chores at home on a regular basis: _____
☐ Student has never worked or volunteered.
☐ If the student has a resume, please attach.

Academic skills
☐ Student's favorite subjects in high school were/are: _____
☐ Student likes to read books for pleasure. The last book read was: _____
☐ Student uses a calculator when doing math problems or for everyday use.
☐ Student likes to read the newspaper and magazines for news, job hunting, and other information.
☐ Student likes to write or keeps a diary/journal.

Computer/electronic skills
☐ Student has basic keyboarding skills and uses correct typing techniques.
☐ Student has basic keyboarding skills and uses only two fingers (hunt and peck).
☐ Student can use Microsoft Word to create letters and other documents.
☐ Student can use Microsoft Excel to create spreadsheets and other documents.
☐ Student can use Microsoft Publisher to create cards, newsletters, flyers, or other documents.
☐ Student can use e-mail correctly.
☐ Student can access the Internet to get information, find services such as Map Quest, and use various search engines.
☐ Student uses a computer to play games, watch TV shows, listen to on-line streaming, and so on.
☐ Student has minimal computer skills.
☐ Student uses a cell phone to talk to others.
☐ Student uses a cell phone for texting.

Additional school and community supports
Student receives Related Services through the school district:
☐ Speech therapy
☐ Occupational therapy
☐ Physical therapy

(continued)

Project | SEARCH

☐ Other
- *Note:* Related Services are only available on a consult basis once the student is enrolled in a Project SEARCH program.

☐ Student has a vocational rehabilitation counselor
Please list: _____

☐ Student is eligible for services from the County Board of MRDD.
Please list case manager/service facilitator: _____

Please list other names and phone numbers of other support people below. It can be anyone in the school or community that helps the student to be successful.

Name	Title	Phone number

Problem solving and conflict resolution
Please give us some examples of the student's problem-solving abilities and/or how they handle conflict:

Home situation:

School situation:

Community or work situation:

Project | SEARCH

Meet Kristen

Kristen is a graduate of the Project SEARCH program at Fifth Third Bank in Cincinnati, Ohio. As a student intern, Kristen impressed the bank staff with her positive attitude and eagerness to learn such that, shortly after she graduated, Kristen was offered a job and subsequently hired in the central file room as a file document specialist. Since then, Kristen has learned her way around this huge facility—the size of several gymnasiums—which houses an array of thousands of files in rows and rows of shelving. Kristen's duties include refiling documents, computer entry, preparing files, and scanning. According to Kristen, "The Project SEARCH program and all the rotations helped me learn business skills."

Outside of work hours, Kristen maintains a whirlwind schedule of social activities, hobbies, and community service. Every week, she studies ballroom dancing at a local studio in a class offered specifically for students with Down syndrome. She plays basketball in a community league, and she studies creative writing in classes offered through the Down Syndrome Association of Greater Cincinnati (DSAGC). Kristen previously served a term on the board of the DSAGC and currently advises that group as a member of the Advocates at the Table Committee. This committee provides the DSAGC board with advice and direction on issues that are pertinent to the lives of adults with Down syndrome. Kristen has also done some public speaking about Project SEARCH and her experience with the program.

As evidenced by her very active lifestyle, Kristen is someone who always wants to do more, learn new things, and advance in her skills. Her supervisors consider her a role model for the department because of her work ethic and her ability to keep her focus and stay on task. As such, Kristen often mentors Project SEARCH interns in her department. Her manager shared the following thoughts about Kristen:

> When Kristen arrived to start work within the central file room, she was a very shy and closed person who did not seem to want to interact with her team members and management. Through the years, and with the help of the Project SEARCH team and the management members within the department, she has grown into a confident and skilled employee. She is always willing to learn new tasks and projects joy on a daily basis in her actions and words. She is a highly valuable asset for management and the department and we would love to have more employees just like her!

Kristen's commitment to her work is reflected in the fact that, over the entire period that she has been an employee at Fifth Third Bank, she has maintained a perfect attendance record. As Kristen puts it, "I'm proud to be a 2005 graduate of Project SEARCH."

7 Complex and Systematic Jobs

> *Disability is a matter of perception. If you can do just one thing well,*
> *you're needed by someone.*
>
> Martina Navratilova

Integrated, competitive employment is the goal for all Project SEARCH® students. But we also strive to stretch and expand on that goal by working against the common misconception that people with intellectual and developmental disabilities can do only the easiest work. We do this by demonstrating that these individuals can excel in a wide range of complex and systematic jobs if they receive the right training. For example, some of the jobs that Project SEACH participants at Cincinnati Children's Hospital have mastered include the sterilization of surgical and dental tools, patient greeting and escort, data entry and data management, supply cart and cabinet stocking, grounds keeping, and laboratory courier services.

Another corollary to Project SEARCH's goal of competitive employment is our commitment to matching program participants with jobs and work environments that are compatible with their particular skills and interests. By zeroing in on high-quality jobs that involve complex and systematic work, by getting to know the program participants as individuals, and by helping them to align their career paths with their interests, Project SEARCH has found that it can expand employment opportunities far beyond the usual expectations that our society holds for people with intellectual and developmental disabilities.

WHAT DO WE MEAN BY "COMPLEX AND SYSTEMATIC"?

We use the term *complex and systematic* in contrast to simple and repetitive work. We consider a complex job to be one in which the worker is engaged in real and necessary work that includes many different tasks that may each have multiple steps. By *systematic*, we mean that there are standardized procedures with a clear sequence of events or systems for prioritization. The concept of complex and systematic jobs was part of Project SEARCH from the inception of the program, but the exact meaning and significance of the term has shifted with time and experience. In the beginning, we were very concerned with avoiding stereotypical jobs for people with intellectual and developmental disabilities. We took a hard line in this regard by adopting a strict policy in which no Project SEARCH student intern would be permitted to work in the cafeteria or on the janitorial staff at Cincinnati Children's. The rationale was that we did not want to reinforce stereotypes; rather, we felt that we needed to break the mold to demonstrate that people with intellectual and developmental disabilities could do complex work. But, even though the intentions were worthy, the dictum's first challenge came from within when one of our student interns, "Carrie," declared her desire to work in the cafeteria. Erin remembers telling her, "Carrie, you can do so much more!" and instead of helping her find a job in the cafeteria, the Project SEARCH staff encouraged her to apply for a job that had opened up in the hospital's linens facility. Erin, Jennifer, and the Project SEARCH teacher all felt that it was a great job for Carrie, with good opportunities for socialization and career advancement, and they felt certain that she would do well and forget all about the cafeteria once she was fully engaged in the work. They convinced her to interview for the job and to accept it when it was offered. She learned the job and did it well, and her co-workers in linens liked her. Nonetheless, she was unhappy. At every opportunity, Carrie would let the Project SEARCH staff know that she was not satisfied with her job and that what she really wanted was to work in the cafeteria. After about 3 years, a job opened up in the cafeteria, and the Project SEARCH staff finally relented and agreed to help Carrie apply and interview for the job. She got the job and, sure enough, as soon as she started working there, it was clear that she had found her niche. Her co-workers in the cafeteria took to her right away; she was a model employee—always coming to work with a good attitude and never showing up late. She started out working at the salad bar and then went on to learn a variety of jobs in the cafeteria. She ultimately settled in the chili parlor within the cafeteria, where she remains successfully and happily employed. With her new-found career contentment and steady income, Carrie was in a position where she could buy a condominium of her own. She was also motivated to hire a tutor, with her own money and on her own initiative, to help her increase her literacy so that she could become even more effective at the job she loved.

The lesson that the Project SEARCH founders learned from their experience with Carrie is that, whereas it is clearly wrong to unthinkingly and routinely channel people with intellectual and development disabilities into food service or housekeeping, the other end of the continuum—to declare that *no* people with disabilities should work in those areas—is equally wrong. It is commendable work that many people take great pride and satisfaction in doing well. What's more, it is far from easy—food service and housekeeping are both areas that require a great deal of decision making and physical stamina. But the key is in the choice, and it's not a real choice if a person has never experienced anything else. Many school-based transition programs focus on cleaning and food service such that, even when students are given the opportunity to try out jobs in the community, regardless of the business they are visiting, the work they are asked to do is essentially the same. One student, before coming to Project SEARCH, had done job exploration through her school in a gym, a retirement home, and a child care center. In each environment, she did basic housekeeping or cleaned up after meals. This sort of thing happens because of a self-reinforcing cycle in which we have become used to seeing people with intellectual and developmental disabilities in these roles, so these are the jobs that job developers are comfortable requesting for their students or clients. Then, when young people leave school and start looking for work, they are predisposed to go for the jobs that are familiar to them and the cycle continues. This is the rut that Project SEARCH works to avoid by exposing student interns to a variety of work environments and job skills.

HIGH EXPECTATIONS DRIVE HIGH PERFORMANCE

The most important thing that Project SEARCH does to promote high-quality employment for people with disabilities is to create an atmosphere of high expectations. Because Project SEARCH is a collaboration with input from all the critical stakeholders, we are able to raise expectations at a system-wide level. For each of the Project SEARCH partners, this is manifested in different ways that make unique contributions to the overall positive atmosphere:

- The student: To gain acceptance into Project SEARCH, a student must demonstrate a commitment to obtaining competitive employment, which sets up a clear expectation at the onset. Once in the program, the camaraderie and support that students receive helps them to internalize that goal, which in turn drives their self-determination in achieving it.

- Parents or caregivers: Of all the things that caregivers do for their children, holding high expectations has the greatest influence on a young person's chances for gaining competitive employment (Carter, Austin, & Trainor, 2011; Wehmeyer, Morningstar, & Husted, 1999; Werner & Smith, 1992). Becoming involved in Project SEARCH is one avenue through which families encounter other young people with significant disabilities engaged in complex work, which expands and gives definition to the aspirations they hold for their own children.

- Teachers/instructors: Teachers have the responsibility to shepherd the process of setting goals for a student's individualized education program (IEP), and those goals drive the planning process for the IEP team. Studies have shown that vague "prevocational" goals that stop short of employment actually have a negative correlation with postschool employment (Carter et al., 2011). In Project SEARCH, the whole team expects that the student will go to work and that expectation is written into the IEP, which guides the team to then set up the scenarios and experiences to reach that goal.

- Community rehabilitation provider (CRP): An agency's outcomes are strongly influenced by the services that it offers. For example, if an agency that coordinates employment services also operates a sheltered workshop, it decreases the likelihood of that agency's clients becoming competitively employed (Timmons, Hall, Bose, Wolfe, & Winsor, 2011). When a CRP partners with Project SEARCH, it becomes a factor that shifts the expectations of the staff involved, and gradually, the sheltered workshop as a fallback option becomes less acceptable.

- Vocational rehabilitation (VR): VR has national policies in place that encourage competitive employment. However, overall low rates of employment persist for people with significant or severe disabilities, and the jobs that they do get tend to be in traditional roles with minimal hours and low pay. One VR representative reported that her first exposure to Project SEARCH immediately opened her eyes to considering a broader range of job possibilities for her clients.

- The host business: It has been shown that employers' expectations for people with disabilities are positively influenced by exposure and that this simple change has a much greater effect than promotional campaigns or other contrived approaches to manipulating perceptions or behavior. Project SEARCH is an effective way to give employers firsthand experience in working with people with disabilities. In turn, the business provides a professional environment that raises the bar for the students, parents, and education and rehabilitation professionals who implement the program.

With regard to raising expectations, Project SEARCH is unique in that it creates a framework in which the sum is greater than the parts. That is, the systematic interdependence of the different parties and their roles in implementing the program results in a thought shift among the entire group. And this shift occurs in a deeper, more extensive way than what could be achieved through individual initiatives.

The Hazards of Making Assumptions

To achieve high expectations, it requires that we let go of our misperceptions about disability and that we carefully assess our actions to be sure that we are not making erroneous assumptions. One common pitfall is the tendency to assume that people with intellectual disabilities are stuck at a certain level. We might make the blanket statement that an individual functions at the level of an 8 year old or decide that a person isn't appropriate for a job because of limited literacy skills. However, when we make these judgments, we are forgetting that, like all people, people with intellectual and developmental disabilities can grow and change and learn new skills. Even individuals with the most severe disabilities are fully capable of learning new things and improving their performance. Indeed, this capacity to learn has been demonstrated through research on methods for teaching a variety of academic and nonacademic skills (Browder, Mims, Spooner, Ahlgrim-Delzell, & Lee, 2008; Falkenstine, Collins, Schuster, & Kleinert, 2009; Farmer, Gast, Wolery, & Winterling, 1991).

Another common error is to look at an individual's performance at one task or in a given environment and then use that information to decide in advance how he or she will perform on a different task. This tendency underscores the importance of giving people with disabilities the opportunity to prove themselves in a business setting. At Project SEARCH, we have seen again and again that people perform differently in different environments. Because of the differences in motivations and expectations, the attitude or level of performance that an individual displays during clinical testing or in a school setting does not always accurately reflect how that person would perform in the workplace. Lena M.'s story (see Chapter 4) is a good example of this. Nonetheless, people with disabilities are still less likely than are people without disabilities to be given the benefit of the doubt in hiring decisions. For example, a job posting might read, "The applicant must be familiar with Word, Excel, PowerPoint, and Access." If a qualified applicant turned up with experience in all of these programs except Access, most managers would be willing to hire that person, assuming that since she or he was able to learn other parts of the Microsoft Office Suite, she or he would be able to learn the other parts on the job. But such assumptions are not usually made for people with disabilities, and as a result, they are routinely denied jobs for which they don't already have all the necessary skills. Or, if an individual with a disability is hired, the job might be "carved" before she or he is given a chance to demonstrate her or his abilities or the opportunity to learn new skills.

It is easy to say that we should have high expectations and that everyone should be given the chance to show their potential, but it takes more effort and focused intentionality than one might expect to truly put this philosophy into practice. At Project SEARCH, we learned early on that, no matter how enlightened a person thinks he or she is, we are all saddled with preconceived ideas about what someone with a significant disability can and can't do. And, when it comes to employment decisions, we tend to limit our expectations accordingly. One of the first Project SEARCH hires at Cincinnati Children's was "David," a young man with Down syndrome, who was successfully employed stocking examination rooms. Erin was approached by a manager in central sterilization who was having trouble with high turnover in a job that involved sterilizing surgical instruments. She had come to Erin because she wondered if the job was something David could do. The initial response from both Erin and Jennifer, the Project SEARCH rehabilitation expert, was, no, David wouldn't be capable of doing the job. They knew that David was not able to locate his locker, nor could he operate the combination lock to open it. To Erin and Jennifer, it clearly followed that, if he couldn't do what, to them, seemed like relatively simple tasks, there was no way he could master the job of clinical sterilization, which involved complex processes such as recognizing and sorting a huge variety of tools, assembling surgical trays, and operating an autoclave. Luckily, they didn't go with their first impulse. Erin and Jennifer literally slept on it and when they met up again the next day, they found that they had both come to the same conclusion overnight: They really didn't know if David could do the job and he should be given a chance to try. Sure enough, with good training and appropriate aids that used photographs instead of words to identify the different implements, David learned the job readily and performed with excellent accuracy. He still had trouble with his locker but that problem was easily solved by labeling the locker with a photo of David's favorite wrestler and by giving him a laser-operated lock that he could open with a push of a button. Erin and Jennifer were glad to be proven wrong about David, who stayed in the job for many years with a great salary and full-time benefits, and they took the lessons of the experience to heart.

But Erin and Jennifer found that, despite David's success, their deeply ingrained beliefs were not so easy to shake. At each step, they kept doubting David and did not expect him to go to the next level. Erin remembers telling David's managers not to expect him to learn the names of the different instruments or to know what they were used for. But, sure enough, over time, David did indeed learn these things. Like anyone else might, he picked up the information through his interactions with co-workers and by paying attention to the conversations going on around him.

Erin likes to tell David's story because it is a cautionary tale that illustrates how easy it is to mistake wrong assumptions for common sense. On the face of

Photo 7.1. Gretchen gathers supplies in the storeroom in preparation for stocking patient rooms.

it, it seems logical to look at David's inability to master the combination lock and conclude that it was indicative of his ability to learn a task that seemed vastly more complex. But the assumption proved to be wrong when put to the test. And, for Erin, the whole experience spoke to the tendency to forget that people with disabilities have the capacity to learn and grow and instead to base our expectations on what they *can't* do rather than on what they *can* do.

This is just one example of the doubts and second guessing that were part of the early days of Project SEARCH as Erin, Susie, and Jennifer learned what worked and what didn't. Another lesson for the team came from a young woman with Down syndrome, Gretchen, who was among the first participants to receive training through the program. The head nurse on a general pediatric inpatient unit was a big supporter of Project SEARCH and inquired about Gretchen's availability for a job opening on her unit. The job was to stock patient rooms with clinical supplies. Erin was doubtful about Gretchen's appropriateness for the job because Gretchen wasn't able to read, write, or count to 10. Erin couldn't get past her belief that the work was too important to entrust to someone with such limited abilities. This time, it was one of the job coaches who convinced Erin to let Gretchen give it a try. The job coach explained that any counting task could be broken down into groups of five and that "there are lots of ways to count to 5." In Gretchen's case, because she came from a family of avid golfers, one of her parents suggested that she use golf beads as an aid in counting (Figure 7.1). Gretchen's job coaches worked around the need to read by providing her with instructions that used photographs of each item. It turned out that she could do the job with great precision by matching the items with the picture while using the beads to get the quantities right. Erin admits that, as an employer, she never would have considered Gretchen for the job if she hadn't had the chance to actually see her do it.

Project SEARCH learned from those early years and has put policies in place to give all participants the best possible chance to reach their full potential. But misperceptions can still create hurdles for our graduates when they leave the program and enter the workforce. One such Project SEARCH graduate, Sarah P., came close to missing out on her dream job, in spite of her relevant training and excellent performance as a Project SEARCH intern, because of assumptions her employer made about her abilities. Sarah is a young woman with Down syndrome who attended the Project SEARCH High School Transition Program at Xavier University in the heart of urban Cincinnati. Sarah's home is in a suburb on the far eastern side of town, so, as a prerequisite to entering the program, she had to learn to navigate the city bus system. Her daily route was a long one that involved two transfers, but she mastered it and, in fact, never missed a day throughout her entire school year in the program. From the start, Sarah expressed a strong interest in food preparation. Accordingly, her teacher, Trish Heim, worked with her to plan a series of rotations in the various dining facilities on campus through which

Training issue	Solution/accommodation	Business benefit
In all the materials management tasks, there are many items that need to be counted in various amounts. Managers often believe that, if a person doesn't have good math skills, then they can't count. There were many situations in which we had to find solutions so that a person could independently count out a variety of items in various amounts for an employee without good counting ability. In one situation, an employee needed to count out 20 bottle nipples and 10 bottles and bag the entire set for delivery to the nursing floors. The employee did not have strong math skills and was in a situation in which she was constantly interrupted to complete other tasks. These other tasks might have priority over the counting. However, when she returned, the process was interrupted and she would have to begin again.	We utilized a traditional cart and created a counting jig on the top portion. Using actual-size digital pictures of the bottle nipples, we taped 20 pictures next to one another on the top of the cart. Also, on the top, we placed large numbers 1 to 10. The employee places a nipple on top of each picture and a bottle on top of each number (imagine filling out a bingo card). When the task is completed, she bags the items and seals the bag with a twist tie, and it's ready for delivery.	The employee is able to do the task with great accuracy, even with interruptions to complete other stocking jobs. When she begins again, it is clear where she left off. This allows the employee to do all of her duties with confidence. The cart is kept toward the back of the storeroom, and her supplies are kept on the bottom of the cart.

Figure 7.1. Materials management: counting aids. Clockwise from upper left: a calculator, a stationary counting board, a cart with counting jig, golf beads.

she could hone her skills in the kitchen. With each internship, she added new skills so that—by the time she finished her year with Project SEARCH—she could confidently operate a range of kitchen machinery, from the salad spinner to the industrial mixers to the professional slicer. By her third rotation, she was given responsibility for all the preparations involved in laying out the salad bar. After graduation, Sarah felt fortunate to be hired by a large grocery store in her neighborhood; a superstore in a large national chain. She was hired as a bagger, which was disappointing for her, but she hoped to use this position as a foot in the door—a starting point from which she could demonstrate her good work ethic and attitude and move up to the produce department (which had a large salad bar) when there was an opening. Sure enough, after several months of success at bagging groceries, the job she was waiting for became available. When she informed her manager that she wanted to apply for a job in the produce department, she was informed that she would not be considered for the position. Luckily, Sarah was not easily discouraged. She refused to take no for an answer and continued to insist that she be given a chance at the job in produce. Eventually, her management became frustrated with her stubborn attitude and told her she would need to take a week off to think about whether she wanted to leave the store or continue to be employed there as a bagger. Sarah took the time off, but her feelings didn't change. Meanwhile, while she was gone, the many regular customers who had gotten to know and appreciate Sarah kept asking where she was. When they heard the explanation, many costumers had the same incredulous response, all saying essentially the same thing: "Really? You're not even going to let her try?" Finally, after hearing from the customers as well as Sarah's job coach, her management got the message and invited her back to work in the produce department on a 1-week trial basis. During that trial period, all of Sarah's experience as a Project SEARCH intern became apparent. She caught on quickly and did well enough at the job that, at the end of the week, she was hired in that position.

Sarah was being held back by the misperceptions of people around her. Although her manager knew that she had completed training in food preparation, it wasn't enough to dislodge his preconceived ideas about the sort of job that was suitable for a person with Down syndrome. If she hadn't been so persistent, and if the customers and her job coach hadn't gone to bat for her, Sarah might never have been given the chance to prove herself.

THE EVOLUTION OF ATTITUDES ABOUT PEOPLE WITH INTELLECTUAL DISABILITIES

The Project SEARCH program evolved with an awareness of the pitfalls of low expectations and misguided assumptions, and the systems and practices that have been put in place are designed to avoid these traps and to create opportunities for participants to demonstrate their abilities. The Project SEARCH philosophy owes a great deal to the work of Marc Gold and other pioneers in the supported employment movement, such as Paul Wehman. Marc Gold was a special education teacher in California in the late 1960s when he began to articulate the set of beliefs that were to influence his life's work. Through his firsthand experiences with students with developmental and intellectual disabilities, and through his interactions with other special education and rehabilitation professionals, he formulated the following core concepts (Callahan, Mast, & Shumport, n.d.):

- [People] with severe disabilities have much more potential than most people realize.

- All people with disabilities should have the opportunity to live their lives much like everyone else.

- Everyone can learn if we can figure out how to teach them.

His ideas were quite radical at the time—an era when institutionalization was still common for people with intellectual disabilities. Moreover, the available services were meant only to meet basic needs such as food and shelter and were often designed with the convenience of the caregiver in mind rather than the quality of life for the person with a disability (Blatt,

1981; Orelove, 1991). Nonetheless, the obvious fairness and justice in the ideas articulated by Marc Gold and others could not be denied for long, and the core concepts began to be put into practice around the late 1970s and the early 1980s. The "try another way" approach to training, which ultimately evolved into the systematic instruction method—a method for teaching complex job skills that involves the analysis and breakdown of a task into discrete parts that can be learned in a precise and predictable way. Around the same time, the related concept of supported employment was established by Paul Wehman and others. Supported employment is defined simply as a framework in which the priority is "to assist persons with severe or significant disabilities in obtaining and maintaining community integrated competitive employment through specifically planned supports" (Brooke, Wehman, Inge, & Parent, 1997). The introduction of systematic instruction and supported employment led to demonstration projects that promoted a shift in perspective and values among people with disabilities, their family members, and service providers. Since then, integrated, community-based employment for people with significant disabilities has increasingly become accepted as a desirable goal by society at large and has, for some time, been recognized as a mainstream concept in academic circles (Wehman, 2003). For example, in 1983, Coughran and Daniels concluded that employment should be considered for all people with disabilities and could only be ruled out for those with the most profound disabilities that are accompanied by devastating loss of function.

In accordance with prevailing opinion, the concept of full inclusion has for many years shaped public policy. In 2001, the federal government formalized its commitment to community integration for people with disabilities and chronic illness with the introduction of the New Freedom Initiative by President George W. Bush. This priority is also reflected in the purpose of the state VR system, as stated on the U.S. Department of Education web site; that is, to provide "services designed to help individuals with disabilities prepare for and engage in gainful employment consistent with their strengths, resources, priorities, concerns, abilities, capabilities, interests, and informed choice." More recently, in July of 2010, President Obama issued an executive order (EO 13548, http://edocket.access.gpo.gov/2010/pdf/2010-18988.pdf), thus directing the federal government, as the nation's largest employer, to set a positive example in the area of employment for people with disabilities. To meet this goal, federal agencies were ordered to provide plans by which they would increase their recruitment, hiring, and retention of these individuals. Indeed, several federal agencies have implemented the Project SEARCH model at their office facilities as part of their strategy to meet this executive order.

SUCCESS IN COMPLEX AND SYSTEMATIC JOBS: THE KEY IS IN THE TRAINING

The expectation of competitive employment forms the overall gestalt in which Project SEARCH participants learn. With this expectation providing the background, the focus can turn to the nuts and bolts of learning job skills—that is, the hands-on learning that occurs between the job coach and the student intern at the worksite. A particular approach to job skills training has evolved in the context of the Project SEARCH model, and this approach is based on best practices in special education and job development, with an emphasis on systematic instruction, which, as we described earlier, is the practical synthesis of Marc Gold's "try another way" approach. The fields of job training and systematic instruction are vast, and it is not our goal to provide a comprehensive review of these topics here because there are many excellent resources already available to anyone who is interested in learning more. Rather, our intention is to discuss the concepts and practices that have particular relevance to the Project SEARCH model and to describe the important innovations that have grown out of Project SEARCH.

Project SEARCH and Systematic Instruction

Systematic instruction and Project SEARCH share many goals and core principles. The expectation of success and the natural tendency for students to live up to that expectation are key

VALUES AND PRINCIPLES OF SYSTEMATIC INSTRUCTION

- **Employability is assumed.** The question is "how," not "if."
- **The employment process begins with the person, not the job opening.** The skills and interests of the individual must be considered. One size does *not* fit all!
- **Differences recede as competence increases.**
- **Systematic instruction is part science, part art.** It is evidence based, but in practice, it is an art—judgment is involved.
- **Learn the task well before you teach it.** Focus on evaluating the learning, not how the task is going.
- **Learning to work is best done in a real workplace surrounded by other working people.**
- **When people are expected to be successful, they will live up to that expectation.**
- **People's potential is frequently hidden until they have an opportunity to shine.** Finding the right opportunity is important because people behave differently in different contexts and with different people.
- **Responsibility for learning rests with the trainer.** Once learning is done, the task is the intern's responsibility.
- **Natural motivation is the best kind.** Know what interests the learner.
- **Local staff are the best source of information for training.** A manager is familiar with the work of a department on a different level from that of a worker. A worker will have up-close knowledge of the work, including most efficient ways to do it.
- **Support needs to be consistent and available.**

From "Training in Systematic Instruction" by Liz Garnham. Presented at the Fourth Annual Project SEARCH International Conference, Miami, FL, July, 2009; adapted by permission.

elements of the Project SEARCH model that are also articulated in the core values underlying systematic instruction. Project SEARCH's single-minded focus on achieving competitive employment sets up an atmosphere of high expectations for the students on the part of teachers, job coaches, managers, co-workers, and most importantly, the students themselves.

Another important aspect of the Project SEARCH method of training is that participants learn complex job skills in the context of their worksite rotations. Moreover, the skills that the student interns learn are carefully aligned with the skills that the employer requires of entry-level hires. This aspect of the program is a direct result of total workplace immersion, which is a core element of the Project SEARCH model that is consistent with the systematic instruction principle stating that learning is most effective when it is done in a real workplace surrounded by other working people.

Lean, Systematic Instruction, and Project SEARCH—Parallels in Practice and Philosophy

Project SEARCH is a business-centered approach to high school transition, and our recommendations with regard to specific job skills training are rooted in that aspect of the model. What Project SEARCH has done is to synthesize established best practices from the fields of special education and job development and to reframe the resulting approach from a business perspective. One way that Project SEARCH has done this is by incorporating the principles and language of Lean (Liker, 2004), a business-based philosophy that overlaps in many ways with the goals of Project SEARCH, systematic instruction, and supported employment in general.

Lean is an outgrowth of the continuous quality improvement movement originated by Toyota. One of the most important underlying principles of Lean is for an organization to create a problem-solving philosophy that embraces people, change, and quality. The Project SEARCH philosophy also embraces people, change, and quality. We welcome change in that we continually grow so that we can serve more people with disabilities and we update our program structure and resources regularly. Moreover, we recognize and actively foster the highest potential in all people.

LEAN AND PROJECT SEARCH: PARALLEL PHILOSOPHIES

Lean promotes the development of each individual as a leader by helping to ensure that everyone is able to contribute to the organization. This is achieved through the following actions:

- Doing work in a standard way
- Recognizing that mistakes occur and being alert to identifying those mistakes
- Fixing the mistakes immediately
- Observing the work when and where it is being done in order to find the root cause of any issue or problem
- Being transparent during the problem-solving process
- Asking questions reflectively and honestly, and not jumping to conclusions
- Creating action plans, carrying out the plan, and evaluating the progress of the plan
- Respecting people

Adapted from the Project SEARCH Lean Curriculum

Among the many components of Lean is the goal of actively looking for and eliminating waste to create the most efficient and productive work flow possible. This Lean concept parallels a prominent part of the work of Project SEARCH instructors and job coaches. These individuals have the critical job of analyzing work processes to find the most efficient way to teach tasks while incorporating the learning style, personality, and specific needs of the person being trained. In fact, many of the accommodations, adaptations, and teaching tools used by job coaches over the years are consistent with the goals of Lean. For example, a job coach might increase the size of the lettering on the labels of shelves or files to help an individual with compromised vision learn a job and then find that this change helps everyone in the department do their work more quickly and accurately. In another example, to help a student with limited literacy skills, a job coach might use photographs instead of words to show which items belong on a given shelf or to help an intern working in clinical sterilization to identify surgical tools. Our experience is that this sort of change has the added benefit of reducing errors for everyone because most people process pictures more quickly and accurately than they do written words. Another common type of adaptation is to make small changes in the organization of the workspace, such as adding drawer dividers to organize items by size or type. These simple changes put in place to help people with cognitive disabilities can make a big difference for a whole organization with regard to increased productivity and reduced waste on the part of all workers.

By incorporating Lean tools, processes, and philosophy into its approach to training, Project SEARCH enhances the learning process while, at the same time, contributing to the goal of creating a more seamless integration of Project SEARCH into the business environment (see Table 7.1). The use of jargon that is specific to the rehabilitation field can be confusing and alienating to the employer (Luecking, 2011; Riehle & Daston, 2006). In contrast, the language and conceptual framework of Lean are understood in a business setting, which facilitates understanding and good communication among business personnel and Project SEARCH students and staff.

Teaching and Coaching for Success

In the 1980s, when systematic instruction was a relatively new concept, it received a lot of attention in the rehabilitation field and it was common for job coaches to learn to use it. But as the prevalence of supported employment grew, the demand for job coaches grew correspondingly, and many people were hired with a variety of educational and professional backgrounds. Because there was no certification or specific training required, the high rate of hiring resulted in a whole generation of disability services professionals with no formal training in systematic

Table 7.1. Lean concepts and rehabilitation terminology: comparison chart

Lean is a continuous improvement and problem-solving philosophy that has parallels in traditional job development and rehabilitation. Utilizing Lean tools bring a common language and credibility to the Project SEARCH® partners. This chart illustrates a comparison of 10 Lean tools with standard rehabilitation processes and concepts. The last two columns provide illustrations of how the different concepts can be applied in the Project SEARCH environment.

Lean tool and definition	Educational/rehabilitation equivalent	Relevance in the Project SEARCH context	Example: when and how to use it
Standing in the circle: Going to the actual place to observe and understand the real situation through direct observation	• Observation • Tour of business to look for potential jobs • Beginning of environmental analysis	This tool is the *first step* in understanding a business environment and work processes. It is a "means to an end" for determining jobs, tasks, flow of work, and so on. Because Project SEARCH is embedded and immersed in the business environment, we have the chance to use this unique tool for a variety of internship and employment opportunities.	• Observe the work in a department to determine core skills for an internship • Observe a student who may be having difficulty to look for possible adaptations • Determine the work flow of a department or specific job in order to begin a task analysis
Waste analysis: Allows an organization to categorize problems into eight types of waste and then focus attention in the appropriate areas for overall improvement, cost reduction, customer satisfaction, and increased value	• Job carving • With permission from the business, waste identification allows the job coach to redesign the work flow with the intention of making it possible for the worker with a disability to be more efficient (and hopefully be hired)	Waste analysis is *part of a process* that looks intently for issues that may be causing problems in an organization. Because they are embedded, the onsite Project SEARCH team has a unique position to look for and identify waste in their internship sites as well as other departments. Once waste is identified, you can begin designing adaptations, accommodations, and identifying an internship and eventual jobs.	In "Untapped or Underutilized Human Potential," the teacher/job coach sees the following: • Nurses stocking supplies • Technicians delivering an item • Copy center technicians loading paper and uses these as opportunities to build an internship and/or eventually a job
Fishbone diagram: Group communication and brainstorming tool to identify **many** possible causes for a problem. Focuses on causes rather than symptoms of a problem (cause and effect)	Team meeting to address problem with employee or intern (trying to determine how to fix the person)	Use the fishbone to identify as many possible causes of the problem as possible and try to find ways to improve the process (not the person). Lean is "hard on problems, easy on people."	**Problem: cafeteria tables not stocked in a timely manner.** Instead of focusing on the person, brainstorm solutions that concentrate on the environment, equipment, supplies, process, and management.
Five Why's: Identifies problem causes that can be corrected by the problem-solving team and forces the question, "What can we do?" It clearly indicates specific corrective actions. To use this tool, the problem statement is posed in the form of a question and the team answers the question and then poses the response as a new question until you reach a solution that can be implemented by the problem solver! This is called the "Five Whys"; however, you may be able to get to the root cause with less than five questions and answers.	Team meeting with all collaborating partners to address problem with the individual. Because team members are not part of the business, it is difficult to identify solutions that involve the business. Your options for improvement are much more limited.	It can be utilized in a specific training or employment situation; because we are part of the business, there are no preconceived ideas of the solutions or assumptions that problems must be related to the person with a disability.	Specific issue: Q 1. Why is Laura not reaching her quota of completing 30 instrument trays a day? A 1. Her speed has slowed down in the last few weeks. Q 2. Why has her speed slowed down in the last few weeks? A 2. She is doing new trays that she has not completed before. Q 3. Why is doing new trays slowing her down? A 3. She has not been trained on these trays and does not have a work aid book in place. Q 4. Why hasn't she been trained using a work aid book? A 4. We made an assumption that she didn't need training because she has been here long enough.

Table 7.1. (continued)

Lean tool and definition	Educational/rehabilitation equivalent	Relevance in the Project SEARCH context	Example: when and how to use it
5 S's: A process that results in a well-organized workplace complete with visual cues. The five "S's" include sort/scrap, straighten, shine, standardize, and sustain.	Supported Employment/Special Education teaching strategies: 1. Examine new workspace for disorder, inefficiency, and any situations that will cause confusion for the learner. 2. Reorder work flow, take photos to reinforce tasks, decide par levels, create jigs, research best accommodations and standard teaching techniques that net optimum performance results.	This step may occur directly after "Standing in the Circle" and any of the 5 S's can be used separately or together. • Discard unnecessary materials. • Organize work area. • Draw current state map. • Establish procedures. • Implement best practices. • Empower employees. • Monitor performance. Again, because we are embedded, the Project SEARCH staff has a relationship with the department staff which enables them to implement the 5 S's in a manner that is seen as helpful versus threatening or bothersome.	This tool can be used in any area that is supplies, materials, and equipment intensive. It also can be utilized to create long-term cues, prompts, and natural supports.
Standard work: To create the best work flow and make it consistent among all workers. It results in the most efficient, highest quality, safest way to perform a process or task (today).	With permission from the business, the job coach observes the work being done and develops a system in cooperation with the department in order to teach the person with a disability the job or elements of the job. Done primarily for the benefit of the person with a disability and used in initial training.	The Project SEARCH staff works in concert with the business and department staff to: • Eliminate random activities and inconsistent methods • Identify the "best way" • Establish expectations for safety and quality • Support with visuals • Use as an audit tool to maintain quality and safety Done primarily to determine the "best way" for the business. Will benefit the employee with a disability as well as all other employees. Used as an ongoing tool to maintain safety, quality, and productivity.	Use it to teach essential skill in internships and on competitive jobs. It allows the trainer and the person with a disability to focus on increasing speed and productivity.
Training matrix: Form used as a communication tool to identify: • The "standard operating procedures" or • "Work instructions" to be included in an employee's training	A similar tool could be a spreadsheet used to track IEP/transition goals.	• As a planning tool to develop internships that teach critical core skills of the department • As a communication tool to track acquisition of core skills that are needed for entry-level employment • As a tool that builds instant credibility with the department/host business as necessary skills are identified and tracked for acquisition and independence	• Demonstrate the gaps between actual and required knowledge levels • Identify champions or knowledge centers • Visual management tool • Identify at a glance individual skills levels within a department or class

(continued)

Table 7.1. (continued)

Error proofing: Any device, mechanism, or process that prevents the mistake from being made or greatly reduces the possibility of error (it shifts the focus of blaming the individual to improving the system). There are two levels of error proofing: 1. Total prevention—error cannot occur when the tool is used. 2. The likelihood of error is greatly reduced when the tool is used.	The disability community has used and understood "universal design" for many years (predating Lean and error proofing). There have been many inventions specifically for people with disabilities that have eventually transferred to the general community. One example is "Sticky Keys," which was invented as a special program (with a cost) for people with disabilities (specifically people with cerebral palsy) to improve their keyboarding skills. Over time, there was a need in the general community. Now, almost anyone can access this free tool. This tool builds credibility and confidence for the job coach. The business relates to "error proofing" through Lean but also recognizes that these devices (accommodations) will allow the person with a disability to be successful as an individual worker as well as allow the department to be successful with the person's skills, productivity, and quality. Over time, the business often benefits from these devices and tools for many employees in addition to the person with a disability. The business often recognizes that the teacher and job coach have expertise in this field. This creates tremendous value for the job coaches and teachers and their skill.	Any time a person with a disability is having difficulty with a specific task, work process, or flow. An example: Level 1 Commercially available temperature gun for a young man who has a difficult time monitoring refrigerator thermometers. This gives an accurate digital printout because the device is aimed at the back of the refrigerator. It can be used by anyone! Level 2 Windex bottle with markings to indicate the optimum usage of product per day to eliminate waste. This was fashioned by the job coach but also creates a self-monitoring process for the employee to build independence.
Action plan: Tool to use to communicate action steps and progress with a team. It holds people accountable for the commitments and provides a timeline for completion of activities. This tool is not specific to Lean and is used broadly in business and rehabilitation.	There are many variations of this tool in the rehabilitation and education fields including Gantt charts, timelines, action plans for project management purposes. Other similar examples include IEPs, IPEs, and internship evaluation forms.	• Project SEARCH implementation plans • Team meeting task list • Special project plans • Vocational service plans for individuals • Once the problem or activity has been clearly defined • When the solutions have been proposed or identified • When the implementation phase has been reached
Measurement/system building: • Provides powerful information using a scientific approach. It is essential for making good decisions to improve performance.	Data collection is used to make sound decisions in: • Training (e.g., task analysis data collection, indicator of need for additional coaching) • Productivity (productivity measurement) • Employment outcomes (job development tracking)	• Offers a way to see a situation clearly rather than relying on assumptions about workers with disabilities • Provides a basis on which to adjust training plans and processes to improve performance and quality • Provides a method to assess whether decisions made led to the desired result and whether activities carried out are yielding expected outcomes To measure the outcomes, results, or effects of processes or projects. To measure/report the actual materials, machines, methods, performance, or environmental factors involved in the process itself. Examples: • Collecting task analysis data during training • Measuring effects of an adaptation or restructuring a task • Tracking the number of compliments and complaints from employers regarding services

Key: IEP, individualized education program; IPE, individualized plan for employment.

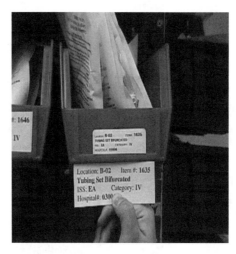

Training issue	Solution/accommodation	Business benefit
We had several employees working in this area, stocking the central storeroom, and on the clinical floors. Several individuals had visual impairments, and the other workers were low readers. It was difficult for them to read the labels and match the words and numbers to the actual items.	We asked permission to create larger-print labels and hang them under the original labels. This made it possible for everyone to be successful in the stocking tasks.	Within a few weeks of installing the new labels, we discovered that the other employees had replaced the larger labels on top of the originals. *Everyone* enjoyed the bigger print and found them easier to read and match items.

Figure 7.2. Central storeroom: increased type size.

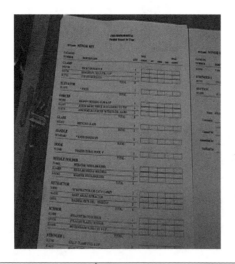 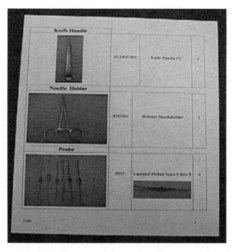

Training issue	Solution/accommodation	Business/department benefit
Surgery kits were assembled from "pick lists." The original lists were entirely text. It is very difficult for a nonreader or low reader to decipher the list and choose the right instrument.	Existing work aids were redesigned to include a photo of the actual instrument. Some of the instruments were pictured next to a ruler to show the angle of the clamp or scissors because many utensils look similar. These aids allow individuals with disabilities to perform the same job as their co-workers without disabilities.	Once the picture books for the surgery kits were in place, it was obvious how helpful they were, not only for the Project SEARCH® employee but also for anyone. The pictures were so much easier to match with the real object. The clinical sterilization department asked whether Project SEARCH could make a picture book for every surgical tray. As a compromise, we created a picture book for each tray that our employee was assigned to. When she is assigned to learn a new tray, we create a new book.

Figure 7.3. Clinical sterilization: photo-based instrument lists for the preparation of surgery trays.

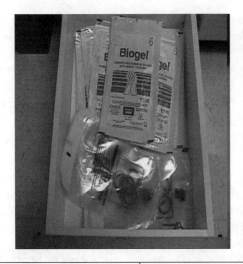
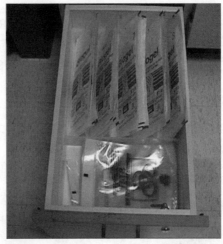

Training issue	Solution/accommodation	Business benefit
Cincinnati Children's Hospital Medical Center has a 58-room emergency department. Before Project SEARCH®, gloves were grouped by size (e.g., small, medium, large), using rubber bands, and placed in the drawer. When a nurse or doctor came into the room, he or she would have to dig through the drawer to find the right size. If he or she accidentally unwrapped the wrong size, the gloves would need to be thrown away. The two young men hired to stock drawers in this department had difficulty with the glove drawers for different reasons. One of the youths had autism and the drawer seemed very chaotic to him, and it was, therefore, very difficult for him to complete the stocking task. The other young man had very large hands and found it difficult to twist and wrap the rubber bands around the gloves. Moreover, the markings on the gloves were not very distinct, so it was difficult to tell them apart to be able to stock to par and check for expiration dates.	Drawer dividers were created to separate gloves by sizes. These dividers also cut down on product loss (each pair of gloves costs over $20.00). Another issue, aside from accidentally taking the wrong size, was that the rubber bands often ruined the packaging, therefore compromising the sterility of the product. The dividers solved this problem and also sped up the work because they created a clear view of the product. Owing to the organization and clear view, the employees were able to establish and stock to par as well as check expiration dates.	Not only did the job redesign result in a more efficient work flow for the employees with disabilities, but it also provided a more efficient work flow for the clinical staff. They could immediately find the needed gloves, resulting in a substantial savings to the hospital. We found similar situations with the diaper drawers and so also redesigned those drawers. Similarly, if a wrong size diaper is chosen and touches a baby, that diaper must be thrown away. Each of these drawer inserts was paid for by the developmental disabilities agency and incurred no cost to the hospital.

Figure 7.4. Emergency department: organizing the workspace to enhance productivity.

instruction. Many learned on the job, but there was no system in place to ensure good preparation (Migliore, Grossi, Mank, & Rogan, 2008). It was in this context that the Project SEARCH leadership team identified a critical need for well-trained job coaches as part of a continuous quality improvement effort. We realized that, in order to promote uniform success in employment and retention in complex jobs across all of the Project SEARCH sites, it was important that the teaching and coaching staff at each program site had access to and familiarity with a battery of effective tools and techniques (see Figures 7.2, 7.3, and 7.4).

With this need in mind, we developed a curriculum that we call "Teaching and Coaching for Success" that formalizes and defines the approach to job training that we have found to be effective in the Project SEARCH setting. The course gives background information and practical tools showing how to apply the principles of systematic instruction and other best

Teaching and Coaching for Success in Action

Cindy Martens-Pitts is a Project SEARCH instructor who embodies the "try another way" philosophy. As the instructor for the program at Wegmans, a food-based retail chain currently in several Northeast and Mid-Atlantic states, Cindy has devised a variety of innovative training methods to help her students be successful.

Many worksite rotations at Wegmans teach skills associated with food preparation and handling. Because many of the students had been discouraged from using sharp utensils in the kitchen at home, they didn't know how to handle a knife. Cindy rectified this situation by bringing knives, protective gloves, a cutting board, and lemons into the classroom where, through copious repetition, students could lose their fear and learn good technique. Cindy used a similar technique to teach students how to use the pizza cutter, where she made "pizzas" out of salt clay for practice.

Karis hones his knife skills.

Salt clay "pizza" used for slicing practice.

In the seafood department, a large part of the work involves using scales. This is something that is unfamiliar to many Project SEARCH students and a particular challenge for those with limited math skills, so Cindy came up with some creative tools to prepare students for this aspect of the internship. First, she found a scale in a back room that she moved into the classroom. Naturally, students couldn't practice on the actual merchandise, so she made some items with the

(continued)

practices in combination with Lean principles in the framework of the Project SEARCH model of high school transition. It is designed primarily for job coaches and teachers, but other Project SEARCH staff members who have input in the job training process find the course useful, as do job coaches and job developers who work in other supported employment or high school transition programs.

Effective Job Coaching—The Big Picture

Good job coaches have a solid understanding of the employer's needs and the specific job tasks that need to be taught. Project SEARCH job coaches have an advantage in this regard because they are embedded within the business. Moreover, there is buy-in from the department from the beginning because managers have voluntarily agreed to host student interns. Thus, the job coach is entering a receptive environment when he or she begins the task of learning about the department. At this stage, the first step is to identify the skills to be learned, and the next step is to break down those tasks into the individual skills that need to be mastered. The teacher and the job coach work with the managers and the business liaison to ensure that items on the task list match the entry-level skills required for employment in the industry sector represented by the host business.

It is important for job coaches to teach specific work-related tasks, but the "soft skills," or employability skills, such as appropriate dress and interpersonal communication, are also critical. In a typical job coaching environment, the coach meets the client at the worksite, teaches the task, and then leaves. In this scenario, there are limited opportunities to teach soft skills, and they are generally brought up only when an infraction occurs in the job coach's presence. For example, if the learner walks by the salad bar and takes a dinner roll, this would give the job coach an opportunity to initiate a discussion about stealing, but after that, she or he would just have to hope it never happens again. But, in the Project SEARCH model, there are multiple opportunities to teach employability skills. First, they are introduced and practiced in the classroom, and then they are reinforced on a daily basis at the worksite during the course of the internship. Moreover, because the learning happens in the context of an internship and not in an actual job, it's a protected environment where the consequences of a mistake are less dire than being fired.

Any good job coach, in any environment, works from day one to achieve independence on the job for the individual he or she is coaching. It's important to steadily back up and gradually give more independence to the learner, but the challenge is in knowing how to gauge when it's okay to step back. To do this, it is critical to have written documentation that clearly and objectively demonstrates that the intern is able to work independently on a given task. This is particularly important in the Project SEARCH model, where it is critical to keep the teacher, manager, and co-workers in the loop.

Monitoring progress is a critical part of systematic instruction, and as we pointed out in the earlier discussion, it's important to have an objective system in place for recording data. This need is also emphasized in Lean principles, which stress the need to become comfortable with data so that one is able to use and learn from them. There are many data collection forms that can be used to track the progress of job skills learning. The important thing is for any group to identify the form that works for them and then make sure that all members of the team use the same form. This is critical to ensure that the job coach, the teacher, the manager, and the student can all look at the chart and interpret the data. The traditional method is a daily log in which the job coach simply writes down observations on the learner's performance in a given task listed on a chart. The problem with this format is that it is relatively time consuming to complete, and the information it contains is strictly subjective and open to different interpretations by different members of the team. The standard work chart is a good example of a more objective data collection tool (a blank chart is provided in Appendix 7.1). With this or a similar tool, the team can see exactly where independence has been achieved so that they'll know where new tasks can be layered on so that learning continues. For example, in the sample chart (Figure 7.5), you can see that the student intern has successfully collected books and magazines and returned them to the bins every day for 4 days in a row. This shows that it might be time to add a new task, such as checking for damaged or out-of-date magazines to be discarded and replaced with new ones. You can also identify areas in which there has been failure to learn a task. In the example provided, it is clear that the student hasn't been successful in checking and replacing the toner in the copy machines. This is a trigger for the job coach to pull that task out of the chain, break it down into smaller parts, and then pinpoint exactly where the problem resides. In this case, the job coach would observe the student and determine whether it was perhaps a problem with opening the printer case, locating new toner cartridges, opening the packaging, and so on. The same standard work chart format can be used for this highly focused training (see Figure 7.6). Once the block is found, the job coach can separate that particular step from the sequence of steps that make up the task, and teach that step in isolation, or perhaps modify it, until it is mastered, at which time it can be inserted back into the chain (a standard systematic instruction training technique known as "forward and backward chaining"). Another advantage of an objective data collection tool is that it makes it easier for students to chart their own progress, which can provide very effective reinforcement.

An effective job coach should encourage co-workers to be involved in training the intern. Indeed,

(continued)

appropriate look and feel to help students get used to handling food items and interpreting the scale's readout. These turned out to be very simple and effective learning tools. She made some surprisingly realistic scallops from salt clay and used cardboard shapes filled with red beans to approximate fish fillets. By weighing these items repeatedly, students became familiar with the approximate size, feel, and heft of different fractions of a pound. They also learned that "half a pound" looks like "0.50" and "three quarters of a pound" looks like "0.75" on the scale's digital readout. In time, the interns were able to transfer these skills to the actual foods and display their confidence as they assisted customers.

Fish models for learning weighing skills.

Karis is a Project SEARCH graduate from the Wegmans program who did two work rotations in the seafood department during his time as a student. Using the training tools that Cindy created gave him the confidence, once he got behind the counter, to focus on the most important part of the job: customer service. When asked what he liked best about the seafood department, Karis said, "I liked to make sure that everything looked good for the customer. If it doesn't look good to me, the customer won't buy it." Even though he admits to having been shy and nervous before entering Project SEARCH, Karis says that being in the Project SEARCH program made him more outgoing and confident, and he liked interacting with customers. As he put it, "I always asked them, 'Do you want anything or need anything?' and they'd say, 'No, I'm just looking,' and I'd say, 'Well, if you need anything just let me know. I'll be right here,' and they appreciated that."

Around the time of his graduation, Karis was offered a job at a Wegmans store near his home. He'll be starting out in the pizza department where he'll use the food preparation and customer service skills he learned in Project SEARCH.

Standard Work - Implemented: 5/2/11

Trainer: Jim Johnson

Intern: Sue Smith   Independent: = +

Job: Reception Family Resource Center   Assistance given: = −

Major Process Steps	5/3	5/5	5/10	5/12
Reception Area 1				
1 Check water coolers (2); replace if less than 1/4	−	−	+	+
2 Gather all magazines - return to rack	+	+	+	+
3 Gather all children's books - return to bin	+	+	+	+
4 Make coffee	−	−	+	+
5 Fill airpot with hot water for tea/cocoa	+	+	+	+
6 Clean coffee/tea bar	−	−	+	+
7 Check coffee/tea supplies - replenish as needed	+	+	+	+
8 Check paper level in copiers (2) - fill as needed	+	+	+	+
9 Check toner in copiers (2) - fill as needed	−	−	/	/
10 Check pads/pens at recept. - replace as needed	+	+	+	+
Reception Area 2				
1 Check water coolers (2); replace if less than 1/4	−	/	+	+
2 Gather all magazines - return to rack	+	+	+	+
3 Gather all children's books - return to bin	−	−	+	+
4 Make coffee	−	+	+	+
5 Fill airpot with hot water for tea/cocoa	−	+	+	+
6 Clean coffee/tea bar	−	−	+	+
7 Check coffee/tea supplies - replenish as needed	−	+	+	+
8 Check paper level in copiers (2) - fill as needed	−	+	+	+
9 Check toner in copiers (2) - fill as needed	−	−	/	/
10 Check pads/pens at recept. - replace as needed	+	+	+	+
Total Time minutes	140	135	132	125
Level of Independence	8/10	6/10	7/10	9/10
	6/10	7/10	9/10	9/10

Notes: Safety, Quality, Efficiency

Reception areas 1 and 2 should be completed in 2 hours by the end of training period.

Figure 7.5. Standard work chart example—reception area.

Task Analysis: Replace toner cartridge

Job: Reception Family Resource Center

Intern: Sue Smith
Trainer: Jim Johnson

Replace toner cartridges - HP 6310 (2011) Date	6/6	6/10	6/16	6/23
1 Gather black and color cartridges from supply	−	+	+	+
2 Place fingers under printer control panel	−	−	−	+
3 Lift control panel slowly until it clicks open	+	+	+	+
4 Place finger on bottom rim of black cartridge	+	+	+	+
5 Apply pressure down and out to remove	−	−	+	+
6 Place old cartridge in container for recycle	+	+	+	+
7 Place finger on bottom rim of color cartridge	+	+	+	+
8 Apply pressure down and out to remove	+	−	+	+
9 Place old cartridge in container for recycle	+	+	+	+
10 Remove black cartridge from package	+	+	+	+
11 Pull tape from cartridge element	−	+	+	+
12 Insert cartridge into recept. - #'s up right side	−	−	−	−
13 Snap into place	−	−	−	−
14 Remove color cartridge from package	+	+	+	+
15 Pull tape from cartridge element	−	−	−	−
16 Insert cartridge into recept. - #'s up left side	−	−	−	−
17 Snap into place	−	−	−	+
18 Close lid firmly - error message if not closed	−	−	+	+
19 Press ok when prompted to align cartridge	+	+	+	+
20 File printed alignment page in copier notebook	−	+	+	+
Level of independence (% of steps correct)	8/20	11/20	15/20	16/20
Speed (time to replace 2 cartridges) minutes	14	12	11	7

Key: Independent = +
Assistance given = −

Notes: Safety, Quality, Efficiency:

Figure 7.6.   Standard work chart example—replace toner cartridge.

one of the important ideas that we like to instill when we train job coaches is that coaching strategies are not secrets—they should be shared with anyone who will be in a position to work with or support the student intern. With a good understanding of the tasks and the functioning of the department, a good job coach is well positioned to identify the co-workers who will act as appropriate natural supports for the Project SEARCH student. The job coach can then model good job coaching and share the strategies she or he uses so that co-workers will know how to effectively provide support when the coach is not around. For example, co-workers might want to encourage the intern with praise, but although praise is an important motivator and source of encouragement, it is effective only when it is specific. It is meaningless to just say, "Good job." It's more helpful to point out precisely what the intern did right. For example, imagine that you're teaching someone to set up audiovisual equipment. If the intern steadies the computer with his or her hand while putting the plug in, you might say, "I really like the way you held the computer in place while you hooked it up so that you could be sure the plug was in securely." Giving specific praise achieves two things—it boosts confidence and, at the same time, it reinforces good performance. Moreover, the trainee's co-workers will pick up on the concept, which is another way to facilitate independence because it becomes something that co-workers can do when the job coach is no longer there. Furthermore, it's a good management strategy for anyone, not just people with disabilities. So it accomplishes a third goal of sharing general training tools with the department staff.

A job coach is responsible for troubleshooting. Part of both systematic instruction and Lean is to correct mistakes early in the learning process so that bad habits and poor skill development aren't reinforced. The Project SEARCH model, in which the teacher and job coach are fully immersed in the business, puts the job coach in a particularly good position to identify issues and respond quickly. More than a traditional job coach, she or he understands the culture and priorities of the business so that she or he has a better understanding of how any transgression or mistake will affect the organization. Moreover, if you've built a good team, it's easier for the job coach to hear constructive criticism. That is, in a partnership in which everyone has a stake in the success of the intern, there is trust and shared goals, so the job coach is less likely to be defensive when getting feedback from the business personnel.

In Project SEARCH, the job coach feels an equal allegiance to the business and to the intern. In typical job coaching, it's more of an 80/20 ratio, but in Project SEARCH, it's 100/100. With the job coach entirely committed to both the business and the intern, it creates a different dynamic. It becomes a symbiotic relationship between the student and the department so one can't succeed at the expense of another.

Project | SEARCH

Standard work - implemented:		Trainer:																			
Intern:		Independent:	=	+																	
Job:		Assistance given:	=	-																	
	Date																				
Major process steps																					
1																					
2																					
3																					
4																					
5																					
6																					
7																					
8																					
9																					
10																					
11																					
12																					
13																					
14																					
15																					
16																					
17																					
18																					
19																					
20																					
21																					
22																					
23																					
Total time																					
Level of independence																					
Notes: safety, quality, efficiency																					

High School Transition That Works: Lessons Learned from Project SEARCH® by Maryellen Daston, J. Erin Riehle, and Susan Rutkowski.
Copyright © 2012 Cincinnati Children's Hospital Medical Center. All rights reserved. Baltimore, MD: Paul H. Brookes Publishing Co., Inc.

Project | SEARCH

Meet Raphael

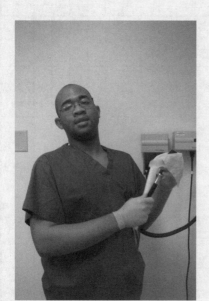

Raphael was a member of the 2010–2011 Project SEARCH class at Cincinnati Children's Hospital Medical Center. His first internship was in the Department of Developmental and Behavioral Pediatrics, where he learned to clean and sterilize clinical and procedural rooms. Raphael learned so fast and worked so efficiently that, when a job opening came up in his department, he was hired in the middle of his Project SEARCH school year. He has made a very smooth and successful transition from student intern to regular employee. In addition to his regular duties, he enjoys helping patients and their families find their way around the clinic, and he loves the daily interactions with his co-workers. His mother, Malaka, finds this outgoing attitude remarkable for a young man who was very quiet as a child—saying only "the bare minimum" of what he needed to get by.

Malaka has seen other changes in her son since his Project SEARCH experience. She says, "I think the program gave him more self-confidence. They gave him the chance to just be able to fit in." And before the program, she admits that she was initially against the idea of his using public transportation on his own. But now she sees that he relishes the independence of getting on the bus every day to go to work.

Being an employee at Cincinnati Children's is particularly rewarding for Raphael because he spent a lot of time there as a child where, at the age of 3, he received a diagnosis of autism with pervasive developmental delays. Some of his co-workers in the Department of Developmental and Behavioral Pediatrics have fond memories of Raphael from his years as a patient, and now they are delighted to have him as a productive and capable colleague. When asked about Raphael's hiring, his supervisor says, "We are the lucky ones to have Raphael on our team!"

8 | Job Retention and Career Advancement

> *Continuous effort, not strength or intelligence, is the*
> *key to unlocking our potential.*
>
> Winston Churchill

C ompetitive employment is the goal for Project SEARCH® participants, but getting a job is just the beginning of reaching that goal. It feels great to be chosen as the right applicant for a job and to be hired, but no job can have a meaningful impact on a person's life unless employment is sustained for the long term. And if a job doesn't last, that loss can be a real blow to self-esteem that can cause setbacks in personal growth from which it is hard to recover. Employee retention is important from the business's perspective, too. Every time experienced workers leave and are replaced by inexperienced employees, there is a disruption in the work flow. High turnover is costly in a strictly monetary sense as well; each time a new hire is brought on board, the business pays roughly $7,500 over and above the salary and benefits of the new employee to cover processes such as advertising the position, reviewing applications, interviewing candidates, and performing background checks.

For anyone, continued success on a job will require perseverance and a supportive environment. But for a person with significant intellectual and developmental disabilities, it will almost certainly require some level of ongoing interaction with disability employment professionals. According to the principles of supported employment, the purpose of that ongoing assistance is to help the individual with a disability "in the identification and provision of supports and extended services necessary to maintain and enhance the person's position as a valued member of the work force" (Brooke, Wehman, Inge, & Parent, 1997). The need for long-term support is addressed in the core concepts of the Project SEARCH approach in the model fidelity component that reads, "Project SEARCH graduates will receive effective follow-along services to retain employment." To meet this requirement, Project SEARCH participants must be linked, prior to graduating from the High School Transition Program, with agencies that provide long-term follow-along. For students who are hired by the host business, continued contact is facilitated by the ongoing presence of Project SEARCH staff at the worksite. Later on in this chapter, we discuss the details of providing long-term follow-along for program graduates employed at the host business and for those hired by other employers in the larger community.

THE LIMITATIONS OF TRADITIONAL FOLLOW-ALONG

There is wide agreement on the value of follow-along services for people with intellectual and developmental disabilities. Nonetheless, there are systemic obstacles in place that can make it a challenge for individuals to get effective services. First of all, in the education and vocational rehabilitation (VR) systems, there is an institutional focus on job placement as an end point. In school systems, job placement can be counted as a successful postschool outcome according to Individuals with Disabilities Education Act (IDEA, PL 108-446) indicator 14, regardless of the duration of employment. In the VR system, the measure of success for a consumer is placement followed by 90 days of employment. When this milestone is reached, the VR counselor considers the case closed and the individual is considered "successfully rehabilitated." At this point, any further services would require a reopening of the case, which can happen only if there is job loss or if there is dissatisfaction with work conditions on the part of the employee or performance on the part of the employer.

In most localities in the United States, funding for long-term follow-along is provided by state DD agencies, and increasingly, funding comes through the Medicaid Home and Community Based Services (HCBS) Waiver program. The different states use different criteria to determine eligibility for services, but in general, it is based on severity of the disability, and this can present a barrier to some Project SEARCH participants. In Ohio, for example, DD agencies utilize a survey called the OEDI (Ohio Eligibility Determination Instrument), to assess independent living skills such as personal grooming and hygiene, written and verbal communication skills, and mobility. Ironically, to qualify for long-term employment support, the individual with a disability must profess a lack of independence in the very same employability skills that Project SEARCH and other transition and supported employment programs work to enhance. The eligibility criteria for HCBS Waiver funds are even more severe. To receive these funds, an individual must demonstrate that the supports are necessary to avoid institutionalization. Needless to say, not all students who are eligible for Project SEARCH are eligible for long-term follow-along through the usual channels. Our experience has been that, in most cases, approximately 50% to 70% of students in a given Project SEARCH class are eligible.

For most individuals who are eligible for long-term employment support, the support that they receive is not as comprehensive or thorough as it could be. In Ohio, for example, an individual receiving long-term support is limited to no more than 4 hours a month with a job coach. What's more, those 4 hours are usually with a job coach who has a very limited understanding of the culture, priorities, or flow of work at the place of employment. This shortcoming isn't because the job coaches aren't smart, resourceful, and dedicated. Rather, it's built in to the way services are provided. A job coach working for a given support agency typically has a case load of 25 or more individuals who are employed in a variety of businesses that are scattered throughout the city or county. They spend their time driving from one business to another checking in on clients, and they can stay only 1 or 2 hours at each worksite. Moreover, the job coach who provides follow-along for a given employee is not usually the same coach who assisted with the initial job training. With this intermittent and brief contact, there is no way for the service provider to develop a real relationship with the staff at the business or to gain a thorough understanding of the business.

THE PROJECT SEARCH APPROACH TO FOLLOW-ALONG

In the Project SEARCH model, we address the weaknesses in the traditional model of service delivery by stipulating that consistent, onsite staff provide follow-along support for student participants once they become employed. Total immersion in the workplace is critical to the job skills and employability training that takes place in the high school transition phase of the Project SEARCH model, and it is equally important to program participants who achieve employment. Having follow-along provided consistently by the same individual, and as an

---

ADVANTAGES OF ONSITE FOLLOW-ALONG
- Follow-along staff understands the business culture and procedures.
- Follow-along staff can respond immediately to changes or problems.
- Business has continuous access to experts in accommodations and adaptations.
- Employees with disabilities receive assistance with feedback, evaluations, and mandatory education.
- Employees with disabilities receive assistance with all benefit questions.
- Follow-along staff has access to information about new openings for career advancement and lateral moves.

---

integral part of the workplace, is ideal for the same reasons that it is beneficial to students in transition. A continuous presence and daily interactions mean that job coaches have a deep understanding of the business and solid relationships with the people who work there. Traditional job coaching is like watching the trailer instead of seeing the whole movie. But with Project SEARCH, job coaches don't just see "the whole movie," they're actually an active part of the crew—they become the "best boys," "gaffers," and "key grips." As an integral part of the workplace, they understand the business priorities, the business culture, and the details of work flow and procedures. This difference is significant to the employers as well as to the recipients of support services. In their responses to surveys, managers make it clear that they appreciate working with job coaches and job developers who understand how businesses function. It is such an important factor that the availability of effective support can have a significant impact on an employer's outlook on hiring workers with intellectual disability (Morgan & Alexander, 2005). Conversely, employers consistently list a lack of understanding and naïveté about business procedures and priorities as a source of frustration in their interactions with disability professionals (Butterworth & Pitt-Catsouphes, 1997; Luecking, 2008, 2011).

Project SEARCH wouldn't be a feasible model without onsite follow-along. But what we mean by *onsite* is "consistent support provided by a single individual," not necessarily that the individual will be onsite full time. The number of hours that a follow-along provider can spend at a given business will correspond to the number of employees who work there who are eligible for long-term support. In most Project SEARCH programs, approximately one fourth of graduating students are hired by the host business in a given year (this number varies widely; e.g., we have found that programs in their first or second year of operation will often hire half or more of the graduating class). With an average class size of 12 students, it is typical for a Project SEARCH host business to add around 3 or 4 employees with intellectual and developmental disabilities to its workforce each year. With a typical case load of 25 individuals per job coach, this means that every five Project SEARCH graduates hired by the host business corresponds to one fifth of a full-time follow-along provider, which equals 8 hours per week onsite. For example, in the early days of Project SEARCH at Cincinnati Children's, the hospital employed 13 DD-eligible individuals. At that time, they arranged with the local DD agency to have Jennifer Linnabary onsite for one quarter of full time, or 10 hours per week. This meant she could be there for several hours in the mornings 2 or 3 days a week, which was plenty of time for her to do more than just drop in and say, "How is everything going today?" She had a name badge and approved access to all areas of the facility, she learned the system at the hospital, and she came to know lots of people in many different departments. As the years went on, more Project SEARCH graduates were hired at the end of each school year. As a result, the number of DD-eligible employees increased and Jennifer's time at the hospital increased accordingly, until eventually the county bureau of DD scheduled her to be onsite at the hospital full time.

FUNDING OPTIONS FOR JOB RETENTION AND CAREER ADVANCEMENT
- Developmental disability agency
- Regional centers
- Plan to Achieve Self-Support (PASS)/impairment-related work expenses (IRWE)
- Medicaid waivers/infrastructure grants
- *New* ticket to work
  - Provides up to $20,000 in additional revenue for long-term follow-along services

---

For many Project SEARCH sites in the early stages, it makes sense to have follow-along services provided by the Project SEARCH teacher and the job coaches who collaborate with the teacher to oversee the worksite rotations. These individuals will already have a familiarity with the supported employees as well as with the business. However, because the High School Transition Program is active only during the school year, the Project SEARCH planning team may need to identify funds to cover job coaching costs over the summer so that the support will be consistent and continuous. The source of these funds would depend on the eligibility profile of the students who were hired by the business.

The scenario described earlier assumes that the Project SEARCH host business is a large one that can hire large numbers of people with disabilities. Whereas this is the typical case, the system can be modified to work in other circumstances as well. For example, the University of Rochester's Institute for Innovative Transition has tailored the mechanisms for providing onsite follow-along for the two Project SEARCH programs that they coordinate to suit the different environments at the host businesses. One program is in a large hospital, Golisano Children's Hospital, and as such, the full-time onsite follow-along is provided in a similar manner as it is at the Cincinnati Children's program site. The other Project SEARCH host business is Wegmans, a food-based retail chain. In this case, the worksite is a series of small stores throughout the county, and not a single campus. With this configuration, there is no avoiding some travel for job coach. But the approach to follow-along is consistent with the Project SEARCH model because support is provided through a coordinated effort from a single agency—in fact, it is the same agency that coordinates follow-along at the hospital. Even though the job coaches may have a more limited presence at each store, they can still be knowledgeable about the business and "in the loop" because the culture and processes are uniform from store to store such that any changes in procedures or required retraining will be the same at all the stores.

The major shortcoming of the Project SEARCH system of follow-along is that it applies only to program participants who are hired by the host business, and as we said earlier, for most businesses, this includes only one quarter to one third of each class. The remaining students receive job-search assistance to find work at other companies in the community. Once they are outside of the Project SEARCH host business, they will receive only the typical follow-along support, depending on their location and eligibility. This remains one of the few difficult-to-solve gaps in the Project SEARCH model, but some Project SEARCH practitioners have found creative ways to address the issue. Among the most successful has been to attack the problem through the use of a Project SEARCH Business Advisory Council (BAC). The Project SEARCH representative at Briggs and Associates (a community rehabilitation partner [CRP] in the Atlanta area) set up such a program in association with the Project SEARCH site at Emory University Hospital. She recruited representatives from several nearby hospitals to form a BAC and brought in other related businesses to support the Project SEARCH program. The organizations represented by the BAC came together to form a follow-along catchment area that can be served by follow-along personnel who have Emory University Hospital, the

Project SEARCH host business, as their home base. This way, nearly all of the eligible Project SEARCH graduates can count on having the support of consistent and knowledgeable long-term follow-along personnel. In fact, one of the most recent hospitals to become involved in the Project SEARCH BAC in the Atlanta area is the Children's Hospital of Atlanta, which has hired many Project SEARCH graduates owing to her efforts. This hospital is able to utilize the standard Project SEARCH in-house method of follow-along because they have hired enough employees to make it feasible.

Integrated Follow-Along Staff Can Respond Immediately to Changes or Problems

When a job coach has only occasional contact with a person in supported employment, the odds are that the job coach won't be at the job site when a problem arises. Small problems that happen between visits are likely to have blown over by the time the job coach is there. As a result, no one mentions it to the job coach, the issue remains unresolved, and when it happens for the second or third time, what started as a small problem suddenly becomes a big problem. This pattern is common enough to have a name among rehabilitation professionals: "fine, fine, fired." Consider the case of an employee with a cognitive disability, "Kevin," who works stocking patient rooms in a hospital. Everyone agrees that Kevin is good at his job; he is very focused and good at ignoring potential distractions. But regardless of how efficiently and effectively he gets his work done, if he misses out on a small procedural change, it will result in errors being introduced into his work. Imagine that, one day, a department-wide e-mail goes out with the message that, for example, there has been a recall on "brand A" size 21 cannulas so the hospital is pulling them all and temporarily switching to "brand B" cannulas. Kevin might have missed the e-mail, or maybe he didn't understand it. A co-worker will correct Kevin's mistake once and think nothing of it. The job coach will come in and get a report that everything's fine. The same thing might happen the following week—maybe this time the hospital has decided to increase the stocking number of a certain item from 10 to 15. Again, it's a small thing and a co-worker corrects Kevin's work. But when it happens a third time, Kevin's co-workers are tired of covering for him, and by the time the job coach comes back, even though she had heard at the last two visits that everything was going fine, Kevin is now on the verge of being fired.

We can teach people with significant intellectual and developmental disabilities to do complex jobs, and we can help them hone their skills so that they become attractive job candidates. The problem is that, once they are hired and on the job, changes will inevitably arise in any complex job, and intermittent job coaching can't support this complexity. A follow-along provider needs to know about those changes and, better yet, to be able to anticipate changes. The "fine, fine, fired" problem can be avoided by having knowledgeable, integrated staff to provide follow-along support. With onsite staff, problems, such as behavioral issues or the need for retraining in response to procedural changes, can be resolved immediately. For example, in Kevin's case, the job coach would have been on the e-mail list and would have seen the e-mail and responded by making sure that Kevin was aware of the change and that he understood and had incorporated the change into his routine.

Onsite Follow-Along Means More Service for the Money

Another advantage of onsite follow-along is that an economy of scale is achieved. Job-support providers can handle much larger caseloads when the majority of their clients are integrated at a single large business because nearly all of their work time is spent actually delivering support services. In the traditional follow-along model, a service provider can easily spend up to 25% of her or his work time driving between job sites; these are all billable hours that the provider agency must pay for but don't in any way contribute to better employment retention for people with disabilities. However, this argument for onsite follow-along can be surprisingly difficult to get across in the context of an agency structure in which services are delivered, and accounting and billing are tracked, based on hours spent with an eligible individual and not on hours spent at a given workplace. This is an area in which the true collaboration that is characteristic of Project SEARCH comes into play. If the DD agency, or other follow-along provider, is part of the planning and implementation team from the onset, that organization will have a partner relationship with the host business and, thus, a better understanding of what will make the program work in that particular setting. They will also have a vested interest in the success of the program, and this can increase their willingness to be flexible in their approach to service delivery.

Integrated Support Personnel Enhance the Business

In the previous chapter, we gave some examples of how the adaptations and accommodations that job coaches devise to enhance their clients' work performance can have the collateral benefit of increasing a business's overall efficiency, and many employers recognize this potential advantage of working with agencies that have expertise in issues of disability employment (Luecking, 2004). In fact, many listed this effect as a motivating factor in the decision to hire individuals with significant disabilities (Luecking, Cuozzo, and Buchanan, 2006). By incorporating Lean principles, Project SEARCH works to maximize this benefit to businesses. Not only are the onsite, integrated follow-along support personnel that are part of the Project SEARCH model knowledgeable about the specific needs of the host business, they are also trained to recognize and eliminate waste to maximize the productivity and efficiency of the work flow.

Follow-Along Personnel Can Coordinate Mandatory Training, Health Screening, and Other Non-Job-Related Work Requirements

Every large employer requires that its employees take part in a number of activities that are critical to performance, workplace safety, or workplace harmony but which are not directly related to job duties. According to Lean terminology, these activities would be categorized as "non-value added but necessary." In most businesses or other employer organizations, these activities include trainings on diversity, sexual harassment, safety rules, disaster response procedures, and other such topics. The nature of the requirements will vary with industry sector. For example, in hospitals or other health care environments, there is the requirement that every employee understand the health information privacy rules associated with HIPAA (Health Insurance Portability and Accountability Act, PL 104-191) legislation, as well as a requirement that every employee receive an annual flu shot and tuberculosis (TB) test. These educational trainings and health precautions are very necessary to the business, but often, DD agencies do not value assistance with these activities as a form of follow-along. Our model allows for these important requirements to be met by employees with intellectual and developmental disabilities because they receive assistance and are checked for understanding and compliance.

The training presentations and the record-keeping procedures used to track the completion of these activities are not designed to be navigated or understood by people with intellectual and developmental disabilities. Nonetheless, it is the manager's responsibility that all personnel working in his or her department complete these trainings and other requirements, which can number as many as 10 or more per year per employee. It would take a huge amount of time and energy for a manager or a co-worker to walk each supported employee through all of these activities. This is especially true at a business such as Cincinnati Children's Hospital, where at any given time we have between 60 and 70 employees with significant disabilities who require workplace supports. Clearly, it is outside the range of what should be expected of a manager or a natural support person, especially considering that designing the necessary adaptations to deliver the trainings is not something that is typically within a manager's expertise. This is an important point because, if the material isn't delivered effectively, it could lead to the firing of an individual with disabilities. Moreover, if it becomes a hassle and a drain on the manager's time, it will color his or her attitudes about hiring people with intellectual and developmental disabilities and is likely to lessen chances that he or she will hire another person with a disability.

Adapting and coordinating the delivery of mandatory trainings and assisting with the logistics of fulfilling the other required activities (such as flu shots or performance evaluations) is a critical role that can be assumed by onsite follow-along personnel. The expertise of a good follow-along professional can make all of these requirements happen in a way that is efficient and effective and easily understandable for the person with a disability. Jennifer Linnabary, in her role as onsite support provider at Cincinnati Children's, developed a system to ensure that none of the Project SEARCH employees missed out on these critical requirements.

For the flu shots and TB tests, Jennifer would arrange a time and location for a nurse from employee health to meet with all of the supported employees to give them their injections. Jennifer would begin by communicating with all of the department directors to ensure that they would allow their employees to attend. Then, Jennifer, or another job coach, would be present to assist the nurse in explaining the procedure to the employees and to make sure that each one completed the necessary paperwork. Similar arrangements would be made to ensure that Project SEARCH participants could make informed decisions concerning their participation in community service activities such as the annual fund drives for United Way or the local fine arts organization.

For trainings on topics such as sexual harassment, diversity, or workplace safety, Jennifer used her expertise in disability employment to assess the standard training, discern the critical points, and create an adapted presentation of the material. Because she was assigned to be at the hospital full time, Jennifer became an integral part of the team and could work closely with human resources (HR) and legal departments to make sure that the adapted trainings met all the necessary standards and legal requirements. She would then arrange a time and place for the employees receiving support through Project SEARCH to take the training together, with Jennifer or another job coach delivering the material in a way that was accessible and appropriate. Taking the training together in a supportive environment was beneficial to the participants and created another way to build community and camaraderie among the supported employees. As we mentioned earlier, not all Project SEARCH students are eligible for long-term follow-along. These group sessions are one way that onsite follow-along providers can have the flexibility to include ineligible employees without adding contact hours. With 50% to 70% of employees eligible for long-term support, it creates a critical mass in which ineligible people can be "absorbed" and served by taking part in group activities.

Benefits decisions that happen around open enrollment periods are handled in a similar way. Again, the managers can't be expected to help every individual with intellectual and developmental disabilities assess their options, especially considering the complex health care needs of some of the employees and the need for a good understanding of the complex interaction between employee-provided benefits and Social Security income. This is another opportunity for the follow-along expert to arrange for sessions in which Project SEARCH participants and their families meet with HR representatives to go over the details and ramifications of the different health insurance options. More than one session should be arranged so that everyone can find an option that fits their schedule, and provisions should be in place to see that the choices that are made can be registered and put into operation at the meeting.

As an example of how complex material can be adapted for trainees with intellectual and developmental disabilities, we have provided a selection from the HIPAA training presentation that Jennifer Linnabary created to be used at Project SEARCH sites located in health care facilities. Figure 8.1 is a sample slide shown alongside corresponding material from standard HIPAA training materials to demonstrate how the concepts were distilled and put into concise language for the adapted version. Another important element was to use plenty of concrete

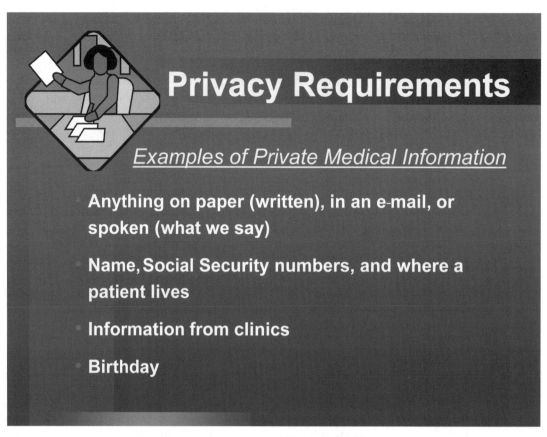

Figure 8.1. Project SEARCH® adapted HIPAA Training: working definition of protected health information.

examples that show how to apply the concepts in the workplace. The material in the resulting document was presented in such a clear, thorough, and entertaining manner that, when it was reviewed by the hospital's legal department, the lawyer who did the review remarked that we should be using it to train all the employees in the hospital. This didn't happen, of course, but we have plenty of evidence that the training is effective. In one example, it was used in a Project SEARCH program in a rural hospital in a small town. When the principal of the local

---

STANDARD HEALTH INSURANCE PORTABILITY AND ACCOUNTABILITY ACT (HIPAA) TRAINING LANGUAGE: WORKING DEFINITION OF PROTECTED HEALTH INFORMATION (PHI)

Basics: What is PHI?

Protected health information is individually identifiable health information, including demographic information, that

- Is transmitted or maintained in any form or medium by a Covered Entity or its Business Associate
- Relates to an individual's physical or mental health or the provision of or payment for health care
- Identifies the individual

U.S. Department of Health and Human Services, Office of Civil Rights. Retrieved from http://www.hhs.gov/ocr/privacy/hipaa/understanding/training/udmn.pdf.

high school became ill and was admitted to the hospital, the mother of a student in the Project SEARCH program asked her daughter how the principal was doing. Her daughter replied simply, "I didn't see him." Clearly, she got the message of the HIPAA training, and there is no doubt that she took it to heart.

Onsite Follow-Along Facilitates Professional Development at the Workplace

When a follow-along provider's entire caseload is located in a single business, it allows for a variety of group activities. Doing things as a group introduces a great deal of efficiency while, at the same time, offering the benefit of building camaraderie and enhancing learning by allowing for the sharing of insights and experiences. Job Club is one such group activity that was instituted at Cincinnati Children's as a way to bring together on a regular basis all of the hospital employees who were hired via their participation in Project SEARCH. Job Club is held weekly on Thursday afternoons from 3:00 to 4:00 p.m. This time works well because it is at the end of the day shift or at the beginning of the second shift. Most managers encourage their employees to attend and even allow the time to attend as professional development when it conflicts with working hours. The agenda can take many forms but usually coincides with an HR or patient services initiative at the hospital that affects all employees. The topics may also stem from a disciplinary action that one of the employees experienced. The following are some sample topics from past meetings:

- Discussion and role playing regarding new HR policies that affect all workers such as new sexual harassment rules

- Preparing for hospital audits and surveys such as Joint Commission visits

- Reviewing hospital emergency codes for fire, evacuations, and so on

- Learning about ways to assist with infection control

- Learning to recognize behaviors that could result in termination such as stealing or high absenteeism

Job Club can also include social activities that coincide with holidays or special events. For example, one year in preparation for Veterans Day, Job Club members researched the history of the holiday and wrote poetry that was dedicated to veterans. The group has also gone on weekend outings and has participated in community outreach activities, partnering with charitable events such as the annual Cincinnati Thanksgiving Feast to feed the homeless and others with nowhere to go on this holiday.

Job Club has also served the purpose of teaching advocacy and public speaking. In one instance at Cincinnati Children's, a nurse in the emergency department contacted the Job Club coordinator, Jennifer, to ask if some Project SEARCH representatives could speak to her daughter's Brownie troop. There had been some teasing and bullying of a girl in the troop who had learning disabilities. Jennifer took three young women from Job Club to speak to the group. They proved to be charming and candid speakers, and they shared many stories about what it feels like to be different and to be teased. One young woman with hearing impairment was accompanied by an interpreter and taught some sign language to the girls.

Another important function of Job Club has been in helping members to deal with difficult personal situations that can disrupt their work life. Most of us can talk to a friend, spouse, or partner about work or personal issues that are bothering us and may be interfering with work performance. But many people with intellectual disabilities don't have the confidence in their relationships or communication skills to reach out to friends or relatives for such help on their own initiative. One such issue that comes up regularly is coping with death and dying. The Job Club group becomes a support system for members who lose a family member or a co-worker. In addition, the group members learn how to manage their grief and how to talk about it and handle it in a mature way. One young woman who had lost a good friend wore a picture of her deceased friend on her work identification badge, talked about her constantly, and cried on the job often. At Job Club, they introduced the concept of dealing with these things in private and not letting them interfere with work. The group found that the lessons learned about handling death and dying were ideas that could be applied in any stress situation. As a result, Job Club acts as something of a "release valve" in which issues that cause stress or grief can be discussed and emotions can be analyzed. When personal problems start spilling over into the workplace, the managers have learned that they can say to the Job Club supervisor, "Can you please discuss this at Job Club, because it's driving us crazy," and the problem would be addressed. In one instance, a young man, "Matt," who had recently started living alone, was unhappy because his parents told him he couldn't ride the bus to the grocery store three or four times a week. Matt was furious; he thought his parents were trying to curtail his freedom because they didn't trust him, and he complained about it at work to anyone who would listen. When it started to get out of hand, he took the issue to Job Club. With the group's input, Matt realized that his parents were really just asking him to be more efficient with his time. They trusted him, but they wanted him to understand that he wouldn't need to shop so often if he would make a list and take care of everything at one time. Once he understood this, his interactions with his parents improved, and the issue no longer interfered with his work performance.

When managers saw that Job Club could have a direct positive influence on work performance, it came to be considered continuing education. With this designation, participation in Job Club became a way that Project SEARCH employees could enhance their performance evaluations. Job Club also provided a format for learning cardiopulmonary resuscitation and first aid. This was not mandatory in the jobs that the Job Club participants held, but when a group decided they wanted to do it, a specialist who could teach an adapted version of the training was brought in. The experience demonstrated to the managers that the participants were dedicated to continued growth and professional development and contributed positively to their evaluations.

Integrated Support Facilitates Career Advancement

In Project SEARCH's formative years, it took the founders a surprisingly long time to appreciate the important role that long-term support providers could play in career advancement. In fact, this is yet another lesson that we learned from our program participants. We were about 5 years into Project SEARCH when we heard from a young man, Tim, who was employed as a laboratory courier. After several years on the job, Tim was bored and wanted to do something more fulfilling. Erin and Jennifer hadn't sensed his discontent and they were not prepared to handle it. In fact, they were even somewhat annoyed with him. After all, they had found him a good job and they expected him to be grateful. Erin remembers thinking, "We don't have time to find you another job. You've already got a job, and I've got 12 students coming up who need jobs." But then, on reflection, Erin and Jennifer realized that it was natural and healthy to become bored in a job. Once again, they had fallen into the trap of forgetting that people with disabilities grow and change like everyone else. By this point, Erin, who had started the program with a business perspective, had become so well versed in the rehabilitation and job development world that she had started to take on that field's focus on placement and successful "case closure" as the desired outcome and had lost sight of the importance of career advancement. But she and Jennifer realized their mistake and Tim's story had a happy ending. They worked with Tim and helped him find and move into a new job where he could use his computer skills as a data-entry technician.

Since Tim paved the way, Project SEARCH has worked to facilitate career advancement for many employees with disabilities. Moreover, this focus has been given high priority and has become an integral part of the overall job retention strategy. In fact, it is so integral to the philosophy that all of the Project SEARCH partners, not just the job coaches, take an active role. One example of this happened at the Project SEARCH program at Fifth Third Bank in Cincinnati. "Andy" was working in a data-entry job but had been keeping his eye open for a new challenge. He applied for a new job that looked interesting to him and was invited to interview. On the day of his interview, he encountered the Fifth Third business liaison. Andy was dressed up for his interview, but the business liaison noticed that his white shirt was worn and dingy. Right away, the business liaison contacted the dedicated follow-along person to track down a new shirt for Andy so that he could look his best and make the best possible impression at his interview. This example illustrates the degree of coordination and trust between the business liaison and the follow-along person and how this close relationship benefits the Project SEARCH participant and the organization as a whole. It helps the bank to hold onto a good employee, and it creates another opportunity to fill a new position with a Project SEARCH trainee.

Tim relishes his work on the data-entry team.

As Andy's story shows, Project SEARCH supports lateral moves as well as career advancements if those job changes enhance the satisfaction of the employee. Another such case involved a young man, Scott, with Down syndrome, who worked in the hospital cafeteria. His job involved cleaning tables in the dining room and stocking napkins, salt and pepper, and other supplies. Scott wasn't good at smiling or interacting with the cafeteria patrons and he didn't enjoy it. The job was not a good match for him, and he wanted to do something different. The Project SEARCH follow-along support personnel helped Scott to move to a job in materials management cleaning shelves in the store room, where he was much happier working in relative solitude. Once he moved, Kristy, another Project SEARCH participant who had been working on a patient unit stocking kitchens and breast-feeding rooms, found out about the opening in the cafeteria and asked if she could apply for the job. Unlike Scott, she was highly social and wanted to be around lots of people. Kristy had felt isolated in her job on the patient unit and was much happier when she moved to the hustle and bustle of the cafeteria. She knew about the job opening because of the cohesive structure of long-term support. Scott's change in position was discussed in Job Club, and Kristy knew right away that the job that would be opening up as a result would be a much better fit for her because, as she put it, she is a "people person."

Kristy prepares the cafeteria for the lunch rush.

Tammy is a young woman who is deaf and has a severe learning disability whose career evolved gradually as she grew and learned with the help of her co-workers and her job coach. She started in a storeroom cleaning shelves. In the beginning, she had a hard time figuring out her schedule, and her job coach had to devise simpler and simpler systems until she found one that she could use to let her know where she needed to be and when she needed to be there. But over time, with continuous attention from follow-along personnel, Tammy learned more and more skills until she eventually moved into a highly complex job where she was required to use a Pyxis machine, a vending machine for medical

Tammy uses the Pyxis machine with confidence to help keep her department running efficiently.

supplies, which requires her to enter patients' medical record numbers into a computer so that supplies are charged to the right account.

To facilitate career changes such as those described earlier, it is critical to have a thorough understanding of the funding system around job training. The need for retraining must be framed carefully because VR is reluctant to fund training for a job change unless it is for the purpose of a "job save" or if it means the employee will be earning significantly more money. For example, when the Pyxis machine was introduced, Jennifer knew about the changes in technology several months in advance and knew who it would affect. She was able to make the case that, if Tammy and others who worked in her department didn't get the training they needed to use the Pyxis machine, they could potentially lose their jobs. Jennifer talked in advance to the appropriate VR counselors and was able to secure 4 to 6 weeks of training for

Figure 8.2. Respiratory etiquette station.

Figure 8.3. Ryan stocks the respiratory etiquette station.

about six people. The structure of the Project SEARCH program allowed the resources to be used efficiently in that the hospital was able to use two coaches for retraining all of the employees who needed it. Most of these employees completed the training successfully and were able to upgrade to the new positions.

In addition to facilitating career advancement, the presence of integrated, onsite follow-along personnel can also result in the creation of entirely new job opportunities for people with disabilities. We began to see this effect as Jennifer's reputation for problem solving spread and departments started approaching her with job ideas in the early stages of the planning process. For example, in anticipation of a particularly bad flu season, the Department of Infection Control decided to place "respiratory etiquette" stations—which would hold tissues and disinfectant wipes—around the hospital and display information about how to prevent the spread of infection (Figures 8.2 and 8.3). Because of Jennifer's prominence in the hospital, the department immediately thought of having Project SEARCH participants take responsibility for maintaining and stocking the stations. They made use of Jennifer's expertise in the planning and design of the stations to ensure that they would be easily usable by people with disabilities who might have challenges with fine motor skills. For example, the tissue boxes are held in place with easy-to-manipulate Velcro straps. What began with three stations has grown to over 60 stations around the hospital. These stations are stocked by three Project SEARCH employees who also have other duties on patient floors. Adding these new job duties to their workloads had the effect of opening up more positions that could be held by people with intellectual and developmental disabilities, so it was a win-win situation for all involved.

Project | SEARCH

Meet Sarah

Sarah is a graduate of the Project SEARCH program at Fifth Third Bank in Cincinnati, Ohio. She was born in India and spent her early childhood there, where a poliovirus infection left her with postpolio syndrome. At age 11, Sarah moved to the United States when she was adopted by her large and loving American family.

Sarah's goal when she entered the Project SEARCH program was to become a receptionist and administrative assistant. So, when she heard about the Project SEARCH program, she applied without hesitation. According to Sarah, "It helped me get the training that I needed." Indeed, she achieved her goal shortly after her graduation from the Project SEARCH program when she was hired as a receptionist at Fifth Third Bank.

By her own account, the job wasn't easy for her at first:

> In the beginning, I was so nervous with everything—like helping the customers and the people that I worked with. But I have gained more confidence through my work. I've also increased the skills needed for my job such as working with Excel, Word, and PowerPoint, too. I love being a receptionist. Without the Project SEARCH program, I don't know where I would be working.

Sarah's increasing confidence and skill level led to a move from the main lobby into the human resources (HR) department. This move was accompanied by an increase in her job duties. Initially, her job involved staffing the front desk, greeting guests, providing directions, and contacting employees when they had visitors. Now, she also assists employees with special projects such as mailings, preparing materials for meetings, scheduling conference rooms, copying, printing, and creating Excel spreadsheets. Sarah also does all her required e-learning on her own (e.g., compliance, security, risk). Another job skill that she has learned from her work in the fast-paced HR department is how to adjust to different supervisors, which she has done several times with grace and confidence. In addition, she works with college student interns and participates in Project SEARCH tours, in which she tells people about her experience in Project SEARCH and about her job.

Sarah is looking forward to getting her own apartment, a long-term goal that will soon be realized. When she's not at work, Sarah likes to go to movies, eat out, shop, and visit with family and friends.

"Sarah is the positive face of Human Resources and of Fifth Third Bank, as our human resources receptionist," says Sarah's job coach and mentor.

(continued)

Every day, she demonstrates that she is committed to her job by increasing her knowledge and skills and by modeling our core values of teamwork and collaboration. Sarah consistently seeks out opportunities to assist with tasks or projects and can be counted on to help others. She takes pride in her work and stays focused on the task at hand, ensuring that she is delivering what was requested. Sarah is an important member of our HR team.

Sarah's manager adds,

In the past year, Sarah has really been engaged in her own development, as well as continuing to help support other departments. Sarah is truly a valuable member of our Human Resources Team.

Workplace Conduct

Project SEARCH as a Real-Life Learning Laboratory

> *Our aim is to discipline for activity, for work, for good;*
> *not for immobility, not for passivity, not for obedience.*
>
> Maria Montessori

For young people with intellectual and developmental disabilities to have a chance at achieving meaningful, integrated, competitive employment, it is critical that they learn relevant job skills. But specific job skills are just one piece of the puzzle. It is equally important for young people with disabilities to learn appropriate social skills. This idea is supported by studies showing that the majority of job terminations for young people with intellectual and developmental disabilities are not related to poor work skills. Rather, jobs are lost because of problems with attitude, inappropriate behavior, deficits in communication skills, or poor grooming and personal hygiene (Wehman, Kregel, & Weyfarth, 1985; Wadsworth & Harper, 1993).

Certainly, poor work ethic, bad attitude, inappropriate attire, and a lack of social graces in the workplace are not unique to young people with intellectual and developmental disabilities. These are complaints that you'll hear from managers about all young people. But young people with developmental disabilities start with a unique disadvantage in that—compared with their peers without disabilities—they have had limited opportunities to observe and practice good

---

WHAT DO EMPLOYERS WANT?

Employees with the ability to

- Get along with others
- Work in teams
- Work independently
- Provide excellent customer service

From NCWD/Youth materials by Curtis Richards, presented by Sean Roy (PACER Center) at the 5th Annual Secondary Transition State Planning Institute, Charlotte, NC, May 18, 2011; adapted by permission.

EMPLOYERS' PET PEEVES—THE JOB INTERVIEW

- Answering a cell phone or texting during the interview
- Dressing inappropriately
- Acting bored
- Acting arrogant
- Talking negatively about a current or previous employer
- Chewing gum during the interview

From NCWD/Youth materials by Curtis Richards, presented by Sean Roy (PACER Center) at the
5th Annual Secondary Transition State Planning Institute, Charlotte, NC, May 18, 2011; adapted by permission.

---

workplace conduct (Carter, Austin, & Trainor, 2011; White, 1997). Indeed, a recent analysis of data from the National Longitudinal Transition Study-2 (NLTS-2) showed that, among youth with severe disabilities, only 27.9% had any work experience within the 12 months prior to the survey. Moreover, among those that had worked, 46% worked only during the school year, suggesting that most of the work experience among this group was school sponsored (Carter et al., 2011). In addition to a lack of work experience, young people with disabilities are less likely to be involved in other opportunities for integrated community engagement that involve contact with people who do not have disabilities, such as participating in church groups, social organizations, and informal socializing (Kessler Foundation/NOD, 2010). Many students with disabilities have not had the opportunity to practice job skills, let alone appropriate social skills, in a real work environment. As a result, they haven't had a chance to prove themselves in either arena—work skills or social skills—and these are both aspects of adult life that young people need to experience and practice in order to have success.

BLACK-AND-WHITE RULES IN A SHADES-OF-GRAY WORLD

Special education programs make an effort to compensate for this shortage of natural opportunities for social interaction by using role-playing and simulation exercises in the school environment. By approximating workplace interactions, such activities are meant to help transitioning students improve their social interactions, improve their overall personal presentation, and develop general employability skills such as punctuality and the ability to take direction (Devlin, 2011). However, the relatively controlled environment of a school does not adequately model the complexity of social customs in the workplace. In the classroom, it is possible to say, for example, "No hugging your co-workers!" And with some practice and reminding, the students will understand that hugging will not be tolerated, and the behavior will be effectively extinguished in the context of the classroom. Thus, the message that is delivered to students in school is, "no hugging" or "never use bad language." But, once those young

---

IMPACT OF DISABILITY ON ADOLESCENT DEVELOPMENT

- Variation in physical development may lead to dissatisfaction with body image.
- Identity may revolve primarily around disability.
- Fewer social opportunities, social discomfort, or peer rejection may lead to social isolation.
- Overprotection and dependence on others may lead to diminished sense of competence and autonomy.
- Fewer educational and vocational opportunities means students may be less likely to have past experience of successes.

people get to an actual job in the less tightly monitored environment of an actual workplace, regardless of what it says in the employee handbook, they will undoubtedly witness hugging and other forms of physical affection at the workplace, and they will occasionally hear foul language. This is confusing for them and, understandably, they might erroneously conclude that these behaviors are okay, which, needless to say, could lead to trouble.

One young man in a Project SEARCH® High School Transition class learned a hard lesson about the subtleties of workplace etiquette. "Charlie" did his first rotation on the loading dock. It was a very physical environment with a lot of friendly pushing and slapping. Charlie liked it because it made him feel like "one of the guys," and he happily engaged in the boisterous give and take. But Charlie's next rotation was on a patient care unit where the staff was predominantly female. When Charlie tried what he thought was a friendly back slap or shoulder punch in this more sedate environment, as you might imagine, it was decidedly not appreciated. It simply wasn't appropriate in his new situation and Charlie was reprimanded. One could argue that roughhousing isn't appropriate in *any* workplace, but the important point is that this is an issue in which there are shades of gray. There may be a clearly written employee code of conduct, but the reality that Project SEARCH students will encounter in the workplace is that rules and limits of acceptable behavior are interpreted and manifested differently in different contexts. It may be simpler to say, "Do this" and "Don't do that," but when we portray a simple, black-and-white world to young people with intellectual and developmental disabilities, we do them a disservice. Like anyone else, they need to understand the subtleties and contextual cues that govern our rules of social engagement.

When we stress that students need to understand subtleties and nuances, we don't mean to suggest that they should be encouraged to bend the rules. Rather, we mean that they need to be prepared to appropriately interpret and respond to what they will inevitably see around them. For instance, if a Project SEARCH intern hears a respected co-worker cursing, that student might reasonably assume that cursing is okay and repeat the behavior. Unfortunately, unlike the co-worker who knows how to be discreet, the student might naïvely use the foul language in a situation in which the results are disastrous—like one student intern who didn't know about using the "hold" button before using a rather rude and unflattering term for a difficult manager on the other end of the phone line. She had often witnessed her co-workers using the same rude term and used it herself in an effort to fit in. To avoid situations such as this, our philosophy is to be honest with students about what they might see and give them the tools to cope with confusing messages. And by having the students rotate through three internships, the students have the chance to experience multiple environments that illustrate a range of variations and shades of gray in workplace culture. In this way, the Project SEARCH participants can experience, imitate, and internalize the rules in diverse settings. The intention is to provide the structure in which student interns can receive the guidance and experience to allow them to function with success in a variety of settings. We have consistently found that, with the right preparation, the student can learn to say to herself or himself, "That person broke a rule. It is not my job to reprimand him or to imitate him. My job is to know the rules and to follow them."

THE PROJECT SEARCH WAY: LEARNING
SOCIAL SKILLS AND APPROPRIATE CONDUCT IN CONTEXT

When a student enters the Project SEARCH program, we recognize that he or she may have limited or no experience holding part-time jobs or attending social activities without parents present. And with this in mind, students aren't expected to be perfect on the first day of the program. The beauty of the Project SEARCH system is that students have a whole school year to learn good social skills and appropriate workplace conduct. Students may come into the program with different levels of experience and social awareness, but once they are in the program, they are all brought up to speed through classroom work and worksite rotations.

Students learn and practice social skills in the classroom, and those lessons are reinforced and expanded during the internships as the students interact with co-workers and observe how other adults interact in the workplace. A cycle of positive feedback is generated when students return to the classroom at the end of each day for discussion and brainstorming with their teacher and their peers about issues and observations that have come up at their internships and then put those new ideas to use when they return to the worksite the next day. Over time, the students gain an understanding of the subtleties of social interaction. But, most importantly, they have the time to make mistakes, to learn from those mistakes, and then to get a second chance and try again.

We firmly believe that total immersion in a real work environment among people with and without disabilities is the best way to learn the soft skills. It's relatively easy to teach the rules—to present a list of do's and don'ts—but the availability of relevant mentors who can model appropriate behavior is even more important. A year of seeing how other people behave has a huge impact. The other advantage of workplace immersion is that students are taken out of the student role and put into a situation in which they must dress and act like adults. In this new environment, students very quickly get the message that they can no longer get away with things that might have been tolerated at school now that they are in the "real world."

STANDARDS OF CONDUCT ARE THE SAME FOR EVERYONE—NO EXCEPTIONS OR ALLOWANCES

Young people in the Project SEARCH program have ample time and are allowed many chances to figure out what is and isn't appropriate at the workplace. But that doesn't mean we are loose about following the code of conduct. Our philosophy of high expectations, which is so critical when it comes to learning specific job skills, is equally important in the context of social skills. The expectation is that Project SEARCH student interns will ultimately meet the same standards of attitude, behavior, and personal appearance as any other worker. Although it might feel like an act of kindness to make allowances and excuses for eccentric or inappropriate behavior, it actually does the young person a disservice. By ignoring or tacitly condoning infractions, we send the discouraging message that we don't believe that the student is capable of learning appropriate conduct and social skills. But, in fact, our experience has shown us that the opposite is true. We routinely receive words of praise from patients and co-workers about the helpfulness and good attitudes of Project SEARCH interns or program graduates who are employed at Cincinnati Children's Hospital. We also often hear from grateful parents of Project SEARCH interns who notice and appreciate the change in maturity and demeanor of their young person.

Educating Managers and Co-workers

Our strict adherence to standards of conduct arises naturally from the business-based foundation of the Project SEARCH model. However, it has been reinforced by our own mistakes, which, in some cases have had painful consequences. For example, in the Project SEARCH experience, there have been several instances in which employees with developmental disabilities have taken things from cafeterias, gift shops, or departmental refrigerators. Often, because of the discomfort that many people feel when it comes to confronting a person with a disability, the theft is overlooked or worse, acknowledged with a friendly greeting and a smile from the cashier. Parenthetically, it is of interest to note that these cases of workplace theft nearly always involve food. Moreover, they predictably are committed by workers who have been put on strict weight-loss regimens at home and sent to work with little food or money in an effort to help them stay on the diet. The "perfect storm" happens when this feeling of deprivation is combined with the abundance of a workplace cafeteria or concession shop and those in a position to offer correction or direction instead look the other way. Nonetheless, when

Project SEARCH follow-along staff learn of a case of theft, they generally spend a great deal of time and effort teaching the individual about what stealing is and why it is unacceptable. But in many cases the teaching is ineffective because it isn't reinforced. The employee can be told to stop stealing, but if the clerk or cashier continues to turn a blind eye, then the theft is likely to continue. Moreover, the person with a disability will receive the not-so-subtle message that they are special and the rules don't apply to them until, of course, the situation gets out of hand and leads to dire consequences.

After some sad experiences in which patterns of theft or other difficult behaviors have led to job loss for otherwise productive employees, Project SEARCH has worked to develop a proactive system of disciplinary action that is tailored to support employees with developmental disabilities and their managers. Ideally, employees with disabilities should receive consistent messages from all of the people around them and should experience real consequences when they fail to act on those messages. This is a simple concept, but it can be difficult for both the employees with disabilities and their supervisors and co-workers to put it into effect. In response to this reality, Project SEARCH follow-along staff Jennifer Linnabary and Anne Wendell have worked with Cincinnati Children's HR professionals Mary Widdowson and Marilyn Martin to create a toolbox for developing a progressive discipline plan for Project SEARCH–supported employees. This pioneering tool reinforces the need for managers to apply the same disciplinary actions when dealing with people with intellectual and developmental disabilities as they would with any other employee. At the same time, it takes into account the need to ensure that people with disabilities truly understand the effect of their misconduct, the reasons behind the code of conduct, and the purpose of the disciplinary action. In addition, it incorporates the need for managers and co-workers to analyze their own contribution to enabling or even promoting the problem behavior.

Recognizing the Difference Between Harmless Eccentricity and Conduct Violations

Sometimes, what seems like a big deal to disability employment professionals really isn't a big deal to others. Managers, job coaches, and providers of follow-along support need to ask some important questions about unusual behavior patterns before intervening or imposing disciplinary action: Does the behavior harm anyone, does it affect the employee's work, does it interfere with anyone else's work, does it disrupt the work flow, and does it create an unpleasant or hostile work environment? If the answer to all of these questions is "no," then it might be fine to step back and simply monitor the situation without taking direct action. This message was brought to life for Project SEARCH through a situation that involves Scott, the young man we discussed in the previous chapter whose job is to clean supply shelves in a hospital materials management department. The work that he does is important; it is mandated by infection control and, as such, must be done at regular, prescribed intervals. It is well recognized that Scott is good at his job and that he is happy doing it. Nonetheless, he exhibits the sort of eccentricities that can give job coaches fits. One of these is an obsession with soft drinks. At one point, Scott was buying 10 1-liter bottles of soda every day. He would carry them to work in a backpack and store them in his locker. He would then open all the bottles and use one to fill the rest of them to the top. When the Project SEARCH follow-along staff noticed that he was carrying up to 21 sodas with him every day, they were concerned that he would injure his back. But more than that, the follow-along team worried that Scott's eccentric behavior would cost him his job. They were so concerned that he was sent for therapy, in which they tried adjusting the medication that he was taking to control his obsessive-compulsive disorder. His job coach would check his bag every day and tried to impose a limit of two bottles, but he got around this by buying more bottles of soda at work. Monitoring Scott's soda bottles consumed a lot of time and energy—for at least 5 years, the follow-along team grappled with various efforts to control this behavior. They even tried to shift Scott's obsession to a collectible item that was smaller and more portable—like shot glasses or postcards—but to no avail. Although it seemed like a

Project SEARCH Employability Skills Curriculum Lesson Plan: Magic Number "3"

Purpose

Students may have difficulty maintaining conversations with peers and co-workers. Like all of us, our students often monopolize conversations or do not like to talk about themselves. This activity will help students understand the "give and take" required for good conversations.

Goal

Students will demonstrate conversational skills with co-workers and peers.

Materials

- Pictures of people holding conversations
- A very large number 3 for a display and a small one for each student

Activities

1. Discuss conversational speech, making note that it is a two-way activity.
2. Discuss some of the cues people give when one person is monopolizing the conversation. (e.g., looking away, turning to leave, nodding, smiling but not paying attention).
3. Tell the students that one way to keep a conversation going is to keep track of how many sentences or "things" we say during the conversation.
4. Tell them to **remember the "magic number 3."** Once we say about 3 things about ourselves, then we should ask a question of the other person.
5. Demonstrate this skill with a job coach. Or, if you have two students who are better at conversation, they can demonstrate a 3-minute conversation using the magic number 3 strategy.
6. Pair students **throughout the year** to practice this skill. Begin by pairing students with similar conversational skill levels and progress to pairing all students.
7. Most students can keep track of saying 3 things about themselves and will learn to stop at that point and ask a question of their partner.

Note: Give the students conversation starters, such as

- What are your hobbies?
- What did you do this weekend?
- Where have you traveled?
- What do you like about your work?

great plan to the Project SEARCH team, the attempt to extinguish the behavior by replacing it with something that meant nothing to Scott was completely ineffective.

Ultimately, the team came to the conclusion that the best solution was to do nothing at all. Scott's follow-along support provider had an "ah ha" moment when she saw the open locker of one of Scott's co-workers who didn't have a disability. It was full of snacks and drinks—no one was checking on the soda consumption or buying habits of any of the other workers in the department. Finally, the job coach had a discussion with Scott's manager who confirmed that the soda-bottle habit had never once affected Scott's work performance. It was agreed that, as long as Scott could fit everything in his locker and was able to get the door closed, he could buy as many sodas as he wanted and could afford. His manager didn't really care, as long as he kept doing his job, and we learned that maybe we don't need to obsess so much about unusual behaviors. Correcting "behavior" is the purview of families and schools. At work, the focus is "conduct," and the concern of Project SEARCH needs to stay focused on actions that disrupt work or violate the code of conduct. In this case, there was nothing in the hospital's code of conduct about how many bottles of soda an employee can buy in a day.

WHAT CONSTITUTES APPROPRIATE WORKPLACE CONDUCT?

Because it is so critical to job acquisition and retention, a substantial part of the Project SEARCH curriculum is concerned with workplace conduct (see Appendixes 9.1 through 9.5.). The host business's "code of conduct" is introduced during the orientation period in the first 3 weeks of the program so that the students clearly understand the policies and the consequences of their actions. If a situation calls for discipline, the Project SEARCH method is to apply the rules of the business, as opposed to the rules and procedures of the school system.

The following are some of the critical lessons for success in competitive employment that we work to instill in student interns during their time in the Project SEARCH program—in the classroom and at the worksite.

Know the Rules of Polite Conversation

Making conversation with co-workers, teachers, fellow students, and job coaches is a struggle for some Project SEARCH students, but it is a critical skill in making friends and establishing good working relationships. Some students are in the habit of doing all the talking, while others might ask inappropriate questions or be too ill at ease to talk at all. Classroom activities centered around conversation are designed to help students recognize that they can find something that they have in common with almost anyone. Students then learn to use these common areas as topics for conversation in practice sessions with their classmates.

Honor Personal Space

Celebrations that happen during the work day, such as retirement parties, awards ceremonies, and receptions for visiting dignitaries, are excellent laboratories for practicing good social skills. At first, our reason for having student interns attend these events was in the interest of being inclusive, and we would encourage them to go without providing much preparation. We began to notice a pattern wherein some student interns failed to pick up on cues indicating that someone wanted or needed to end a conversation. The students would spend too long at the front of a reception line or fail to understand what it meant when one member in a conversational grouping looked at her or his watch or said, "Great talking with you." Also, some students persistently stood way too close to the person with whom they were talking. In response to issues like this, we now consider receptions to be part of the curriculum. As such, we prepare the students in advance. By the time they get to the reception, they know what to do, what kinds of things to talk about, how close to stand, how to greet people, and how to recognize the sign that it's time to end a conversation.

Know When, Where, and How Much to Eat

Many social interactions revolve around food, so it's critical for student interns to understand the rules of etiquette associated with eating. Some common mistakes that we've noticed are for students to approach a buffet table at a reception too eagerly and to take too much food. In response to this issue, part of the Project SEARCH classroom curriculum is to learn the difference between meals and refreshments. They learn clear guidelines like "Don't rush to the buffet table," "Talk with some people before you head to the food," "Take no more than two or three cookies or crackers," and "Make no more than two trips to the buffet table." Also, as they move through the hallways of a business, students are likely to encounter tables laden with food set out for a meeting. We make sure that students understand that, if they are not attending that meeting, then the food is not for them—even if it is left over from a meeting that has ended. Also, if their department is hosting a luncheon or reception, the Project SEARCH students are expected to attend and contribute an appropriate snack.

The end of internships is another opportunity to practice appropriate social skills. Internship departments celebrate the end of each training period in different ways. Some have parties and give a simple gift to the intern on the last day; others might sign a greeting card and take the intern to lunch, whereas other departments may do nothing. This presents a wonderful teaching opportunity to discuss the variety of ways each department behaves to recognize the interns and that all are acceptable!

Another important lesson that students learn in the Project SEARCH year is that, when they are at work, they need to eat only what they can manage. This directive became part of the Project SEARCH training after an incident in which a student intern who had some difficulties with motor control went to the cafeteria for lunch and ordered a double cheeseburger with all the trimmings. The cheeseburger ended up everywhere—all over her face, the table, her clothes, the floor—the mess was so extensive that it reached the point of spoiling the meals of the patients and hospital workers seated around her. In addition, her clothing was no longer clean enough for her to return to the worksite. Since then, we have asked students to be mindful about what they choose to eat while they're at work. It may seem unfair to ask young people with disabilities to limit their food choices, but it's really no different from what we all do. Everyone modifies what they eat on the basis of the activity that they're engaged in or on the impression they want to make. There isn't anyone who wouldn't avoid eating something messy—like a big plate of spaghetti or a bowl of cheesy French onion soup—when on a job interview or a first date. Or one would most likely forego the raw onions at the salad bar before giving a seminar or attending a meeting with the boss. Likewise, young people with disabilities need to keep in mind their circumstances and their physical limitations when they choose what to eat at work.

Nutrition is another aspect of the food discussion that takes place as part of the Project SEARCH curriculum. The students aren't told what to eat, but they do use classroom time to discuss their choices. Students learn what it means to eat a balanced diet. For example, one student chose mashed potatoes, French fries, and potato chips for his lunch, and the class discussed what was wrong with that meal and how he might have made a better choice. Project SEARCH students also discuss food choices with respect to budgeting, with an emphasis on such things as how much it is reasonable to spend on lunch each day. We try and keep in mind that many of our students have never had the opportunity to make their own food selections. So when they find themselves in a large business, with a cafeteria, a gift shop, and vending machines, it is natural that some will have a tendency to go a little wild with all of the choices. In the very first year of Project SEARCH, Erin remembers meeting up with an intern in the cafeteria who had chosen for her lunch a small pizza and five packages of cream-filled chocolate cupcakes. She had never before had the chance to buy food that she liked, and the temptation was too great to resist. Because of experiences like this, we have learned to work with our students to help them learn how to make good choices. And when we talk with groups of parents and families, we recommend that they give their children opportunities to choose their food and order in restaurants from an early age so that they'll be prepared to respond with moderation to the smorgasbord that they're bound to encounter once they're out in the world independently.

Another food-related issue that we've encountered occurs when parents try to put their young adult children on strict diets by sending them to Project SEARCH with healthful but unappealing lunches and taking away their spending money. What we've found in these cases is that the young people start asking for money or taking candy and soda from other people's packed lunches. In fact, our experience in general is that theft is often related to changes that occur in the home. We ask parents to think about how the rules that they enforce at home will affect their student's conduct at work. Sometimes, a program of strict discipline imposed at home can translate into conduct issues at work when pent-up desires are released in the absence of a parental authority figure to monitor the student's choices.

Don't Play the Sympathy Card

It is human nature to take advantage of the effect one has on people. We all know pretty girls who use their looks to get what they want or large, muscular people who use their size to intimidate. Likewise, people with disabilities have been known to make improper use of the fact that people tend to feel sorry for them. We have had multiple experiences with student interns and Project SEARCH graduates who have become employees asking their co-workers for money and other favors. Normally, an employee who was constantly asking his co-workers for money wouldn't get very far at all. But, unfortunately, for young people with disabilities, this tactic works surprisingly well. In the beginning, co-workers and other workplace acquaintances feel good about helping out. They think they are being kind, but in fact, they are enabling and reinforcing behavior that will ultimately get the young person with a disability in trouble. Indeed, Project SEARCH staff often don't hear about issues like this until they have gotten out of hand. Project SEARCH tries to avoid situations like this by educating all of the important parties in advance. We make sure that families, co-workers, managers, teachers, and employment support providers all understand that people with disabilities have to follow the same rules and social conventions that everyone follows.

Remember that Work Isn't Home

One of the most important messages that we impart to Project SEARCH students is to remember that the boss gets to set the rules. We stress that students can do what they want outside of the workplace, but at work, they need to go by the rules. Students need to understand that it doesn't matter whether or not they like the rules, because they don't get to change them.

For some Project SEARCH participants, the place of business becomes almost too comfortable for them. It becomes the center of their lives because it is where they have friends, and can shop in the gift shop, eat in the cafeteria, and talk to people with whom they share common experience and interests. When a student's whole social life revolves around work, it becomes her mall, her restaurant, and her familiar hangout. Many people feel a sense of camaraderie and comfort at work, but it can become a problem for Project SEARCH students because they don't always have a good feel for the appropriate limits and boundaries. Some Project SEARCH graduates who become employees at the host business have been known to arrive at work several hours early to socialize. Some even return to the hospital after hours for dates. Because of this, Project SEARCH has found that it is important to stress that participants should be at the workplace only during working hours.

Don't Bring Your Parents to Work

Parents and families play a tremendously important role in the Project SEARCH program, and their support has an enormous influence on a young person's chances for success. But, as it should be for any young person who is trying to take on an adult role, the parents' place should be behind the scenes and not at the workplace. Whereas this might seem like common sense, it's a message that some parents have an easier time grasping than do others. Indeed, one mother of a young lady in a Project SEARCH program on the West Coast had to be told repeatedly that she needed to stay away from the workplace. But she was so determined to keep an eye on her child at work that she actually went to the extreme of sneaking into the workplace wearing a disguise.

Parents sometimes have blind spots when it comes to their children, but they also have valuable insights. This was certainly true in one case of a young man who was perpetually coming back to his internship site 5 minutes late after his break. His job coach suggested to his parents that he get a watch, but the mom was confused because she knew that he already had a watch and that normally he was reliably punctual. The team made an exception and had her come into the worksite to see whether she could figure out what was going on. What she discovered was that he would put away the food and other items that he used on his break at 3:15, which was when his break was over. But because of his autism, he was very fastidious about putting everything in exactly the right order, which meant he was 5 minutes late getting back to work. Once they understood what the real issue was, his job coach had him set his watch alarm for 3:10 to allow him the time he needed to clean up and be back on the job at 3:15 sharp, and the problem was solved.

Learn to Take Direction Gracefully

One of an employer's most basic expectations of their employees is that they will be able to take and follow directions from someone else. Taking direction is a hard concept for many young people right out of high school—with or without disabilities. This is a time in life when people are trying to establish their identity *and* assert their independence. Taking orders can feel like an insult to a young person's fragile sense of self confidence, and as a result, those orders are sometimes met with defiance. This is a common reason in that young people lose jobs or quit jobs (National Collaborative on Workforce and Disability/Youth, 2011). Project SEARCH teaches students that taking direction is an important aspect of being part of team. Students can see that the work of the business gets done only because everyone is doing what they are asked to do.

Practice Good Hygiene and Personal Grooming

Project SEARCH programs often have to deal with students who come to work with dirty clothes, hair, and nails. This is something that parents and other caregivers often neglect to

---

PRACTICING GOOD HYGIENE

- Wear clean clothes.
- Make sure your hair and nails are groomed.
- Shower every day.
- Use deodorant.
- If you know you have a tendency to spill food, carry an extra shirt.
- If you have a tendency to drool, wear a sports wrist band.

---

enforce. Clearly, the families of young people with significant disabilities have a lot to cope with and it is understandable that they will "choose their battles" and let certain things go unchecked. But poor grooming and hygiene is never acceptable at work, especially in a health care setting. High standards of cleanliness are strongly enforced in Project SEARCH programs. For the first couple of weeks, if someone shows up unclean, they will be asked to go to a locker room and take a shower, if such facilities are available, or wash up in the restroom if that is the only option. In addition, the teacher could work with the family and possibly with community social services to locate resources that will enable the student to be successful.

Students must also follow the dress code of the business as opposed to that of the school. Students need to be made aware that the dress codes go beyond clothing to include things such as limits on the size of earrings and bans on facial piercings, exposed tattoos, sleeveless shirts, and open-toed shoes. The dress code of the host business should be shared with the students before they enter the program and must be strictly enforced from the first day of orientation.

Sometimes, issues of hygiene and personal care cannot be resolved; this is one reason that students might be exited from the program. However, the more common experience for us is to find that students rise to the high expectations for personal care, just as they do for job skills, and discover capabilities and determination that they never dreamed they had. One such example is Sarah P. who was diagnosed with type 1 diabetes in the year before she entered the Project SEARCH program at Xavier University. Because there was no one available at the site who could help check her blood sugar levels throughout the day, Sarah almost wasn't accepted into the program. But her special education instructor worked with the family and the diabetes clinic at the local children's hospital to provide extensive (but appropriate) training on how to test for blood sugar and properly use the equipment. A team approach was utilized so that everyone could support Sarah. By the time she began Project SEARCH, she was travel trained to take three public buses from her home to get to the Project SEARCH site by 8:00 a.m. Once she arrived at the Project SEARCH classroom, she tested her blood sugar (independently), called her dad to agree on the dosage of insulin, gave herself the injection, changed her clothes, and walked across campus to her internship site.

Don't Express Your Sexuality in the Workplace

Many young people with intellectual and developmental disabilities have never been taught about appropriate sexual behavior. They are often treated by parents, teachers, and other important adults in their lives as though they are asexual beings. But young people with disabilities have the same sexual desires as any other young adults. Unfortunately, because this simple fact is too often denied, many arrive in the working world with no clue as to how to handle those sexual impulses. Not surprisingly, when those impulses are expressed in inappropriate places, or toward the wrong person, this is a nearly certain start on the path to termination.

We tell young people in the Project SEARCH program to refrain from holding hands, kissing, or any other intimate contact at the workplace. We try to emphasize that it's not a bad thing, in general, but that it doesn't belong at work. Students also learn about sexual harassment so that they can recognize it if it happens to them, and understand how unwanted sexual or romantic advances can feel threatening and be destructive to working relationships. They also learn that unwanted advances can include things that may seem innocent, like note writing or phone calls. Students also need to understand that, if they experience sexual or romantic encounters outside of work, these are things that should not be discussed at work.

For the students, their Project SEARCH experience may be the first time that they have worked in an inclusive situation with peers and supervisors in their age group. A common occurrence is for the students to develop crushes on a fellow Project SEARCH student, co-worker, or even the business liaison. This can become very uncomfortable for all involved. From the beginning, there should be rules restricting any workplace relationships other than the typical peer friendships that happen naturally in a workplace.

Project SEARCH Employability Skills Curriculum Lesson Plan
E-mail mentor project

PURPOSE

Just about all of our students use e-mail for personal communication with friends, but few have used e-mail for business purposes. This activity helps them practice business e-mail with your oversight. It also connects them to community business leaders and host business managers. Possibly the best part of this activity is that it gets a variety of people involved with your program. Think internships, recruitment, and job placement!

GOAL

Students will demonstrate skills to read and write effective business e-mail messages.

MATERIALS

E-mail access, computers, people who will be mentors, list of weekly assignments

ACTIVITIES

1. Procure enough people to have an e-mail mentor for each student. Our programs at Great Oaks have Advisory Committees, and I ask the people serving on our Project SEARCH Advisory Committee. Other possible sources are managers in your host site, human resources (HR) people from other businesses, Transition coordinators from local schools, DD case managers, vocational rehabilitation counselors, special education, career technical or typical teachers, or your friends. Let the mentors know that you will instruct the students to e-mail them weekly and that all e-mails should be brief and to the point and utilize proper punctuation. Ask the mentors to respond in a timely fashion to the student e-mails and to model good business e-mails.

2. Discuss business e-mail with students.

3. Let the students randomly choose a mentor. It is best to have the mentor be someone they do not know.

4. Complete a practice e-mail together, demonstrating how to put in an appropriate subject and use proper e-mail format.

5. Post the weekly assignments in the classroom. It is the responsibility of each student to complete the assignment during class time of that week. Monitor and assist students as needed. **Always have them cc a copy of the e-mail to you.**

6. Student e-mails can be graded using a rubric.

7. You can build on this activity by arranging job shadowing with the mentors, asking them about potential jobs at their place of business or inviting the mentors to a brown bag lunch with the students.

EXAMPLE OF WEEKLY ASSIGNMENTS

Week 1—Write a letter to your e-mail mentor to introduce yourself.

Include: Name, Project SEARCH student, worksites, home school, job goal, and other things related to your program.

- *Do not include*: Girlfriend/boyfriend information, favorites, gossip or other things that you might talk about with your friends.

- Ask your mentor to tell you about his or her first job.

Week 2—Write to your mentor and describe your ideal job—what it pays, what are the hours, where it is. Ask her or him about her or his ideal job.

Week 3—Write to your mentor and ask him or her to tell you about his or her worst job.

Week 4—Ask your mentor how she or he got her or his current job and if she or he knows of any job openings in her or his company.

Week 5—Ask your mentor to tell you about his or her favorite part of his or her job and what he or she does not like.

Week 6—Write your mentor and ask her or him to give you tips for interviewing. Ask her or him if she or he would do a practice interview with you over the phone or in person.

EXAMPLE OF BUSINESS E-MAIL

Dear Mrs. Rutkowski,

My name is Linda Emery. I am a student in the Project SEARCH program at Clinton Memorial Hospital. I am working in the Financial Services office right now. I am from Hillsboro High School. My job goal is to be a teacher some day. Can you tell me about your first job? Thank you for being my e-mail mentor.

Sincerely,

Linda

Project SEARCH Employability Skills Curriculum Lesson Plan
T-Charting your course

Project | SEARCH

PURPOSE

Students will understand what appropriate work behaviors look like and sound like. T-Charts are a way of writing down information in a concise form, describing what a certain behavior "looks like" and "sounds like." Students will be more in tune with that behavior. This will also teach them how to act in certain situations on the job.

MATERIALS

Positive work behaviors to "chart your course to success" handout

Blank "T-Chart" handout

"Listening T-Chart" example

"Keeping Your Cool T-Chart" example

"Staying on Task T-Chart" example

IMPLEMENTATION STRATEGIES

1. Review one of the blank T-Chart examples with the students.

2. Create a T-Chart on the board and have the students provide the information. Make sure that they use "observable" descriptors. For instance, while completing a T-Chart for "Good Attitude," the student's response is "teamwork"; that is not descriptive. A better answer is "working beside other people." The description on the right side of the chart must be something you can actually see or visualize and the descriptions on the left side must be something you could actually hear.

3. Then have the students use the blank form provided and create a T-Chart using one of the suggested positive work behaviors.

4. Have everyone share their T-Charts with the whole group.

VARIATIONS

Feel free to use your own examples. Use a T-Chart to help students understand your host business site's core values and mission statements.

POSITIVE WORK BEHAVIORS TO CHART YOUR COURSE TO SUCCESS

1. Listening

2. Keeping your cool

3. Staying on task

4. Working fast

5. Being on time

6. Making good decisions

7. Asking appropriate questions on the job

8. Learning and following company rules

9. Getting along with others

10. Keeping busy

Project | SEARCH

T-Chart

Looks like	Sounds like

LISTENING

T-Chart

Looks like	Sounds like
Making eye contact with the speaker	Quiet
Nodding your head	Hmm, hmm
Taking notes	Sounds of agreement or understanding ("I see," "I understand," "OK")
Concentrating	Occasional questions
Standing or sitting still	Pen writing or clicks on the computer if you are using technology to take notes
Not interrupting	

KEEPING YOUR COOL

T-Chart

Looks like	Sounds like
Taking a deep breath	Counting to 10 in a calm manner
Having a calm exterior – not a red face	Speaking in a low voice
Being relaxed	Talking it over with supervisor or teacher
Having your hands and arms relaxed (no clenched fists)	Asking to go somewhere to calm down if necessary
Keeping your hands to yourself	Discussing with co-worker from "I" perspective-
Excusing yourself appropriately from situation (restroom, break room, locker, getting a pop if allowed)	I feel overworked because…
Having patience	I am upset that…
Having a smile on your face	I feel ignored when…

STAYING ON TASK

T-CHART

Looks like	Sounds like
Being busy	No unnecessary conversation
Keeping your hands moving	Equipment running
Working steadily	Noise of "tools of trade"
Concentrating	Quiet
Not socializing	Asking questions if you need more work or direction
Staying in your work area	
Arranging your work area efficiently	
Having the machine on and running (if necessary for job)	
Having a stocked work area	

Project SEARCH Employability Skills Curriculum Lesson Plan
How attendance affects the team

Project | SEARCH

GOAL

The students will list the ways absenteeism affects teamwork and production.

MATERIALS

20 beanbags or something similar

This activity works well outside or you need a large indoor space.

PROCEDURES

1. Discuss how most companies make a product that is then shipped to the marketplace. If possible, use a video of a factory assembly line production.

2. Form two teams with the same number of people on each team.

3. Give each team 10 beanbags and let them choose a company name.

4. Their goal is to move the beanbags from point A (their company) to point B (their marketplace). Make point A and point B at least 30 feet apart if possible.

5. There are three rules for moving the beanbags.

   - If a beanbag is dropped, it must be returned to point A and the contest must start all over.
   - A student may carry only one bean bag at a time.
   - Every student must touch all of the beanbags before they reach point B.

6. Have the teams race against one another to see who can deliver all 10 beanbags to the marketplace first.

7. Then have one student on the winning team call in sick and redo the contest.

8. Then have two students call in sick on the winning team and redo the contest.

9. Then have three students call in sick on the winning team and redo the contest.

10. Discuss the impact of attendance on the ability of a company to beat the competition.

High School Transition That Works: Lessons Learned from Project SEARCH® by Maryellen Daston, J. Erin Riehle, and Susan Rutkowski.
Copyright © 2012 Cincinnati Children's Hospital Medical Center. All rights reserved. Baltimore, MD: Paul H. Brookes Publishing Co., Inc.

Thinking on Your Feet
By Mary Jo Alstaetter

Project | SEARCH

PURPOSE

Many students have difficulty responding to questions. This activity lets them practice this skill in a fun way. Simply use 3×5 cards with questions or statements requiring a response. The teacher reads the question/statement, calls on a student, and he or she answers the question using a complete sentence. Students often love this to the point that they come up with questions to include on the cards. The only rule is that the question needs to be general knowledge for the student population. Some of the questions are factual whereas others do not have a specific answer. Also it is a good idea to put questions on different color cards based on the difficulty of the question.

GOAL

Students will demonstrate the ability to use complete sentences when speaking and to respond to questions in a timely manner.

MATERIALS

- Index cards with questions

ACTIVITIES

1. Discuss the importance of clear communication in the workplace.

2. Explain to students that they will need to give the answer using a complete sentence and within a reasonable amount of time, such as 30 seconds.

3. Create questions for information that students would typically know.

4. Choose a question or have students draw a card.

5. Have students add questions to the game as the year goes on.

SAMPLE QUESTIONS

- What is your favorite color?

- Who was your favorite teacher in high school?

- What month follows the current month?

- Name your favorite holiday and tell why.

- Name someone on the staff with whom you would like to eat lunch.

- How are clouds like paper?

- Name a meal you could prepare without assistance.

- Share a memory about one of your grandparents.

- Tell two reasons why you want to have a driver's license.

- What is one item of advice you could give a 10-year-old?

- What is one item of advice you could give a parent?

Project SEARCH Employability Skills Curriculum Lesson Plan
Conversation small talk worksheet

PURPOSE

Students often have difficulty having conversations with co-workers, job coaches, and other students. Sometimes, they do all the talking, ask inappropriate questions, or don't talk at all. This activity will help students recognize that most of us have a few things in common. They can learn to use the "common area" as topics for conversation.

In order to be able to have conversations with others, you must find "common topics." To find out what you have in common with another person, try a Venn diagram. A Venn diagram consists of two or more overlapping circles that show common characteristics. You may have used it in math class.

1. List some of your interests in the left circle—be specific. For example, don't just write "music." Name the specific type of music. The same goes for books, movies, and so on.

2. Then have a classmate do the same on the right circle.

3. Next, write the things you have in common in the middle, overlapping area.

4. The things listed in the overlapping area are good topics to talk about in conversation with each other. Conversation requires taking turns. Change partners and repeat the activity.

5. Practice conversations about the topics in the overlapping area. Remember that conversation requires taking turns talking.

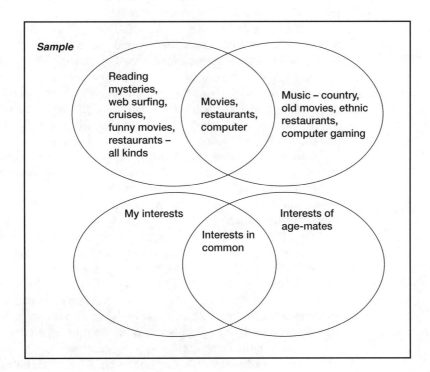

page 1 of 1

Project | SEARCH

Meet Justin

Justin was a member of the first Project SEARCH class at the National Institutes of Health (NIH) Clinical Center in the Washington, D.C., area. He became an employee with that organization shortly before he graduated in June 2011.

Justin works in the Office of Clinical Research, Training, & Medical Education. His job title is office automation clerk. Justin currently works 20 hours per week and receives full benefits as a federal employee. His job duties include routine clerical and administrative work such as duplicating and distributing materials, filing, and preparing memos and other documents; developing databases and other web-based applications using various Microsoft platforms and other tools; data entry; and developing and editing presentations using PowerPoint, Flickr, and other tools.

Justin came to the NIH Project SEARCH program from the Ivymount School—a school that serves children and young adults with special needs from throughout the Washington metropolitan area. Having the opportunity to participate in Project SEARCH completely transformed Justin. Prior to entering Project SEARCH, he was a very shy young man who found it extremely difficult to interact with people. He would make little eye contact and, when he did talk, his voice was barely audible. He often wore his jacket zipped all the way up, creating a "cocoon" to shield him from the world.

Throughout his Project SEARCH experience, Justin became a confident, engaging young man. He now interacts with others regularly and was even able to put together a PowerPoint presentation about himself and his disability (autism) that he presented to his whole department at one of their monthly department meetings.

When Justin isn't at work, he enjoys learning about Japanese culture and video game design. He also likes to cheer for the Georgetown Hoyas men's and women's sports teams. His long-term goal is to go to college so he can be a game designer. In the immediate future, his goal is to keep learning additional skills at his job at the NIH. Justin is very aware of his strengths and also the areas in which he could improve. He is working on enhancing his communication skills by being an active participant in departmental meetings. He also plans on learning more computer programs that he can use in his job. Justin is confident that he can do this because, as he puts it, "I'm comfortable with technology so I can learn new programs or projects quickly." Justin is proud of his work, and he is an accepted and contributing member of his team.

10 Adapting the Project SEARCH Model to Different Environments

> *Action and reaction, ebb and flow, trial and error, change—this is the rhythm of living.*
>
> Bruce Barton

Project SEARCH® originated in a large hospital in a dense urban center. When we started the program, it was specific to Cincinnati Children's Hospital, and we had no thought of taking it anywhere else. But after Project SEARCH was up and running and becoming established in the Cincinnati area, people began to hear about what we were doing—in part, through an article that appeared nationally in *Family Circle* magazine (Sonnenberg, 2002)—and interest started growing. For the first few years, we were primarily contacted by schools and rehabilitation agencies that were interested in beginning a program. When advising these organizations on how to identify an appropriate business partner to establish a new Project SEARCH site, we'd steer them toward hospitals or other health care facilities because that was the arena in which we were comfortable. It was only later, when we began to be approached by employers in a variety of fields and regional settings, that it occurred to us to move the Project SEARCH model into other business sectors and geographic settings. Thus, it was the inquiries that we received from employers that drove us to start thinking about what it meant to adapt our model to different environments. That, in turn, started us on the path to defining and distilling the core elements of the Project SEARCH model, which helped us to define the range and limits of our adaptability.

Since those early days of Project SEARCH, we have carried out an active program of replication and dissemination of our model that has brought us from a single program at Cincinnati Children's Hospital to an international program operating at more than 230 sites throughout the United States and abroad. Through this program expansion, the Project SEARCH model has been successfully implemented in a number of different environments. In fact, every time we go to a new site to provide technical assistance, we are entering a new situation with unique opportunities and distinct challenges. This experience has taught us to operate within a dynamic framework of change and continuous quality improvement while, at the same time, staying true to our core mission. Our program originated at Cincinnati Children's Hospital where the tagline is "Improve the Outcome," and we strive to embody this message by always

Tips for Successful Implementation of Project SEARCH in any Environment

- **Select the right instructor (teacher):** The instructor wears many hats, and teaching is actually a small part of the job. The person needs to know that she or he does not have autonomous control of the program. This is a partnership, and the school staff and students are guests in that host business facility. The instructor must be someone who is interested in job coaching, job development, public speaking, communication, and facilitating partnerships. Job development and some case management skills are also critical for the job. A willingness to learn a new skill set in supported employment, as well as Lean principles, is also critical to align with the business partners and reach the goal of 100% employment.

- **Select appropriate students:** There is a process that makes use of a variety of tools to work with all of the partners to select the student cohort that is most likely to benefit from Project SEARCH. This process involves utilizing the Project SEARCH entrance criteria and rubric for selection purposes. Another recommended tool is to establish a skills interview day. At this event, each of the partners has a chance to observe candidate students as they perform basic tasks and also interview students to discern their communication skills. Afterwards, all the partners score the students on the rubric based on what they have learned about the candidates' strengths and verbal skills. One of the most important selection criteria is choosing students who want to work and have the independence to work toward competitive employment.

- **Locate resources for job training:** Vocational rehabilitation (VR) typically funds the job coaching and job development for eligible students; however, they do not usually provide direct service. It is imperative to identify a qualified community rehabilitation partner that provides good job coaching services, has experience with transition-aged students, and is willing to work as part of the team effort.

- **Gain commitment from your host business to provide a liaison:** It is important to have someone inside the business who is committed and passionate about Project SEARCH. That person needs to be available to the program staff approximately 5 to 10 hours per week and should have a history with the business, respect within the organization, and the authority to make decisions for the program.

(continued)

seeking a better way to do things so that more young people with disabilities can have fulfilling work lives.

Continuous change is nearly a mantra in the business world, and it's an important aspect of supported employment as well. Marc Gold stressed that, for supported employment to be successful, it's important not to get stuck in patterns, but to recognize that there's always another way (Gold, 1975). We try to apply the "try another way" philosophy at every level—from the systems we create for program implementation to the hands-on training of individuals with disabilities. We are always assessing where we are in relation to the current environment and then thinking of how we need to adapt so that the program continues to move forward toward our goal of maximizing employment for young people with disabilities. We use a process of planning, implementing, evaluating, and acting (also known as "plan, do, check, act"), which is a common tool for continuous quality improvement in the business world. In this way, we continuously assess the situation and explore new directions so that we can be in a position to respond and anticipate changes rather than falling prey to them. We pay attention to shifts in education law, changes in vocational rehabilitation (VR) payment procedures, new state education guidelines, funding patterns, technology advances that affect jobs in that industry sector, and other factors that influence our work; we improve continuously by adapting to change.

NAVIGATING IN A SHIFTING POLICY MILIEU WHILE STAYING TRUE TO OUR CORE VALUES AND PRINCIPLES

Project SEARCH strives to be adaptable and comfortable with change; however, our principles, mission, target audience, fidelity indicators, and outcomes measures always remain constant. Project SEARCH is a business-led program, and part of the business perspective is to accept that change is the rule and not the exception. We expect to encounter changes in the disability world related to policy, practice, and funding, much of which is mandated by state or federal government. For example, VR in a given state might change from payment points to lump sum payments, or a state education system might decide to deemphasize deferred graduation and encourage young people to leave high school at age 18. We recognize that there are going to be changes in how the different agencies function and that this is something that we can't control. Our job is to find a way to make Project SEARCH work in light of continuous change in the systems around us; we don't give up or change course.

When we replicate the Project SEARCH model, an important part of the planning is to ensure that each program site is self-sustainable. We achieve this by building the program on the basis of existing funding streams. The specifics of the funding plan can vary somewhat from site to site, but typically, the instructor is provided by the education system, VR pays for job coaching and job development, and the developmental disabilities (DD) agency provides long-term support. Self-sustainability means that we don't rely on soft money; this is another factor that helps us to stay focused on our core mission. Our reason for adapting and changing is to do what we do better in the context of each unique situation. It is not to create a new fidelity model each time there is a shift in policy or funding priorities. It is difficult for organizations to move forward when they are forced to change direction with every new trend. We recognize and respond to changing policy, but we stay on course and keep our focus on training and employment for young adults with significant disabilities.

EVERY TIME WE ADAPT TO A NEW ENVIRONMENT, PROJECT SEARCH IMPROVES

Project SEARCH has the privilege of working with smart people throughout the United States and around the world who are very knowledgeable about transition and disability employment. Our interactions with these groups are an important part of our continuous improvement program. Usually, if a group brings us in for technical assistance, it's because they already have good practices in place. What we offer is technical assistance, a "toolbox," and core model fidelity components that provide a template that can be adapted for the specific environment. Sometimes, the adaptations that implementation teams come up with are innovations that have value for all the program sites. The international Project SEARCH team, based at Cincinnati Children's, maintains a network of communication and sustained connection among all the program sites. We do this through our annual Project SEARCH conference, the web site, and ongoing training and technical assistance. Through these channels of communication, innovations that one group creates can be introduced to all the sites. With this constant dissemination of ideas that originate all over the country, the Project SEARCH model improves at an accelerated pace, and all the program sites benefit from being part of a dynamic network of innovative and dedicated people. As part of our technical assistance for program replication, we provide all of our materials and tools and allow each site to adapt them to meet their individual needs. This has a double benefit: once a new site signs the licensing agreement, they are welcome to all of our materials and, thus, can concentrate their time on such activities as creating great internships and strengthening their partnerships. In addition, having similar documents in use at every site helps to ensure adherence to the model and generates many examples that can be shared more widely among all the Project SEARCH sites in different settings.

One example of a programmatic improvement came from the Project SEARCH team in New Hampshire who established a program site at St. Joseph's

(continued)

- **Recognize that you may not be popular in your own community at first:** Project SEARCH is a single-point-of-entry model, meaning that the host business is providing training and employment for interns with disabilities from a single vendor. Other community-supported employment agencies may feel left out of this opportunity. As time goes on, there may be additional Project SEARCH programs developed and a way for other community agencies to become involved. For example, in Columbus, Ohio, there are several Project SEARCH programs with a variety of school districts and at least five different supported employment vendors each linked with a specific program.

- **Continually find new internships for the students:** This is an exciting challenge. It means that, as the program grows and interns are hired into the departments in which they did their internships, new training sites may need to be developed. Some departments may not want to host an internship more than once or twice for many reasons. Their priorities or work flow may change such that a student internship is not always possible. It is important to continually develop relationships within the business and find new managers willing to host these unique training sites.

- **Choose internships carefully:** Internships must teach marketable skills that lead to competitive employment. It is tempting to say "yes" anytime a department offers to host an internship. However, we need to select internships based on their ability to teach core competitive skills that are transferable to a variety of jobs and employers. There also have to be an adequate number of internships to fit the number and interests of the students.

- **Plan and implement independent transportation if at all possible:** Project SEARCH works best when students travel independently. Family members are sometimes skeptical and want to rely on school transportation, but once the students are successful and traveling independently, parents realize that this is helpful in many other areas of the student's life.

- **Establish a process for student recruitment and selection:** Utilize existing Project SEARCH tools and timelines and adapt them to your team and community. It is ideal to have at least 4 months for the entire process, beginning with an information session and continuing through selection and development of a new individualized education program (IEP) for each student. Ensure that the business is involved in the process because the students will be spending an entire year in their facility.

(continued)

(continued)

- **Secure classroom space:** Space is always at a premium in the host business. However, it is critical to have a dedicated classroom training space for the students and staff. Having a "home" in the host business adds to the positive impact of the program and allows for a physical space for delivering the curriculum, holding the monthly employment-planning meetings, and problem solving and planning.

- **Secure cutting-edge classroom and worksite technology:** Students with disabilities will be competing for jobs against their typically abled peers. They need to know how to utilize and be proficient using mainstream (as well as assistive) technologies. It is important that the students have adequate computers, Internet access, and other technology relevant to their career goals. Using iPads and smart phones instead of low-tech tools adds skills, confidence, and "cool."

- **Involve VR and the local developmental disability agencies from the beginning of planning:** Eligibility for these two agencies is critical for Project SEARCH students, for both the services and the funding they provide. Involving these agencies from the beginning creates "buy-in" and ownership in the process and program. It is important to have a single VR counselor to secure funding for job coaching and development as well as a long-term support person. As the partners work together to plan and implement the program, the team will find strategies for needed services.

- **Define partner roles:** Project SEARCH is a partnership and everyone needs to understand the scope of their roles and responsibilities. The Project SEARCH planning tools include detailed written and visual job descriptions that can be adapted for individual teams. It is important that teams spend time reviewing these and agree to the activities as well as how to fund them. Even after the program is implemented, it will be important to revisit roles and responsibilities for clarity and continuous improvement. It is equally important to recognize your partners and have an agreement in place to do this. For example, the partners could design a visual image (e.g., a jpg image) with all of the partner logos that can be used in every document and communication about the local program. In this way, the partners are always visually represented.

- **Project SEARCH is business led:** It is important that the host business be represented and involved in all major decisions regarding students, internships, and other important programmatic issues. Our experience shows that the more involved the business, the better our employment outcomes.

(continued)

Hospital in Nashua. Because the host business was relatively small, the implementation team developed the Business Advisory Council (BAC) concept as a means to improve their program and to expand the number and variety of job opportunities for their program graduates. They recruited representatives from other health care facilities and related businesses in the region to take part in their BAC. The Nashua BAC now works with the local Project SEARCH team on various aspects of program development such as identifying critical job skills, designing internships, looking over student resumes and portfolios, and helping students with interviewing skills. For example, Dartmouth-Hitchcock might have an ongoing need for coders. The Project SEARCH instructor can use that information to develop internships that teach basic clerical and coding skills with the intent of making the students marketable. In general, members of the BAC take an interest in the student interns and consider them as job candidates when positions become available within their own institutions. In fact, the Nashua team achieved 100% employment in their first year as a result of the BAC partnership. The BAC concept was so successful that the Nashua team worked with the Project SEARCH leadership team in Cincinnati to create a how-to manual and accompanying DVD. This material is now available through the Project SEARCH web site so that other teams can benefit from the Nashua innovation.

Another innovative Project SEARCH partner is Fifth Third Bank, a host business based in Cincinnati. Like the New Hampshire group, Fifth Third Bank has developed resources with broad applicability to other Project SEARCH sites. One of these is a handbook for department heads with information and advice on how to work with people with disabilities. Another resource they created is a business liaisons handbook. It was created to fill a need that arose when Fifth Third Bank expanded their Project SEARCH initiative to additional sites within Cincinnati and beyond, to their Michigan branch offices. The bank wanted to promote the success of their new Project SEARCH sites by being very clear about the role of the business liaison. The resulting handbook is now a resource that we can share with any Project SEARCH site that is interested. In addition, Cincinnati Children's and Fifth Third partner to host a monthly 2-day tour that demonstrates the model for prospective sites from all over the world. Fifth Third is committed to using their resources to show the "banking version" of Project SEARCH, which includes their classroom, internships, curricula, and jobs in the Fifth Third environment.

The Project SEARCH curriculum is another example of continuous improvement that happens through input from our network of program sites. The first version of the curriculum was created by Susie and Erin. Linda Emery—then Project SEARCH instructor at Clinton Memorial Hospital in Wilmington, Ohio—added lesson plans to complement the various curriculum units. Now we give those away as part of the implementation packet. After 3 years with the original curriculum, the syllabus was due for an update. At that time, we had five program sites in Cincinnati, and drawing from these sites, we put together a curriculum team consisting of the teachers from all five programs. By 2010, there were 30 programs in Ohio, and Tony Huff, the supervisor for Project SEARCH programs at Butler Tech in Fairfield Township, Ohio, led a team of the Butler County Ohio Project SEARCH sites (and Susie) in an extensive curriculum overhaul. Every year since the very beginning of Project SEARCH, more people have gotten involved with improving and updating the curriculum so that now the quality of the document is enhanced by the input of a group of talented curriculum experts who also have a thorough understanding of Project SEARCH.

(continued)

- **Constantly communicate about your Project SEARCH program:** This is critical for marketing of the program, promoting recognition of the host business and other partners, spreading awareness that people with disabilities can work competitively, enhancing student recruitment, and creating employment opportunities.
- **All partners need to keep in mind the goal of the program—competitive employment for each intern:** Reaching the goal is everyone's responsibility including the students, staff, families, host business, VR, and supporting agencies. Every lesson plan, activity, and internship task should relate to and support this goal.

WHAT DOES PROJECT SEARCH LOOK LIKE IN DIFFERENT ENVIRONMENTS?

When we meet with a new group that is interested in starting a Project SEARCH site, we often hear things like, "You don't understand, we're different, our bureaucracy is much more complex than anywhere else," or "We're a rural district, we don't have tons of money like *they* do." It is true that there are a lot of differences across the United States. But as we've worked in different regions, we have found that the similarities are of far greater consequence than the differences. If a committed group of people can be brought together in a given locality, we've found that there is always a way to work out a plan for effective partnership. Challenges and barriers can always be used as excuses not to move forward. What we like to ask our replicating groups is, "Do we want to look for a reason to move forward, or for a reason to do nothing?" Our intention for this chapter is to illustrate the ways we've adapted to some of the most significant differences that we've encountered.

Project SEARCH in Rural Areas

There are certain challenges to implementing the Project SEARCH model in a rural environment, but there are no insurmountable barriers. Typically, the biggest challenge is to find a single host business that is large enough. Many rural areas have small hospitals, and we have several examples of successful programs in such environments. In addition, another option that is often available in a rural area is a retail business. But for program sites that go this route, it's important to avoid stereotypical roles such as greeters and grocery baggers for student internships and, instead, focus the internships on widely transferable skills such as food preparation, inventory management, and cashiering.

A small company might have many attributes that make it a suitable host business, but because of its size, it will most likely not be able to accommodate all of the student interns with adequate options for worksite rotations, and it certainly can't be expected to hire the same percentage of Project SEARCH graduates as a large company would. To compensate for a host business's small size, the local Project SEARCH team can consider having students do one or more of their three worksite rotations outside of the host business in other businesses in the community. The BAC is more important than ever in this scenario. Training student interns in worksites outside of the host business requires a degree of coordination among companies that makes strong community buy-in essential, and the BAC concept is a good way to achieve such buy-in.

If a region has no single business that is large enough to host a Project SEARCH site, the partners might consider asking two or three small business to share the role of host business. If this route is chosen, it is critical that the businesses be located in close proximity to one another—perhaps in a shopping mall, within a block or less in a small business district, or in a small office park. Another issue with this type of replication is making sure that one of the businesses is the lead "host" business because it is important that the host business has a sense of ownership of the program. An Ohio example of this sort of collaboration is in a rural county in which the YMCA, a medical office building, and a retirement center all within a few blocks of each other are working as a group to provide internships. In this case, the YMCA is acting as the primary host business because they have the greatest number of potential internships.

Locating the program in a smaller business can make it difficult to find space for a dedicated onsite classroom. Some programs have solved this problem by looking to the neighborhood for an available space such as a church basement or Kiwanis Club headquarters. In our Ohio YMCA example, the classroom space is being provided by a community college branch campus that is in the same complex as the YMCA. Having the program spread out over more than one building creates some logistical issues, but in a rural or small-town environment, the distances between the different facilities are apt to be walkable.

Another challenge in rural areas is that, because there may be only one Project SEARCH site in the area, students will have more limited training options than they do in urban settings. In Cincinnati, for example, we have five different Project SEARCH programs so that young people with disabilities can choose to train in a health care setting, a bank, a university, the administrative offices of a large urban public school district, or a law enforcement agency. A rural program can't offer such an array of choices, so in marketing the program to parents, teachers, and students, the Project SEARCH team should focus less on the specific business setting and instead emphasize the broad applicability of the skills that the student interns will be learning. When site choices are limited, it is particularly important to stress the concept of the business site as a microcosm of the working world. For example, if the local business is a small rural hospital, it doesn't necessarily mean that a student intern must plan on working in the field of health care. In addition to the health care–related internships, even a small hospital can offer training opportunities in a range of areas including food service, grounds keeping, building maintenance, and clerical work.

Rural areas are notoriously lacking in public transportation of any sort, and this can make for some difficulties. But the challenge is not so different from what we find in suburban locales where students often end up carpooling with family members or neighbors. The same solutions generally apply in rural settings. But because of the particular challenges around transportation in rural areas, we do offer some flexibility with regard to our policies on independent travel. Normally, we strongly recommend that students complete their travel training the summer before beginning their year in Project SEARCH. However, in some rural settings where students are drawn from a large catchment area and may travel relatively long distances, we have conceded that it sometimes works best to have the school provide bus transportation from the high school to the business in the beginning of the year. In such cases, travel training can happen during the school year instead of insisting that travel training occur before the school year starts. By the time the students are ready to start travel training, there has been time to get to know the students, and we will know more about where each one might end up working, so we can be sure to teach relevant travel skills. Many rural areas offer transportation programs for older citizens and people with disabilities, and our students would qualify for this resource.

Sadly, poverty is another significant issue in our rural programs, as well as at our inner-city sites. Oftentimes, the entire Project SEARCH class will be made up of students who qualify for free lunch. This causes logistical challenges because, whereas the partner school is obligated to provide lunch for the students, they don't have the means to deliver the lunches to the business. Regardless, this is an issue that must be worked out because, if students aren't able to eat during the day, it could preclude their participation in the program. One solution is for a volunteer from among the Project SEARCH staff to go to the school and pick up student lunches. At Clinton Memorial Hospital in Wilmington, Ohio, the hospital stepped up in their role as business liaison and gave lunch vouchers that could be used in the cafeteria to all the students who needed them. Having access to appropriate clothing is another challenge for youths living in poverty. In some such cases, we've been able to negotiate with VR to provide uniforms. In other instances, we've worked with groups such as Dress for Success to provide students with interview outfits and other work-appropriate attire.

Cultural competency is an issue in all environments, but certain cultural groups are particularly prominent in rural settings. For example, Ohio has more Amish citizens than any other state, and in fact, the first year we had a program in rural Ohio, one of the participants was a young man from an Amish family. Maintaining contact with his family was a challenge because they couldn't be reached directly by phone. To reach them, Project SEARCH staff had to call a nearby family. In addition, without a car, it was not possible for parents to attend every monthly meeting. There was also some adjusting to typical work attire for the Amish young man, but he was willing to step outside of his familiar clothing comfort zone to follow the hospital dress code.

Pregnancy and parenthood among students are issues that we've encountered most frequently in rural areas, although it is not confined to these regions. Indeed, pregnancy and parenting are challenges in large districts also. For example, the District of Columbia Public Schools has the highest percentage of teen pregnancy among students with disabilities in the country, and this issue has been prevalent in our programs in Washington, D.C. Many schools have programs aimed at teen parents that can be adapted and added to the Project SEARCH curriculum. The instructor needs to be aware of these services and the circumstances of the students in this regard to address any individual situations before the program begins so that each student has the best possible chance for success. For instance, our program at Avera St. Luke's Hospital in Aberdeen, South Dakota, has a high percentage of students who are also parents. The instructor at this site makes sure the students are eligible for community services such as WIC (Special Supplemental Nutrition Program for Women, Infants, and Children) and other federal programs before the school year begins. Another rural program at the Wal-Mart Distribution Center in North Platte, Nebraska, helped a young intern to adapt his work and school schedule so that he could best support his young family.

Large School District versus Multiple Small Districts

A key element of the Project SEARCH transition model is an onsite classroom that is staffed by a full-time special education teacher. This is often easier for large school districts to manage because they have adequate resources and personnel to move a teacher from their home school to an off-site location. Large school districts also have responsibility for large numbers of students, so it is not a challenge to recruit a full class of students with the necessary interest and eligibility for Project SEARCH. They also generally have the resources to implement travel training and are often in a position to staff the Project SEARCH classroom with a teaching assistant or paraprofessional in addition to the teacher.

Whereas there are clear advantages, there is also a downside to working with a large school district. First, it means dealing with a large bureaucracy that, because of its size, is prone to being frustratingly slow moving and rule bound. For example, when choosing a teacher to staff the Project SEARCH classroom, the school system may be inclined to assign the teacher with most tenure as opposed to interviewing to find the teacher with the greatest interest and most appropriate skill set. Also, in a large system, small things can fall through the cracks, such as making sure all young adult nondrivers have the state identification (ID) cards necessary to get an employer ID badge.

Small schools or school districts may have only two or three teachers with training in special education, which can make it difficult to spare an instructor for the Project SEARCH site. Also, with a limited student body, it can be a challenge to identify enough eligible students to fill a classroom while still taking into consideration the Project SEARCH selection rubric. There are a couple of ways to address these issues. First, the Project SEARCH site can work with an education organization that draws from a large group of school districts, such as a local education agency (LEA) or a career and technical center. This will increase the student pool and allow for the consolidation of sufficient per-pupil funding to hire the teacher. Another solution is to bring multiple school districts together in a more informal organizational structure specifically around Project SEARCH. In this arrangement, one school district must serve as the fiscal and hiring agent while the others contribute at a level based on the number of students from their school system participating in the program. A problem that might be encountered when this sort of system is used is that the school districts would want to parcel out and designate Project SEARCH slots a priori so that each district can send an equal number of students to the program. We discourage this practice because we feel strongly that student selection should be strictly about identifying the best candidates, regardless of their home school district. By "best candidates," we do not mean the most "high-functioning" students but, rather, the candidates who are most committed to achieving competitive employment. This concept is more easily accepted by the school districts once they understand that they need contribute to the cost of the teacher only if a student from their district is accepted and that the source of this funding is the per-pupil funding that follows the student.

Project SEARCH in Different Business Sectors

With our origins in Cincinnati Children's Hospital, we started out with an image of Project SEARCH as a health care training program. But in 1998, only 2 years after the birth of Project SEARCH, Susie and Erin were invited to speak at Virginia's Transition Forum in Richmond, Virginia. The talk generated a lot of interest and, as a result, Susie and Erin started getting calls from companies other than hospitals. This was the first time it occurred to Susie and Erin to expand to other industries, and it was the event that planted the seed for the intensive replication and dissemination effort that followed and which is still going strong. Our first foray outside of a health care setting was to establish a Project SEARCH program within Provident Bank in downtown Cincinnati.

Now that we have accumulated many years of experience in replicating Project SEARCH in different companies and different business sectors, we have identified the general characteristics of an ideal host business:

- The host business should have at least 200 employees at a given location. If there are fewer, it is probable that there will not be enough opportunities for varied internships.

- The business should be easily accessed through public transportation. Obviously, this is not always an option, but when given a choice, we suggest choosing a business close to a bus route, subway, or light rail line.

- Ideally, the host business should have a cafeteria or some other type of food service. Many young adults with disabilities desire to live independently, but one common obstacle to doing so is a limited ability to prepare meals. If we focus on businesses with food service, it becomes possible to ensure that our program participants have access to one or more good meals a day.

- An onsite exercise facility is highly desirable. People with disabilities are three times more likely to die from secondary conditions as the general population, and this often has to do with a lack of opportunities for physical activity (Kailes, 2002; National Center on Physical Activity and Disability, 2001). Even if they live in close proximity to a gym, difficulties with transportation, or other problems related to access, reduce the likelihood that they will attend. Exercise facilities located within a Project SEARCH host business will decrease these barriers and increase the likelihood of participation.

- We encourage Project SEARCH implementation teams, if they have a choice among several potential host businesses, to select a business with a turnover rate of 7% to 10%. A business with no turnover may be a great environment in which to train, but it is unlikely that such a business would hire many Project SEARCH graduates. Conversely, a business with a turnover rate higher than 10% may not be in the best position to welcome and support the program.

For a Project SEARCH site that is looking to expand by establishing an additional program site in the same city or region, it is very important to diversify by industry sector. The reason for this is to avoid creating a situation in which too many Project SEARCH graduates trained in a given field saturate the local job market. For example, if a city already has a Project SEARCH program in a hospital, we don't advise putting a second program in another hospital in that city. To maximize the chances that program graduates will be hired, it's best to have only one hospital program and to involve the other hospitals as potential employers for program graduates. Diversifying with respect to business sector also helps to expand the choices available to transitioning students with disabilities, just as students without disabilities have a variety of postsecondary training options.

A primary issue when adapting Project SEARCH to a new business environment is the need to modify materials. For example, the curriculum and student selection rubrics will need to reflect the priorities of the business—hygiene and hand washing will not be as important in a county park system or at a zoo as it is in a hospital. Confidentiality, which is critical at a hospital to protect the privacy of patients and their families, will have a different interpretation at a university or a bank, who will value confidentiality of their customers and accounts. Filing, counting, and reading skills will be more important at a bank or other office environment than it would be in an environment with more varied job opportunities. Manager handbooks are another resource that will vary with business sector. Fifth Third Bank created a handbook that is geared toward the banking industry. A single handbook works well for a bank in which the nature of the work is more uniform from department to department. But in a hospital, the work varies considerably among the departments, so it would not make sense to use a single set of guidelines for all managers—from the loading dock to the patient floors.

Different businesses will have different processes, dress codes, and requirements for mandatory education, and it is important that Project SEARCH be aware of those differences and willing to adapt our procedures to meet the business's needs. For instance, at the food-based retail chain, Wegmans—an enthusiastic and highly successful Project SEARCH host business—students need to learn knife skills and understand how to use scales, but in a hospital, the students will be required to understand Health Insurance Portability and Accountability Act (HIPAA, PL 104-191) rules. We need to honor those needs and make sure that our curriculum is responsive. For instance, we couldn't say to Wegmans, "We don't let students use knives," or to the hospital, "We aren't HIPAA experts, so we're not going to do that training" or "Our school doesn't require background checks for students, so we're not going to do that." Instead, we need to learn what we need to know to adapt to the business and find a way to meet that need and deliver those lessons in a way that is safe and meaningful for our students.

Project SEARCH in Agencies of the Federal Government

In recent years, we have been invited to establish program sites within agencies of the U.S. federal government, which has been a very exciting development for Project SEARCH. This initiative has offered many fabulous opportunities as well as unique challenges. By the very nature of these organizations, there are additional layers of bureaucracy in the form of security and scrutiny. Processes such as badging, locating space, and utilizing computers become considerably more complex than in standard commercial or not-for-profit enterprises. The primary education partner, the Washington, D.C., public school system—one of the largest in the nation—is also quite different from other school districts in their culture and structure. That said, there are many agencies within the District of Columbia that are extremely excited to share their resources in order to offer programming and improve transition outcomes. The Washington, D.C., Department on Disability Services and their related organizations have extended both human and financial resources to support planning, technical assistance, staff training, and problem solving. Their assistance, along with technical assistance from the Project SEARCH leadership team, created the impetus necessary to establish functioning programs.

Being in the public eye of federal departments such as the Department of Education, the Department of Health and Human Services, the Department of the Interior, the Department of Labor, and the National Institutes of Health has been exciting for the staff and students. It has afforded them many unique opportunities such as a trip to the White House, internships in very prestigious agencies, and graduation ceremonies with assistant secretaries of those agencies as guest speakers.

Employment within the host agencies has also been a double-edged experience. On one hand, the President's executive order to increase hiring of people with disabilities within the federal government gives the Project SEARCH program some additional advantage and priority. Each federal department that hosts a Project SEARCH program has written in our program as one strategy to meet the executive order. On the other hand, navigating the federal hiring system is very difficult, even with these diversity initiatives in place.

The highlight of our experience in the federal government is that there have been wonderful staff members in each department who have helped to navigate through the red tape and to embed the program and create a culture in which young people with disabilities have high expectations for training and careers. Other initiatives that have grown out of our association with the federal government have been extremely productive. One example is the development of an official guide to replication of Project SEARCH within the federal government. This planning tool provides specific information and will ease the planning process as we move forward with other federal organizations.

Even with the challenges we have encountered, we feel that it is important to have transition programs like Project SEARCH within the federal government. We have already seen that our presence has challenged some aspects of the organizational structure and has initiated a shift in the outlook with regard to having young people with developmental disabilities as employees within their agencies. It also helps the federal departments in charge of disability policy see the real-life outcomes of the policies they create. In essence, the abstract laws take on concrete form.

Project SEARCH in a Union Environment

There is nothing inherent about a union environment that makes it difficult to establish a Project SEARCH program. However, the program is often met with resistance from union leadership because of suspicions that the program is actually an effort by management to, in some way, undermine contract protections or devalue the status of the union. It is important to dispel these fears by educating union representatives about what Project SEARCH is and making sure they understand that the program is really about integration and diversity, about righting historic wrongs, and about improving working conditions for all employees. Indeed, unions have formally expressed specific support for encouraging and facilitating the employment of people with disabilities (see Appendix 10.1).

It is extremely important to bring the union leadership into Project SEARCH early in implementation so that the union membership can feel ownership. However, the most difficult part about keeping union staff in the loop is that they are very busy and it is hard to get their time and attention. When there is an opportunity to meet, it's important to keep the message short and to the point. The following are claims that are genuinely true and that will resonate with the unions:

- The purpose of Project SEARCH is to bring people with disabilities into the workforce.

- The program will have a positive impact on the experience in the workplace for union members.

- We want to address union concerns up front.

- Project SEARCH expects that program graduates who are hired will become union members. We expect the union to extend solidarity to young people with disabilities.

Another critical aspect of working with unions is to make it clear that Project SEARCH interns will not be displacing union employees. East Bay Innovations (EBI), a community rehabilitation partner (CRP) in the San Francisco area that partners in the operation of a Project SEARCH program at Children's Hospital Oakland, devised a creative approach to this issue (Witzler, 2011). One of their graduates wanted to work in a hospital near his home where he had been a volunteer. The young man's former manager wanted to hire him but said that, because the hospital staff was unionized, there were no job classifications that would be suitable. On hearing this, EBI worked to forge an agreement between the hospital management and the union to create a job classification reserved for people with developmental disabilities. The Project SEARCH graduate is now working in that position and is making $14.50 an hour as a proud union member.

Differences Among the States

Every state in the United States has essentially the same disability-related government, public, and private organizations sanctioned to assist people with disabilities in gaining employment. The names may vary, but each state has entities that represent education, VR, DD, and community rehabilitation agencies with federal and state mandates. Because of this, regardless of the state, Project SEARCH involves collaboration among essentially the same agency partners. However, although they are quite similar, they also have unique features. Most often, the corresponding entities within different states go by different names and have different funding systems and different organizational structures. Regardless of the policy and funding structure and climate, when providing technical assistance to a new site, Project SEARCH advisors will sit down with the same complement of partners and figure out how to work together under those particular circumstances (Table 10.1). We make broad recommendations such as, "VR should support job coaching" and "The education agency should pay the teacher's salary," but we don't tell them how much to spend or what payment points to use. We don't impose policy

Table 10.1. Project SEARCH® agency partners: State-to-state variations

Examples of 2011 vocational rehabilitation funding arrangements for Project SEARCH® by state

State	Funding arrangement
Colorado	VR completely funds job coaching for internships by regular fee schedule. Job development is partially covered. VR has a wait list, which means the PS team must make arrangements to expedite eligibility.
Georgia	Regional VR person attends statewide PS meetings. VR has a separate funding plan for PS ($4,000 for each student in PS). That rate is a little higher than the average for transition-aged students ($3,500 for other students). The first $500 is paid when the student begins the program. The additional $3,500 is not paid until that individual has a competitive job. This causes issues in cash flow for the CRP, especially in the first year of the program. The Georgia Council on DD is working to get the PS curriculum approved for adult education by the Georgia DOE. If this could be done, it would allow VR, or other potential funders, to help fund PS for adults by paying for the instructor.
Idaho	As in many states, VR didn't meet their federal match, so some money goes back to the federal government every year. The CRP has partnered with VR through a VR public-private partnership to provide match to pull down federal funds. This assists VR in meeting their goals, and the dollars can be used to provide job coaching for PS.
Indiana	VR funds a statewide PS initiative. They add approximately two new programs per year through an RFP process. Once selected, PS programs receive $9,000 per student to provide job coaching via the supported employment agency. They support job coaching through a structure that incorporates performance measures with payment at enrollment, the start of each of three internships, individualized job placement, and independence on the job.

(continued)

Table 10.1. *(continued)*

Examples of 2011 vocational rehabilitation funding arrangements for Project SEARCH® by state

State	Funding arrangement
Kansas	No VR funding. Entire program funded by school systems and Kansas Council on Developmental Disabilities.
Michigan	VR will soon be under an "order of selection" process. There is no consistency across the state with regard to VR funding. Some regions have been very supportive; others have not wanted to be involved.
Nebraska	VR funds job coaches through the school districts, as well as technical assistance to replicate Project SEARCH. School districts hire the job coaches. Schools receive $5,000 per student for a maximum of $25,000 per program.
New York	Each site has a slightly different funding model. ACCES NY supports three or four PS sites. Funded sites have contracts, which are negotiated every 5 years. Contracts must have a line item for PS in the UCS. There is a particular line in the UCS that is required for ACCES NY to reimburse agencies for PS because the participants are high school students. Contracts are negotiated only every 5 years, so if PS underestimates the number of students served or adds new programs in the interval, there will not be enough hours or dollars to cover the costs. In New York, the DDSO used a special regional level discretionary fund to make up the gap. Thus, the PS programs in New York are funded through a variety of sources including ACCES NY, DDSO, school districts, and private dollars.
Nevada	VR already had a system of contracting with a CRP to hire a person to assist with opening cases for transition-aged youth. That funding stream is used to allow the CRP to hire a job coach to be allocated for PS.
Ohio	PS has strong support from the state VR commissioner: (http://www.ohiochannel.org/MediaLibrary/Media.aspx?fileId=132523) VR uses payment/performance points, but the amount varies per region, ranging from $4,000 to $6,000 total with the following payment points: program intake, coaching for each internship, individualized job placement, and independence on the job. Currently, Ohio is under order of selection, which means that some students who may be very appropriate for PS are not eligible for VR and therefore not eligible for the needed job coach funding.
Oklahoma	VR funds 30% of the state PS coordinator's salary. They also pay $750 per student per month, plus $2,500 for placement and closing fees.
South Dakota	VR is very supportive of PS. They pay for all job coaching and job development. In addition, they provide a monthly stipend of $200 to each student if the students keep up attendance and participation.
Texas	VR is the lead agency in a statewide PS initiative so there is consistent funding across the state. They use a benchmark system to provide a total of $6,000 per student for job coaching.
Virginia	VR uses a uniform milestone payment plan across the state to pay a total of $4,900 per student for job coaching. Currently, VR is in order of selection, and as a result, they are having a difficult time making students eligible. Students interested in PS are put on a waiting list with all other VR clients.
Washington, D.C.	VR is very involved in PS in the District of Columbia. They fund job coaches for each of the D.C. programs. VR also provides a stipend to students for transportation, lunch, and clothing according to need.
Wisconsin	VR uses consistent fee schedule across the state: $500 per month, $1,400 at placement, and a $1,200 bonus for long-term assistance.

Partner organizations have different names in different states

State	VR	Education	DD
Minnesota	Vocational Rehabilitation Services	Community Transition Interagency Committee (CTIC). School districts are required by DOE to have CTIC, but role varies widely. The school districts provide the teacher.	DDS Developmental Disability Services (DDS)
New York	Was VESSID, but changed name to ACCES VR in 2011	PS programs in New York are run through Board of Cooperative Educational Services (BOCES) and city school districts.	Statewide agency is Office for People with Developmental Disabilities (OPWDD). Regional agency is DDSO.
Nevada	Bureau of Vocational Rehabilitation (BVR)	School districts only	Regional centers
Ohio	Rehabilitation Services Commission (RSC)	Career and technical schools, school districts, regional support teams (special education only), and Education Service Centers (ESC; special education and other services)	County Boards of Developmental Disabilities

(continued)

State	VR	Education	DD
Pennsylvania	Office of Vocational Rehabilitation (OVR)	School districts or intermediate districts (county entity that provides services related to special education)	County boards of Mental Health-Intellectual and Developmental Disabilities (MH-IDD)
Texas	Division of Rehabilitation Services and Division of Blind Services both fall under Department of Assistive and Rehabilitation Services	Regular schools are considered Independent School Districts (ISDs). ISDs can combine and become CISDs (Consolidated Independent School District). Texas also has ESCs that serve as a resource and training center.	County boards are mostly called MRDD but are in process of changing names. Statewide DD is DADS (Department of Aging and Disability Services)
Washington	Division of VR	Educational Service Districts and Office of Superintendent of Public Instruction.	Division of DD, Department of Human Services (Division of DD for each county)
Washington, D.C.	Rehabilitation Services Commission	DCPS: District of Columbia Public Schools, as well as many charter and private schools.	DDS: Department on Disability Services

Key: CRP, community rehabilitation partner; DD, developmental disabilities; DDSO, Developmental Disabilities Service Office; DOE, Department of Education; MRDD, Mental Retardation Developmental Disabilities; PS, Project SEARCH; RFP, Request for Proposal; UCS, universal contract services; VR, vocational rehabilitation.

changes; rather, we analyze the existing system and make suggestions as to how to make it work within that system.

All states have departments of education and statewide VR agencies, but not all states have DD services to provide long-term follow-along. Moreover, service delivery and funding patterns for DD tend to be the most variable from state to state, as compared with other agencies. For example, DD in most states, but not all, will pick up young adults upon graduation, regardless of their age. But Project SEARCH programs in some states, including New Hampshire, can only accept students of ages 20 or 21 because, currently, DD in those states will not work with anyone until they have completed all available years of secondary education.

Project SEARCH in the United Kingdom

Although there are considerable differences in the systems for education and social services in the United States and the United Kingdom, Project SEARCH has been well accepted and successful in the United Kingdom. This is in large part due to a concerted effort by the British government to introduce the Project SEARCH model as a job training and employment option for their young people with intellectual and developmental disabilities.

From 2000 to 2010, the public sector in the United Kingdom led the way toward increasing inclusion of people with intellectual and developmental disabilities. Consistent with this, Project SEARCH is active in 15 large, public sector organizations in England. However, with a government change and global recession, the private sector now appears better placed to act on this promise. A highly active corporate social responsibility (CSR) movement, which is actively encouraged by the British government, is another motivating factor. Indeed, most large companies have a commitment to increasing diversity in their workforce, and this is reflected in their CSR policies and summaries. Several industries are working to implement Project SEARCH in their operating centers, and they clearly see this initiative as a critical part in fulfilling their CSR commitments.

Both the public and the private sectors in the United Kingdom have been very welcoming and enthusiastic about the Project SEARCH model. However, there have been several challenges in adapting to differences in the way things are done in the United Kingdom. One of the first differences that we encountered when we began working in the United Kingdom was the unfamiliar terminology. For example, in the United Kingdom, they refer to a plan as a "scheme," which has rather nefarious connotations in the United States. Another important difference is that, in the United Kingdom, individuals that we would identify as people with significant intellectual disabilities are referred to as "people with learning disabilities," which could be a source of great confusion. We have learned to be aware of these differences and to be careful to ask for clarification often to avoid unfortunate misunderstandings.

The structure of the education system also has an impact on Project SEARCH implementation. Many Project SEARCH teams in the United Kingdom partner with Further Education (FE) colleges instead of high schools. FE colleges are programs located in higher education institutions that are analogous to community colleges in the United States. FE colleges are for young people with intellectual and developmental disabilities who have graduated from high school. They offer an independent living curriculum that is very similar to what is offered through standard high school transition programs in the United States. Students are taught things like how to tell time, how to make a bed, how to make change, and how to cook for themselves. The FE colleges are required, according to British government regulations, to teach to certain qualifications, and this has posed a problem with regard to funding instructors for Project SEARCH classrooms. To fund a teacher, the teacher has to be teaching to the qualifications. However, there is no employment-focused qualification specified in the government regulations on the FEs, and thus, the Project SEARCH curriculum doesn't meet the requirements for funding. This problem has pointed out the fact that, by having these qualifications, the government was effectively limiting what FE students could learn. The national Ofsted report, published in September 2010, has recommended changing the qualifications to include topics related to employment. The British government chose to import the Project SEARCH model because they recognized that it would push systems to change, and this is one example of how it has lived up to that expectation.

According to the core fidelity components of the Project SEARCH model, student interns must be allowed to leave Project SEARCH at any time during the academic year if they are offered and choose to accept suitable employment. Complying with this provision has been difficult for some U.K. FE colleges whose funding is dependent on curriculum completion. Project SEARCH programs have typically sidestepped this problem by negotiating an agreement in which the new employee can continue his or her qualification while going to work.

For some Project SEARCH programs in England, the education partner is one of a network of schools, often called "special schools," whose sole purpose is to educate children with disabilities from primary school through secondary school graduation. These schools have their own funding challenges, but in many ways they seem to provide a more seamless fit with the Project SEARCH model than do the FE colleges. Their scheduling priorities and qualifications (i.e., graduation requirements) tend to be more closely aligned with the Project SEARCH structure and outcome goals. They also have access to a pool of transition-age candidates for the program, as well as staff with the appropriate expertise and familiarity with the students to promote successful outcomes.

The greatest challenge with regard to implementing Project SEARCH in the United Kingdom is that there is no dedicated funding stream for job coaching. However, the Project SEARCH initiative has done a lot to raise awareness of this gap between policy and practice and has led government officials to begin to rethink policy in this area, which is another example of Project SEARCH setting the stage for systemic change in the United Kingdom.

Project | SEARCH

Resolution 119A
Service Employees International Union (SEIU)
supports good union jobs for persons with disabilities

SEIU International Convention

ADOPTED June 4, 2008

Whereas, the Service Employees International Union (SEIU) recognizes that the ability of individuals to contribute to their communities through productive work for which they are paid a living wage is a basic human right, and this basic human right should never be denied based on gender, race, religious belief, sexual orientation, or physical or mental disability; and

Whereas, as part of its organizing goal SEIU has been working with members of the disability community to bring members of this community into our union; and

Whereas, according to 2000 U.S. census data only 55.8% of adults with disabilities in the U.S. are currently afforded the dignity of employment; and

Whereas, persons with disabilities who are employed are often placed in segregated work settings, paid less than the minimum wage, and denied access to promotion; and

Whereas, persons with disabilities often place their public health benefits at risk when accepting employment[a]; and

Whereas, the loss of health benefits when losing employment can lead to increased hardship and more severe disabling conditions due to lack of access to medical services; and

Whereas, access to employment for persons with disabilities is often limited by misguided assumptions and lowered expectations of the value and productivity that persons with disabilities bring to the workplace, in spite of repeated, recent studies showing that workers with disabilities are just as productive and valued by their employers as their non-disabled co-workers[b]; and

Whereas, numerous artificial barriers to employment of persons with disabilities persist as the result of public policy and labor management agreements that end up excluding disabled workers from the marketplace. These barriers include public and private health care benefits policy at the state and federal level; civil service testing and hiring procedures; job classification requirements; federal Social Security Disability Insurance and Supplemental Security Income benefits policy and work incentive rules that don't work[c] and few understand; and

Whereas, the Americans with Disabilities Act (ADA) and Family Medical Leave Act (FMLA) are laws that were enacted to give equal access to the workplace to people with disabilities but employers often fail to meet existing requirements under the ADA and FMLA, and many union rank and file members and stewards are unaware of how to inform and protect members' rights under the ADA and FMLA.

Therefore be it resolved:

SEIU will take an ongoing leadership role to contribute to policy change that removes artificial barriers to the employment of persons with disabilities and emphasizes the abilities and innovations of people with disabilities who engage in any paid work.

SEIU will work in partnership with other groups to develop initiatives and policy that support employment of persons with disabilities in good union jobs with access to benefits.

SEIU will support health care policy such that no individuals lose insurance when they lose a job, change jobs, or lose existing insurance when they get a job.

---

[a]For example, a 2001 Urban Institute study found that 20.1% of nonworking adults with disabilities cited "fear of losing health insurance or Medicaid" as a reason for not looking for work.
[b]De Paul University, Exploring the Bottom Line: A Study of the Costs and Benefits of Workers with Disabilities, 2008.
[c]For example, the Social Security Administration reports that, in 2003 and 2004, just 0.5% of Social Security Disability Insurance (SSDI) beneficiaries had a change in cash benefit because of employment.

(continued)

SEIU staff and membership will be given the information they need to work with employers with respect to health benefits, COBRA health continuation protections, HIPAA, and pre-existing condition exclusionary policies and protections.

SEIU will develop and provide training and training materials for staff, stewards and members on:

- Federal laws on inclusive employment and relevant state initiatives

- Americans with Disabilities Act and reasonable accommodations

- Family Medical Leave Act

- Information on protecting and retaining access to benefits for persons with disabilities who are employed and/or self-employed

SEIU through its publications, web sites, and other communications with staff members, employers and policy partners will address cultural barriers and misinformation that limit the acceptance of persons with disabilities in the workforce. These will include highlighting:

- The positive contributions made by disabled workers who are SEIU members

- Innovative initiatives and best practices that support the employment of persons with disabilities in good union jobs with access to benefits.

SEIU will work with employers to create more flexible job descriptions and work rules that facilitate the employment of persons with disabilities. SEIU will create and share contract language that facilitates employment of persons with disabilities.

SEIU locals will reject contract language that would create unnecessary barriers and *de facto* systemic exclusions that limit the employment of persons with disabilities.

SEIU will support the establishment and operation of worker with disabilities caucuses or committees at the levels of chapters, locals, the International, and Change to Win.

(From SEIU Developmental Disabilities Council. [2008, June 4]. Resolution 119A: SEIU International Convention. SEIU supports good union jobs for persons with disabilities [p. 2]. Retrieved from http://seiudd.org/ files/2012/01/Resolution119A.pdf; reprinted by permission.)

Project | SEARCH

Meet Lisa

Lisa is a nontraditional Project SEARCH graduate. She came to the program as an adult after working 20 years for a fast food franchise. When the restaurant where she worked changed owners, all of the employees with disabilities were let go. The new owner didn't even observe their work or give them an opportunity to interview. It still angers Lisa to think about it. "I know it's against the law," she says, "but people with disabilities are discriminated against."

But after unexpectedly finding herself unemployed, Lisa landed on her feet. In fact, she has a much better job now. Her first step toward her new career was to apply for the inaugural Project SEARCH class at the Children's Hospital and Research Center in Oakland, California. Lisa impressed her future manager right away when she was touring a potential internship site in the materials management department. While walking through the storerooms, she started spotting damaged and expired items and pulling them off the shelves. The manager noticed and said, "I really, really want you to come intern with me. I could really use the help."

Lisa accepted the offer and excelled in her internship, particularly because of her unusually acute attention to detail. Lisa is proud of her careful work and likes to tell people that she has "identified instruments with expiration dates that were written so tiny that no one else had seen." Moreover, she and her job coach developed a system by which each bin was marked so it was easier to know which bins to inspect for expired and damaged items. This system helped everyone in the department work more efficiently.

While Lisa was doing her internship, the hospital received accolades for having so few expired items. This made it clear that the work Lisa was doing was essential, and as a result, the hospital created a modified distribution clerk position and hired Lisa to fill it. She now earns $20.54/hr and has access to all of the retirement, health care, and other benefits that come with employment at the hospital. According to Lisa, "It's not an easy job. I have six or seven stock rooms and I have to take care of all of them."

Outside of her work at the hospital, Lisa has become an advocate for people with disabilities. She enjoys educating people about her disability and talking to members of Congress, employers, and other people in positions of power, about the rights of people with disabilities. Lori Kotsonos, the coordinator of the Project SEARCH program at Children's Hospital in Oakland, says of Lisa, "As soon as I met her, I knew she was amazing!"

11 | Where Do We Go from Here?

> *When we do the best that we can, we never know what
> miracle is wrought in our life, or in the life of another.*
>
> Helen Keller

The history of Project SEARCH® to date has been a story of rapid growth and expansion with respect to both geography and business sector. In the beginning, Project SEARCH was just Erin, Susie, and Jennifer working together to figure out what worked at Cincinnati Children's Hospital. In those days, the mode of operation was more reactive than strategic, and the planning didn't go beyond the next year. But now that we are an international organization with over 200 program sites, we've outgrown that structure. Our goal now is to continue growing in a strategic and planned way through a system that can best be described as not-for-profit franchise management. Our highest priority is to maintain consistent quality across our entire network of program sites so that young people with disabilities have excellent experiences, acquire competitive skills, and gain employment with Project SEARCH, no matter where their program is located. Thus, one of the first structures that we put into place when we started realizing the potential for program expansion was the licensing agreement. Growth is important because it allows us to reach more young people with disabilities, but the quality of each program site is critical—we'd rather have five good programs than 500 mediocre ones—and the licensing process is a key element in ensuring quality. Through the licensing agreement, the Project SEARCH leadership team in Cincinnati—which is often represented by one of our team of consultants located throughout the United States and the United Kingdom—is highly involved with start-up at each new site. Moreover, we develop an ongoing relationship with all of our sites so that we can maintain contact and two-way communication throughout program development and beyond.

After developing the licensing agreement, our next big step toward forming a more structured organization was to institute an annual Project SEARCH National Conference. It was after our first conference in the summer of 2007 that we realized the tremendous value of getting Project SEARCH practitioners together to share experiences, best practices, and lessons learned. It quickly became obvious that what was meant to be a one-time happening needed to become an annual event. At the 2010 conference, we instituted our Outcomes Awards to

215

recognize program sites that had achieved competitive employment for 60%, 70%, 80%, 90%, or 100% of their participants in the previous school year. This was another turning point that clearly defined our goal for all of the hundreds of professionals involved in carrying out the Project SEARCH model. It clarified for everyone that everything we do needs to be done with a single-minded focus on employment for young people with disabilities.

In 2008, the rate of successful competitive employment upon completion of Project SEARCH High School Transition Programs in Ohio dropped from 75% to 62.5%. Although this drop was, in part, a result of the economic downturn and a more focused definition of employment, the Project SEARCH management team at Cincinnati Children's Hospital Medical Center realized the need to identify some strategies to enhance the Project SEARCH process to meet the demands of the troubled economy, recognizing that this programmatic improvement would also contribute to improved employment outcomes after economic recovery. Toward this end, the Project SEARCH directors, Erin and Susie, as well as six members of our team of national Project SEARCH consultants, received funding through the Mayerson Foundation in Cincinnati to complete the Lean Healthcare Certificate Program offered through the University of Michigan College of Engineering Center for Professional Development. Lean is an outgrowth of the continuous quality improvement movement originated by Toyota. It has been adopted by health care, manufacturing, banking, and many other large organizations and systems (Spahlinger & Kin, 2006). An important Lean component is to actively look for and eliminate waste in order to have the most efficient and productive work flow and final product. As part of their certification training, the Project SEARCH group carried out a value-stream mapping of the processes and practices involved in implementing and carrying out the Project SEARCH High School Transition Program. This involved examining the way recruitment, admissions, orientation, internships, job development, and employment was carried out at program sites, as well as the way the leadership team delivered technical assistance for program start-up. With facilitation by a member of the University of Michigan faculty, the group identified areas for improvement and a systematic plan for growth. The rest of this chapter discusses that systematic plan.

CENTRALIZED MULTISITE PROGRAM DEVELOPMENT

When we began replication efforts, it was typically at the request of an individual school or agency, and we established new program sites one at a time. There was almost no strategic consideration as to where new sites would be located. New sites were chosen strictly on the basis of who happened to call us. We considered each new program to be a separate entity (even if they were in the same city or region), and there was no coordination among the sites.

Statewide Initiatives

Our approach to replication began to change in 2006 when we received a grant from the Ohio Developmental Disabilities Council with the goal of replicating Project SEARCH throughout the state of Ohio. With this experience, instead of treating each site as a totally independent player, we recognized that our "single-point-of-entry" philosophy could be used to bring about statewide coordination, collaboration, and systems change in a way that was much more effective and efficient. We found that having a statewide initiative brings with it the following benefits:

- Statewide consistency in areas such as funding plans, payment points, and curricula

- Greater understanding and support from state directors of vocational rehabilitation, education, and developmental disability

- Increased buy-in at the regional and local levels

- Diversity among site settings and strategic planning around program site locations via a Request for Proposal (RFP)–based site selection process

- Enhanced collaboration and accountability from all partners

- Synergy among the programs so that it becomes a movement that is hard to ignore

- Increased opportunity for systems change at the state, regional, and local levels

- Increased interaction and shared learning among all sites through quarterly meetings and ongoing communication

- Shared knowledge of tools and strategies that lead to better employment outcomes

- More efficient delivery of technical assistance from the Project SEARCH leadership team that is less expensive owing to streamlined travel and cost sharing

- Enhanced camaraderie and increased knowledge among all stakeholders

- Possibility of incorporating Project SEARCH into the planning process in states that are initiating Employment First Initiatives

- Enhanced long-term planning on a statewide basis

For all these reasons, we have found that statewide initiatives, whether directed by vocational rehabilitation, the Department of Education, developmental disabilities councils, or the Department of Developmental Disabilities, are the best way in which to replicate Project SEARCH. As such, we are moving toward a system in which we will begin any new replication as part of a statewide initiative. For states that already have individual Project SEARCH sites, this will involve creating cohesive teams from the multiple individual sites within that state. For states that do not yet have a Project SEARCH presence, it means that we will work to establish a coordinated statewide initiative and then implement any new sites within that framework.

Corporation-Wide Initiatives the statewide replication project initiated through the Ohio Developmental Disabilities Council Grant caused us to rethink our model of replication. Likewise, our work with small-scale and large-scale state, national, and multinational companies has also inspired changes in the way we expand the Project SEARCH program. The first inkling of the need for a change came several years ago when we were approached by the national office of a large bank interested in replicating Project SEARCH. Unbeknownst to us, an existing Project SEARCH site in Georgia was simultaneously approaching a regional office of the same bank. The left hand had no idea what the right hand was doing, and it caused confusion and angst for the bank and for all parties involved. Since that time, we have made an effort to follow the single-point-of-entry approach in all of our work with business partners. Toward that end, we have recently assigned a specific member of the Cincinnati-based Project SEARCH team (or one of our national consultants) to work with each of our business partners that have multiple operating centers. With one person as the point of contact, our goal is to facilitate clear channels of communication to ensure consistency across locations. Our experience with businesswide initiatives to date has revealed the following advantages:

- Like the statewide initiatives, central control and planning of replication efforts ensure efficiency and consistent quality.

- Standardized rollout procedures facilitate seamless start-up.

- Materials such as templates, tools, and policies that are individualized to the specific business can be used at all sites because policies and procedures are uniform across all branch locations of the business.

- Maximum efficiency in the delivery of large-scale staff education, marketing, and communication is possible.

- Dedicated Project SEARCH national support personnel are assigned to the business.

- Regional rollouts with simultaneous start-up at several sites lead to efficient use of technical assistance.

- Program graduates trained at one location are qualified for employment at any of that business's locations.

- Culture change within the business becomes embedded at local, regional, and national levels.

- Expanded business leadership and commitment with regard to program development and advocacy for employment of people with disabilities is assured.

A businesswide initiative brings with it considerable practical advantages with regard to efficiency and cost effectiveness. But there are other advantages that are more difficult to measure, but which are just as dramatic. It has been our experience that being involved with Project SEARCH allows business people who may already feel passionately about diversity to become actively involved in changing outcomes. Taking direct action, as opposed to years of "admiring the problem," inspires these leaders within the Project SEARCH host businesses to become our champions of the future. Like a pebble in the pool, the ripple effect caused by their passion and their status in their organizations creates a tidal change.

INTERNATIONAL PROGRAM DEVELOPMENT

No matter the country, the issues young adults with disabilities face are surprisingly similar. A lack of meaningful training opportunities; obstacles to achieving gainful, integrated employment; and inadequate transportation options seem always to top the list. And whereas government policies, educational practices, and the terminology we use might differ, the overall language of disability remains the same. People with intellectual disabilities are capable of being outstanding employees, but the necessary opportunities for training and employment are few and far between.

Each time we work with another country, we are forced to adapt our model and we evolve in ways that we might not have dreamed of, but which are applicable in many settings. Our goal over the next few years is to expand by one country per year, not so much because we believe everyone must follow the Project SEARCH model but, rather, because we recognize that with each new country we visit, we are exposed to new and creative ideas. And those new ideas allow us to maintain our focus on outcomes for young adults with disabilities even as we continuously seek new ways to improve those outcomes. To date, we've had interest from South Korea, Israel, Portugal, New Zealand, Finland, Denmark, Hungary, and Ireland and are eager to see where the future leads us.

One of the most pleasant surprises that came out of the substantial work we've done in the United Kingdom has been the discovery of a new vocabulary and way of talking about disability. Often, the United Kingdom is further ahead in the words they use to describe the disability condition, and it helps us by forcing us to pay more attention to the words we use and to refine our language accordingly. Businesses understand that the first battle in marketing a product is in framing the message. Project SEARCH works diligently to move beyond the stigma of a specialized disability vocabulary and, instead, frame the message of young adults with disabilities in normal language that emphasizes the similarities in the conditions and concerns of all young people making the transition to adult life. Yet, even when we think we're doing a good job, we're brought up short when the practices of others point out our inconsistencies in this regard. For example, in England, they would never say, "Where was Billy placed?" or "Did you get a placement?" They wouldn't say, as we did in the last paragraph, "We our constantly seeking new ways to improve our outcomes." Instead, they would say, "We are constantly seeking to increase the number of people with disabilities who are employed" or "Did Billy find a job?" These might seem like small differences, but words are powerful tools and those used in the United Kingdom tend to remove the aura of separateness or second-class citizenry from people with disabilities and focus instead on the universal nature of their humanity. Another great example is the way we talk about "behavior." In the United States, we frequently write about and discuss "student behaviors" as though "behavior" is always a problem. In England, they use the word "conduct" instead. We all have behaviors, good and bad, but it's how we conduct ourselves in a given situation that makes the difference. Oddly enough, our experience working in the United Kingdom also forced us to take a hard look at our name, "Project SEARCH." It is a historical reality that this is our branded name, and there is little to be done to change that now. But, over time, we have become uncomfortably aware that the word "Project" carries with it the connotation of a program that is run by "us" to elevate the condition of a group that we think of as "them," be it people with disabilities, people living in poverty, or at-risk youth.

Another informative and enlightening difference between England and the United States is that, in England, everyone leaves high school at the same age. Those who want to continue their education, whether or not they have a disability, go on to college. It's not a perfect system, and they have many of the same problems as those we encounter in the United States: Transition services provided through the colleges are often delivered in a disjointed manner with no clear focus on a career plan. Funding programs that focus on training for competitive work seems difficult as opposed to funding for more generalized academic training. However, the shift in location from a high school to a college setting has some advantages over the deferred graduation that is practiced in the United States. That is, it results in an age-appropriate change in atmosphere that has the effect of normalizing the transition experience for young people with disabilities. With this option, young people with disabilities, like their peers without disabilities, can move on to college as opposed to being left behind in their high school. Indeed, most of our Project SEARCH programs in England are affiliated with colleges, and this is something that we are interested in encouraging in the United States. That is, instead of extending the high school career, we would like to explore some creative alternatives for students that would allow them to spend their last few years of educational eligibility in the most appropriate, integrated setting possible in which to prepare them for adult life, give them meaningful training, and prepare them for work. We don't know yet exactly how this would look, but we do know that it would involve an unprecedented level of flexibility and collaboration among high school special education programs, community colleges, adult services such as vocational rehabilitation, and state education funding systems.

STANDARDIZED SYSTEMS FOR STRUCTURED REPLICATION

The only reason for Project SEARCH to exist is to create strong transition programs that prepare students for competitive employment. We currently have more than 200 programs all over the world, with more starting all the time, and we hope to be replicating Project SEARCH programs throughout the United States and abroad for many years. Certainly, our current level of interest suggests that this will be the case; not only are we being asked on a regular basis to work with programs in new locations, but many of the areas in which there are existing Project SEARCH sites are also eager to expand to additional industry sectors. Whereas we are thrilled with this enthusiasm and support, we are aware that rapid expansion heightens the need to ensure quality and maintain model fidelity. We do this by making sure that all new program sites sustain a connection to the Project SEARCH leadership team in Cincinnati. Our primary means for maintaining that connection is through the licensing agreements that we require all programs to sign. Through these agreements, Project SEARCH National ensures model fidelity and manages continuous improvement. In return, the licensed sites receive a comprehensive resource guide that includes a detailed implementation plan, sample agreements, roles and responsibilities of partnering agencies, job descriptions, the Project SEARCH curriculum, internal and external program marketing tools, and access to password-protected areas that are available on the Project SEARCH web site (http://www.projectsearch.us. This web site area include a national database of Project SEARCH outcomes, resource guide materials, and more. In addition to the resources that come with the license, full program implementation requires a minimum amount of hands-on consulting and start-up assistance from members of the core Project SEARCH team and periodic model fidelity audits.

Project SEARCH is a branded, copyrighted program because it is important to us that the Project SEARCH name, intellectual property, and years of experience and development be respected. In this regard, we will pursue action to limit "Project SEARCH–like" programs or unauthorized replication or use of the name. We also ask that any articles, publications, videos, or other public communications that mention Project SEARCH acknowledge Project SEARCH in Cincinnati as the founder and refer all interested parties back to our national offices. In addition, active sites may not offer tours or take part in research or publication as a "best practice" without first having an official audit to ensure model fidelity. Although these rules may sound harsh, the intention is not to be punitive. Rather, the goal is to make sure that the meaning of the name "Project SEARCH" is clear and consistent and that any young person with a disability who takes part in Project SEARCH, no matter where he or she is, will benefit from the collective experience and wisdom of the many talented people involved in operating Project SEARCH sites around the country.

Many individuals have been running Project SEARCH programs for quite a while and have developed a high level of expertise with regard to our model and practices. To give those experienced and successful program directors the opportunity to expand to new industry sectors in their communities, we have developed the following regulations, centered on program audits, to provide leeway for strong programs to replicate without using technical assistance from the Project SEARCH International support team:

- The first step is to contact the Cincinnati-based Project SEARCH International support team to ensure that there is no duplication of effort or multiple partner contacts.

- Ensure that all partners involved in local replication have been active on the core planning team and have practical experience.

- Replication must be led by an experienced team and be limited to the same local community. That is, if Agency A is part of a successful Project SEARCH program, Agency A could begin another Project SEARCH site at a different industry in the immediate community. They could not teach Agency B how to create a Project SEARCH program. Programs in different cities or involving different partner organizations will require technical assistance from Project SEARCH National.

- Partner organizations that have affiliations in other cities and states are not permitted to independently market or expand Project SEARCH.

- Before engaging in replication activities, an existing site must be audited to ensure compliance with the fidelity model.

- If the audit shows model fidelity, the partners can proceed with replication using their own team expertise.

- Each new site must sign a licensing agreement with Project SEARCH National.

- All replication materials will be provided to each site by Project SEARCH National. Partners may not share registered and copyrighted Project SEARCH materials with any other sites or new partners without prior approval.

- There must be a first-term review of the new program and an audit at the end of the first year performed by Project SEARCH National.

- Large federal grants built around Project SEARCH must work with Project SEARCH National to develop budgeted roles for the Cincinnati-based Project SEARCH leadership team.

Model Fidelity Audits

As part of our continuous quality improvement, we have created a fidelity audit tool that is based on our core model fidelity components (see Chapter 2). The purpose of model fidelity audits is to ensure that all of the programs are using the same model of transition and to limit the variability between sites. We have begun performing audits at the request of individual program sites, but we are in the process of developing a more systematic approach to auditing sites that incorporates the following reasons that a given site would be audited:

1. An individual Project SEARCH program site might request an audit for their internal continuous improvement process.

2. Project SEARCH National might initiate an audit in cases in which there are indications that a program site is not following one or more of the core model fidelity components.

3. We plan to initiate our own quality improvement study, perhaps working with external funders and researchers. The goal would be to audit all programs that achieved 100% employment and an equal number of the programs with the poorest employment outcomes. The findings would be used to compare and contrast practices between the two groups to assess the relative impact of the different core fidelity components. With this information, we would develop across-the-board programmatic recommendations to improve outcomes on a national and international scale.

4. An individual site might request an audit as a condition of initiating an independent replication project, as discussed in the previous section.

The audit process is not meant to be a disciplinary action. Rather, it is a growth and learning experience for the team whose site is being audited as well as for the auditing team. We have found that we routinely learn of many new and productive enhancements of the Project SEARCH model components that have been developed at the program sites. We also have noticed that there are certain areas in which we are most likely to find that groups are not in compliance:

- The most common of these is that there is not a consistent teacher on site every day. Some sites want to have class just once a week, whereas others have classes 5 days a week but use different teachers on different days.

- Many sites don't have a consistent business liaison that gives 2.5% to 5% of his or her time. In some cases, this is because the host business has been reluctant to designate someone, whereas in other cases, there is a dedicated liaison who is committed to the program but that individual is having a hard time finding the time to be involved to the extent needed.

- Some sites do not have an active Business Advisory Council. Again, the barrier is most often finding the right person to organize it and keep it active.

- It is fairly common to see issues with the monthly employment-planning meetings that are meant to track the progress of each student. The problems that we find indicate that the program in question has not incorporated a thorough appreciation of the purpose of the meetings and the significant advantages that they can bring to the students if they are done correctly. In some cases, the students aren't leading the meetings or aren't even there, and in other cases, the teacher will be under the impression that calling the parents on a regular basis is an acceptable substitute for a full team meeting.

- In many programs that we audit, we find that they are having difficulties in figuring out how to fund long-term follow-along for employed program graduates. The mechanisms for achieving this goal vary greatly from state to state and the solution for each site will be highly specific to that region.

- The auditing process has revealed some instances of programs that are not routinely creating a job development plan for each student before she or he starts the program. Again, this is something that will be done differently at each program with regard to the agency and individual who is best positioned to take the lead in this activity.

- Another repeated bit of guidance that we often give as part of the auditing process is to remind programs to review roles and responsibilities of partner organizations on a regular basis. Once a program is up and running, people do their jobs as a matter of course and it is easy to overlook this process. Also, as the program evolves, new needs emerge, and people change roles, the process of reviewing responsibilities becomes crucial. This process is an extremely useful exercise for optimizing procedures and renewing a sense of commitment for all parties involved.

THE PROJECT SEARCH TRAINING INSTITUTE

As we described earlier, the Project SEARCH leadership team carried out a value-stream mapping process with the overarching goal of improving the rate of employment for youths with intellectual and developmental disabilities. One outcome of this process was to identify a need to enhance the preparedness of the professionals at each site that carries out the Project SEARCH model (see also Wehman, Barcus & Wilson, 2002). Toward this end, we created the Project SEARCH Training Institute to offer specialized course offerings for the special education teachers, job coaches, and job developers who work in Project SEARCH High School Transition Programs. Specifically, we developed training curricula on systematic instruction as a tool for teaching complex job skills, which we called "Teaching and Coaching for Success," and another course on Lean principles as they apply to the Project SEARCH model.

Our next goal for the Project SEARCH Training Institute is to continue to refine the curricula and then to enhance availability by using web-based systems. We will translate the curricula from traditional face-to-face training sessions to an innovative blended-learning system that encompasses online learning, web-based discussion forums, and facilitated lessons through webinars.

An important development in the rehabilitation field is that APSE (a national organization with an interest in integrated employment and career advancement opportunities for

---

TEACHING AND COACHING FOR SUCCESS

Teaching and Coaching for Success is a two-day training session on educational and supported employment strategies presented in the context of the Project SEARCH environment. We discuss sound, research-based techniques and how they can be used to help meet the high expectations of the Project SEARCH program, which starts with the assumption that every intern will gain competitive employment. We demonstrate how to design meaningful internships in which students can learn systematic and complex work starting with job analysis at the level of the business community (the 5,000-foot level) to the hands-on teaching of complicated tasks at the internship site (the 5-foot level). The training describes some new ways of tracking skill acquisition that make use of Lean tools and customized student profiles. Creative ways to teach employability ("soft") skills are also presented in light of their demonstrated importance in the success of any young worker. Job coaching strategies that incorporate systematic instruction techniques are shared. The workshop also highlights the role of each Project SEARCH partner as well as successful strategies to achieve collaboration among all the partners.

LEAN TRAINING IN A PROJECT SEARCH ENVIRONMENT

Lean is an outgrowth of the continuous quality improvement movement originated by Toyota. It has been adopted by health care, manufacturing, banking, and many other large organizations and systems—the same industry sectors where we have Project SEARCH programs. An important Lean component is to actively look for and eliminate waste in order to have the most efficient and productive work flow and final product. "Value added" is a term embedded into Lean thinking. Every part of a work process should add value to the organization, product, or outcome.

A main task for Project SEARCH instructors and job coaches is to analyze a job and work process and find the most efficient way to design and teach the tasks while incorporating the learning style and personality of the person being trained. This work is embedded in the Lean training which will ultimately help to meet our goal of a competitive job for each intern. People with disabilities, when trained properly with competitive, marketable skills, add value and help meet a business need. Many Lean terms and tools are analogous to systematic instruction strategies used by many job coaches and job developers. Aligning this knowledge base brings credibility and increases communication between the business community and Project SEARCH staff. Recognizing these parallels, we want to incorporate Lean tools, processes, and philosophy into our Project SEARCH program and give this knowledge to our staff. The Project SEARCH Lean Training is a 2-day workshop in which we introduce a problem-solving philosophy based on 10 Lean tools and strategies that support continuous improvement in people, systems, and performance.

individuals with disabilities) is working on creating a certification program for job coaches as a means to promote a consistent level of expertise and a universal knowledge base among these professionals. Our aim is to have our Training Institute support this development by monitoring APSE's progress with this project and ensuring that our course offerings are relevant to the resulting certification process.

ENHANCED FAMILY INVOLVEMENT

Research has shown, and the experience at Project SEARCH sites has confirmed, that families and other caregivers have a critical influence on employment outcomes for young people with intellectual and developmental disabilities (Hanley-Maxwell, Whitney-Thomas, & Pogoloff, 1995; Hanley-Maxwell, Pogoloff, & Whitney-Thomas, 1998; McNair & Rusch, 1991; Weymeyer, Morningstar, & Husted, 1999; Whitney-Thomas, 1995). The transition process is daunting for parents as their children leave the school system and transfer to a new set of services, providers, and guidelines. Project SEARCH can impart knowledge that will help smooth this transition. In turn, we recognize that we have a lot to learn from our families. Their intimate understanding of the preferences, interests, learning strategies, and unique challenges of their young adults, as well as their connections within the community, are extremely valuable to the success of the program. To structure and formalize this two-way exchange of information, we have developed a Family Involvement component of the Project SEARCH High School Transition Program. We have begun to roll out this feature, primarily in our Ohio sites, and our goal is to expand to all of our sites. In addition, we would like to adapt what is now a series of traditional face-to-face sessions to include web-based learning and online discussion groups to increase access and flexibility of use. The goal is to create positive relationships with our families, firmly embed them in the Project SEARCH process, and utilize their connections in the community to enhance employment opportunities for the young adults with disabilities that participate in Project SEARCH.

RESEARCH ON THE PROJECT SEARCH MODEL

Our work has always been informed by best practices and current thinking in special education, high school transition, and supported employment. However, Susie and Erin, the founders of Project SEARCH, are by nature doers more than they are analyzers. As a result, our program has been developed largely through an essentially empirical, hands-on, trial-and-error approach. Nonetheless, we have come to a place where we have methodically defined and delineated the core fidelity components that our experience suggests are the features critical to achieving our good outcomes. We feel that the next necessary step to continue to improve our outcomes, and to do it in the most efficient way, is to carry out research with the purpose of rigorously testing the impact of the various components of our model as well as the effectiveness of new initiatives.

As the first step in developing a research program, we have developed a web-based, password-protected database, which will allow us to readily track program outcomes on a national, and ultimately international, scale. The information that we will gather will include the numbers of Project SEARCH interns who participate in the program, complete their training, and gain employment; the salary, hours worked per week, and benefit status of the student interns who gain employment; and the range and variety of jobs.

As part of our effort to put the necessary resources in place for an effective research program, we have initiated a partnership with the University of Cincinnati UCEDD (University Center for Excellence in Developmental Disabilities) to plan and carry out studies in the future. This group has the experience, facilities, and expertise to work with us to rigorously test the effectiveness of various components of our model.

Our intention is to use the results of our studies for program improvement and for dissemination of best practices through publications. We also hope that we can achieve a cost-benefit analysis so that we can compare the cost effectiveness of our programs with other models for high school transition.

SUMMARY

When we think about where we want to take Project SEARCH in the future, all of our plans revolve around improving our employment outcomes. We have achieved excellent results: Project SEARCH in Oklahoma achieved competitive employment for their program participants at a rate of 73.5% in 2010. Several programs in Georgia, New Hampshire, and Virginia have achieved 100% employment 2 years in a row. In the first year of giving Outcome Awards, we had 29 recipients who achieved greater than 60% employment, with 9 of those programs achieving 100% employment. In 2011, we had 30 programs that achieved 60% and over. Although these rates may be good compared with the overall rate of employment for transitioning youths with intellectual and developmental disabilities, it still means that we are failing our program participants roughly 25% to 35% of the time. If you're one of those young adults, the parents, or the vocational rehabilitation counselor associated with that student, you might not think we're a good program. That is why the new programs and directions that make up our plan for the future were conceived with the goal of increasing the numbers of young people with intellectual and developmental disabilities who achieve and maintain competitive employment. We always keep in mind an ultimate goal of 100% employment for every Project SEARCH participant. It may not be achievable, but it is a goal that keeps us moving forward and thinking innovatively.

Project | SEARCH

Meet Stephanie

Stephanie (Steph) is a member of the first Project SEARCH class at the Royal United Hospital (RUH) in Bath, England. She became an employee at the RUH shortly after her graduation from Project SEARCH in 2010. Working at RUH has special significance for Steph and her family because, as a premature infant with a birth weight under 2 pounds, Steph spent the first 8 weeks of her life in the neonatal unit there.

Before applying for Project SEARCH, Steph, who has multiple disabilities, attended a local special school, where she rarely spoke. Because of her extreme shyness and difficulties with communication, there was some concern on the part of both her family and the Project SEARCH teacher with regard to her readiness for Project SEARCH. But, even though she entered the program with some trepidation, Steph proved to be up to the challenge. As her mother says, "We're so glad we made the decision. I know it's given other people confidence to [try Project SEARCH]. Steph has led the way."

Now Steph is excelling in a permanent, full-time position at RUH. She is an assistant technical officer in the sterile services department. The job was advertised on the open market and Steph was chosen from among a very large field of applicants. Steph's willingness to learn, her motivation, and her great attention to detail are qualities that helped the department in their decision to select her as the best candidate for the job. And, as Steph's confidence in her work grows, her reluctance to engage in verbal communication is disappearing. Steph speaks easily to her colleagues in the workplace now.

Sterile services is a busy department, which has responsibility for inspecting, cleaning, and processing surgical instruments for operating rooms, clinics, and patient wards. Steph is involved in the assembly of procedure packs as well as the technical tasks involved in using and testing autoclave machines. She also works in other departments where sterile services has satellite areas, such as gastrology, where she cleans endoscopes for a variety of procedures. Steph has shown that she is quick to pick up technical tasks in the area. Kim Stuart, Steph's department manager, considers her to be a great colleague.

References

Benz, M.R., Lindstrom, L., & Yovanoff, P. (2000). Improving graduation and employment outcomes of students with disabilities: Predictive factors and student perspectives. *Exceptional Children, 66,* 509–529.

Blatt, B. (1981). *In and out of mental retardation: Essays on educability, disability, and human policy.* Baltimore, MD: University Park Press.

Brassard, M., & Ritter, D. (2010). *The memory jogger 2* (2nd ed.). Salem, NH: GOAL/QPC. (Available from www.MemoryJogger.org).

Brooke, V., Wehman, P., Inge, K., & Parent, W. (1995). Toward a customer-driven approach of supported employment. *Education and Training Mental Retardation and Developmental Disabilities, 30*(4), 308–320

Brooke, V., Wehman, P., Inge, K., & Parent, W. (1997) Supported Employment: A Customer-Driven Approach. In *Supported Employment Handbook: A customer-driven approach to persons with significant disabilities* (pp. 1–20). Eds. Valerie Brooke, Katherine Inge, Amy J. Armstrong, and Paul Wehman. Richmond, VA: Rehabilitation Research and Training Center on Supported Employment, Virginia Commonwealth University,.

Browder, D.M., Mims, P.J., Spooner, F., Ahlgrim-Delzell, L., & Lee, A. (2008). Teaching elementary students with multiple disabilities to participate in shared stories. *Research and Practice for Persons with Severe Disabilities, 33,* 3–12.

Bruyère, S. (2000). *Disability employment policies and practices in private and federal sector organizations.* Ithaca, NY: Cornell University, School of Industrial and Labor Relations Extension Division, Program on Employment and Disability.

Butterworth, J., & Pitt-Catsouphes, M. (1997). Employees with disabilities: What managers, supervisors, and co-workers have to say. *Employment in the Mainstream, 22,* 5–15.

Butterworth, J., Smith, F.A., Hall, A.C., Migliore, A., & Winsor, J. (2009). State data: The National Report on Employment Services and Outcomes. Institute for Community Inclusion (UCEDD). Boston: University of Massachusetts.

Callahan, M., Mast, M., & Shumpert, N. (n.d.). *Technology evolves: The story of MG&A. What happened when "try another way" met the real world.* (Available at http://www.marcgold.com/technologyevolves.html).

Carter, E.W., Austin, D., & Trainor, A.A. (2011). Factors associated with the early work experiences of adolescents with severe disabilities. *Intellectual and Developmental Disabilities, 49,* 233–247.

Certo, N., & Luecking, R. (2006). Service integration and school to work transition: Customized employment as an outcome for youth with significant disabilities. *Journal of Applied Rehabilitation Counseling, 37,* 29–35.

Certo, N.J., Luecking, R.G., Murphy, S., Brown, L., Courey, S., & Belanger, D. (2008). Seamless transition and long-term support for individuals with severe intellectual disabilities. *Research and Practice for Persons with Severe Disabilities, 33,* 85–95.

Certo, N.J., Mautz, D., Pumpian, I., Sax, C., Smalley, K., Wade, H., et al. (2003). A review and discussion of a model for seamless transition to adulthood. *Education and Training in Developmental Disabilities, 38,* 3–17.

Chamalian, D. (2001) Teens with disabilities find life after high school tougher. *The Exceptional Parent.* (Retrieved from http://findarticles.com/p/articles/mi_go2827/is_4_31/ai_n28891642/?tag=content;col1)

Chater, V. (2002). Act three: Walkout. From episode 207: Special edition, originally aired 3/8/02. *This American Life*© 1995–2011 WBEZ Alliance, Inc., & I. Glass. *This American Life* is produced by Chicago Public Radio and distributed by Public Radio International.

Coughran, L., & Daniels, J.L. (1983). Early vocational interventions for the severely handicapped. *Journal of Rehabilitation, January/February/March,* 37–41.

Dembo, T., Leviton, G., & Wright, B. (1975). Disability spread. *Rehabilitation Psychology, 22,* 1–100.

De Paul University. (2008) Exploring the bottom line: A study of the costs and benefits of workers with disabilities. Chicago, IL.

Devlin, P (2011). Enhancing job performance. *Intellectual and Developmental Disabilities, 48,* 221–232.

Diamant, M. (2010). *Unemployment nears record levels among people with disabilities.* (Available at http://www.disabilityscoop.com/2010/08/06/july-jobs-10/9671/).

Dixon, K.A., Kruse, D., & Van Horn, C.E. (2003). *Restricted access: A survey of employers about people with disabilities and lowering barriers to work.* New Brunswick, NJ: Heldrich Center for Workforce Development, Rutgers University.

Falkenstine, K.J., Collins, B.C., Schuster, J.W., & Kleinert, H. (2009). Presenting chained and discrete tasks as nontargeted information when teaching discrete academic skills through small group instruction. *Education and Training in Developmental Disabilities, 44,* 127–142.

Farmer, J.A., Gast, D.L., Wolery, M., & Winterling, V. (1991). Small group instruction for students with severe handicaps: A study of observational learning. *Education and Training in Mental Retardation, 26,* 190–201.

Fraker, T., & Rangarajan, A. (2009), The Social Security Administration's youth transition demonstration projects. *Journal of Vocational Rehabilitation, 30,* 223–240.

Garnham, L. (2009). Training in systematic instruction. Presented at the Fourth Annual Project SEARCH® International Conference, Miami, FL.

Gold, M. (1975). Vocational training. In J. Wortes. (Ed.). *Mental retardation and developmental disabilities:*

An annual review (Vol. 7) (pp. 254–262). New York, NY: Bruner/Mazel.

Hanley-Maxwell, C., Pogoloff, S.M., & Whitney-Thomas, J. (1998). Families: The heart of transition. In F. Rusch & J. Chadsey (Eds.). *Beyond high school: Transition from school to work* (pp. 234–264). Belmont, CA: Wadsworth.

Hanley-Maxwell, C., Whitney-Thomas, J., & Pogoloff, S. (1995). The second shock: Parental perspectives on their child's transition from school to adult life. *Journal of the Association for Persons with Severe Handicaps, 20,* 3–16.

Harbison, J.R., & Pekar, P.P. (1998). *Smart alliances: A practical guide to repeatable success.* San Francisco, CA: Jossey-Bass.

Hershenson, D.B. (1981). Work adjustment, disability and the three r's of vocational rehabilitation: A concept model. *Rehabilitation Counseling Bulletin, 25,* 91–97.

Hill, M. (1998). *Project EMPLOY final report.* Richmond, VA: Employment Support Institute, Virginia Commonwealth University. (Retrieved from http://www.ed.uiuc.edu/sped/tri/final385.html#_Toc427549244).

Kailes, J.I. (2002). *Can disability, chronic conditions, health and wellness coexist?* Chicago, IL: The National Center on Physical Activity and Disability. (Retrieved from http://www.ncpad.org/wellness/fact_sheet.php?sheet=106&view=all)

Kaye, H.S. (2010). The impact of the 2007–2009 recession on workers with disabilities. *Monthly Labor Review,* 19–29. (Retrieved from http://www.bls.gov/opub/mlr/2010/10/art2full.pdf).

Kiernan, W.E., Hoff D., Freeze, S., & Mank, D.M. (2011). Employment first: A beginning not an end. *Intellectual and Developmental Disabilities, 49*(4), 300–304.

Kessler Foundation/NOD. (2010). *The ADA 20 years later: Survey of Americans with disabilities.* (Retrieved from http://www.2010disabilitysurveys.org/pdfs/survey summary.pdf).

Kohler, P.D., & Field, S. (2003). Transition-focused education: Foundation for the future. *The Journal of Special Education, 37,* 174–183.

Lakoff, G. (2006). *Thinking points: Communicating our American values and vision.* New York, NY: Farrar Straus Giroux.

Larson, S.A., Goldberg, P., McDonald, S., Leuchovius, D., Richardson, V., & Lakin, K.C. (2011). *2010 fast family support survey: National results.* Minneapolis: PACER Center; Minneapolis, University of Minnesota, Research and Training Center on Community Living, Institute on Community Integration (UCEDD).

Liker, J. (2004). *The Toyota way.* New York: McGraw-Hill.

Liptak, G.S. (2008). Health and well-being of adults with cerebral palsy. *Current Opinion in Neurology, 21,* 136–142.

Luecking, R.G. (2011). Connecting employers with people who have intellectual disability. *Intellectual and Developmental Disabilities, 49,* 261–273.

Luecking, R. (2008). Emerging employer views of people with disabilities and the future of job development. *Journal of Vocational Rehabilitation, 29,* 3–13.

Luecking, R. (2004). *Essential tools: In their own words: Employer perspectives on youth with disabilities in the workplace.* Minneapolis: University of Minnesota, Institute on Community Integration, National Center on Secondary Education and Transition.

Luecking, R., Cuozzo, L., & Buchanan, L. (2006). Demand-side workforce needs and the potential for job customization. *Journal of Applied Rehabilitation Counseling, 37,* 5–13.

McInnes, R. (2006). The Power of Presence: Increasing Workplace Receptivity. *Diversity World* (Retrieved from http://www.diversityworld.com/Disability/DN06/DN0611.htm)

McNair, J., & Rusch, F. (1991). Parent involvement in transition programs. *Mental Retardation, 29,* 93–101.

Migliore, A., Grossi, T., Mank, D., & Rogan, P. (2008). Why do adults with intellectual disabilities work in sheltered workshops? *Journal of Vocational Rehabilitation, 28,* 29–40.

Morgan, R., & Alexander, M. (2005). The employer's perception: Employment of individuals with developmental disabilities. *Journal of Vocational Rehabilitation, 23,* 39–49.

Murphy, K.P., Molnar, G.E., & Lankasky, K. (2000). Employment and social issues in adults with cerebral palsy. *Archives of Physical Medicine and Rehabilitation, 81,* 807–811.

National Alliance for Secondary Education and Transition. (2005). *National standards and quality indicators: Transition toolkit for systems improvement.* Minneapolis: University of Minnesota, National Center on Secondary Education and Transition.

National Center on Physical Activity and Disability. (2000). *NCPAD's Mission Fact Sheet.* (Available at http://www.uic.edu/orgs/ncpad/index.htm).

National Collaborative on Workforce and Disability/Youth. (2011). Tapping into the power of families: How families of youth with disabilities can assist in job search and retention. *NCWD for Youth InfoBrief, April,* 2011. (Available at http://www.ncwd-youth.info/sites/default/files/infobrief_issue27.pdf)

National Council on Disability. (2007). *Empowerment for Americans with disabilities: Breaking barriers to careers and full employment.* (Available at http://www.ncd.gov/newsroom/publications/2007/NCDEmployment_20071001.htm#2a).

National Secondary Transition Technical Assistance Center. (2011). Developing soft skills: The role of family. Presented at the 5th Annual Secondary Transition State Planning Institute. Charlotte, NC.

Niemiec, B., Lavin, D., & Owens, L. (2009). Establishing a national employment first agenda. *Journal of Vocational Rehabilitation, 31,* 139–144.

NOD/Harris Survey of Americans with Disabilities. (2004). (Available at http://www.nod.org/research_publications/nod_harris_survey/).

Ofsted (Office for Standards in Education, Children's Services and Skills). (2010). The special educational needs and disability review: A statement is not enough. Ofsted, Manchester, England.

Ohio Rehabilitation Services. (n.d.). Finding a job should be about ability. (Available at http://www.rsc.ohio.gov/docs/internet-documents/s-1-for-internet-final-8-11.pdf)

Orelove, F.P. (1991). Educating all students: The future is now. In L.H. Meyer, C.A. Peck, & L. Brown (Eds.).

Critical issues in the lives of people with severe disabilities (pp. 67–87). Baltimore, MD: Paul H. Brookes Publishing Co.

Pekar, P., Jr. (2001). Alliance enterprise strategies destroying firm boundaries. In L.W. McKnight, P.M. Vaaler, & R.L. Katz (Eds.). *Creative destruction: Business survival strategies.* Cambridge, MA: The MIT Press.

Peraino, J. (1992). Post-21 studies: How do special education graduates fare? In P. Wehman (Ed.). *Life beyond the classroom: Transition strategies for young people with disabilities* (pp. 21–70). Baltimore, MD: Paul H. Brookes Publishing Co.

Piercy, M. (1982). To be of use. In *Circles in the water* (p. 73). New York: Alfred A. Knopf, Inc., & Middlemarsh, Inc.

President's Commission on Employment of People with Disabilities. *WDC. Project Employ.* July 6, 1998.

Rehabilitation Research and Training Center on Disability Statistics and Demographics. (2009). *Annual compendium of disability statistics: 2009.* Rehabilitation Research and Training Center on Disability Demographics and Statistics, Hunter College. (Available at http://www.disabilitycompendium.org).

Riehle, J.E., & Daston, M. (2006). Deficit marketing: Good intentions, bad results. *Journal of Vocational Rehabilitation, 25,* 69–70.

Rogan, P. (2001). The impact of the revised VR regulations. The advance. *APSE, 11*(2–4), 3.

Rogan, P. (2007). Moving from segregation to integration: Organizational change strategies and outcomes (pp. 253–272). In P. Wehman, K.J. Inge, W.G. Revell, Jr., & V.A. Brooke (Eds.). *Real work for real pay: Inclusive employment for people with disabilities* (pp. 253–272). Baltimore, MD: Paul H. Brookes Publishing Co.

Rogan, P., & Rinne, S. (2011). National call for organizational change from sheltered to integrated employment. *Intellectual and Developmental Disabilities, 46,* 248–260.

Rutkowski, S., Daston, M., Van Kuiken, D., & Riehle, E. (2006). Project SEARCH®: A demand-side model of high school transition. *Journal of Vocational Rehabilitation, 25,* 85–96.

Salembier, G., & Furney, K.S. (1997). Facilitating participations: Parents' perceptions of their involvement in the IEP/transition planning process. *Career Development for Exceptional Individuals, 20,* 29–41.

Sharee, C. (2009). Outlook for employment opportunities looks brighter. *Making a difference: A quarterly magazine of the Georgia Council on Developmental Disabilities, 10,* 19–21.

Siegel, S., Robert, M., Greener, K., Meyer, G., Halloran, W., & Gaylord-Ross, R. (1993). *Career ladders for challenged youths in transition from school to adult life.* Austin, TX: Pro-Ed.

Simon, S.H. (1998). Extracurriculars impact job success after college. *ADA Quarterly, A Supplement to the Ohio Rehabilitation Services Commission NewsNet, 21,* 1–2.

Siperstein, G., Romano, N., Mohler, A., & Parker R. (2006). A national survey of consumer attitudes towards companies that hire people with disabilities. *Journal of Vocational Rehabilitation, 24,* 3–9.

Sonnenberg, E. (2002). Women who make a difference: Working wonders. *Family Circle Magazine* (Available at www.FamilyCircle.com).

Spahlinger, K., & Kin, B. (2006). Lean health care: What can hospitals learn from a world-class automaker? *Journal of Hospital Medicine, 1,* 191.

Stevenson, C.J., Pharoah, P.O., & Stevenson, R. (1997). Cerebral palsy—The transition from youth to adulthood. *Developmental Medicine and Child Neurology, 39,* 336–342.

Szymanski, E.M., Hershenson, D.B., & Power, P.W. (1988). Enabling the family in supporting transition from school to work. In P.W. Power, A. dell Orto, & M.B. Gibbons (Eds.). *Family interventions throughout chronic illness and disability* (pp. 216–233). New York, NY: Springer.

Test, D.W., Fowler, C.H., Richter, S.M. White, J., Mazzotti, V., Walker, A.R., et al. (2009). Evidence-based practices in secondary transition. *Career Development for Exceptional Children, 32,* 115–128.

Timmons, J.Q., Hall, A.C., Bose, J., Wolfe, A., & Winsor, J. (2011). Choosing employment: Factors that impact employment decisions for individuals with intellectual disability. *Intellectual and Developmental Disabilities, 49,* 285–299.

United States General Accounting Office. (2001). Special minimum wage program: Centers offer employment and support services to workers with disabilities, but labor should improve oversight (Report to congressional requesters, GAO-01-866). (Retrieved from http://www.gao.gov/assets/240/232264.pdf)

Wadsworth, J.S., & Harper, D.C. (1993). The social needs of adolescents with cerebral palsy. *Developmental Medicine and Child Neurology, 35,* 1019–1022.

Wagner, M., Blackorby, J., Cameto, R., Hebeler, K., & Newman, L. (1993). *The transition experiences of young people with disabilities: A summary of findings from the National Longitudinal Transition Study of special education students.* Menlo Park, CA: SRI International.

Wagner, M., Cameto, R., & Newman, L. (2003). *Youth with disabilities: A changing population. A report of findings from the National Longitudinal Transition Study (NLTS) and the National Longitudinal Transition Study-2 (NLTS2).* Menlo Park, CA: SRI International.

Walker, A. (2011). CHECKMATE! A self-advocate's journey through the world of employment. *Intellectual and Developmental Disabilities, 49,* 310–312.

Wehman, P. (2003) Workplace inclusion: Persons with disabilities and coworkers working together. *Journal of Vocational Rehabilitation, 18,* 131–141.

Wehman, P., Barcus, M. &Wilson, K. (2002) A survey of training and technical assistance needs of community-based rehabilitation providers. *Journal of Vocational Rehabilitation, 17,* 39–46.

Wehman, P., Kregel, J., & Weyfarth, J. (1985) Transition from school to work for youth with severe handicaps: A follow-up study. *Journal of the Association for Persons with Severe Handicaps, 10,* 132–136.

Wehmeyer, M.L., Morningstar, J., & Husted, D. (1999). *Family involvement in transition planning and implementation.* Austin, TX: Pro Ed.

Werner, E., & Smith, R. (1992). *Overcoming the odds: High risk children.* Ithaca, NY: Cornell University Press.

Westat. (1998). *Report on findings of significant issues and trends.* Westat: Rockville, MD.

White, P.H. (1997). Success on the road to adulthood: Issues and hurdles for adolescents with disabilities. *Pediatric Rheumatology, 23,* 697–707

Whitney-Thomas, J. (1995). Packing the parachute: A survey of parents' experiences as their children prepare to leave high school. *Exceptional Children, 63,* 75–87.

Wittenburg, D., Rangarajan, A., & Honeycutt, T. (2008). The United States disability system and programs to promote employment for people with disabilities. *La Revue Française des Affaires Socials.* (Retrieved from http://www.mathematicampr.com/publications/pdfs/labor/usdisabilitysystem08.pdf)

Witzler P. (2011). *Stories from the field: Employment of people with disabilities.* (Available at http://spsc.seiu.org/2011/05/17/stories-from-the-field-employment-of-people-with-disabilities/).

Wright B. (1996). Teens say job training their top need. *Point of Departure—A Publication on the Technical Assistance About Training on the Rehabilitation Act Project.* PACER Center, 2(8).

Online Disability Resources

The following is a list of online resources that Project SEARCH® practitioners have found to be very useful. It is not a comprehensive list.

CAREER PLANNING

America's Career Info Net
   http://www.careerinfonet.org/
Assess Yourself, Employment & Training Administration (ETA)—U.S. Department of Labor
   http://www.doleta.gov/jobseekers/assess_yourself.cfm
Career Cruising
A commercial web site; resources must be purchased.
   http://www.careercruising.com/
The Career Game by Rick Trow Productions
A career game based on Dr. John Holland personality-based career matching.
   http://www.careergame.com/index.htm
Career Games
   http://www.careergames.com/
Career Interest Game
   http://www.missouriwestern.edu/careerdevelopment/cig/
Career Services: Western Illinois University
   http://www.wiu.edu/student_services/careers/decision/interestgame.php
Careers and Career Information: Career One-Stop
   http://www.careeronestop.org/
CareerShip
   http://mappingyourfuture.org/
Connecticut Connect-Ability
   http://www.connect-ability.com/
Guideposts for Success NCWD/Youth
   http://www.ncwd-youth.info/guideposts
JobHuntersBible.com
   http://www.jobhuntersbible.com
New York CareerZone
   http://www.nycareerzone.org
Ohio DJFS Online Office of Workforce Development
   http://jfs.ohio.gov/owd/WorkforceProf/SCOTI-Home.stm
Oklahoma Career/Tech Career and Academic Connections Homepage
   http://www.okcareertech.org/cac/Pages/assessment/specpops.htm
Tulare County Career Center (California)
   http://www.tcove.org/career_center/interest.htm
Welcome to JIST Publishing—America's Career Publisher or Occupational Outlook Handbook
   and Career Publications
   http://www.jist.com/shop/web

GOVERNMENT AGENCIES ON DISABILITY

Center for Universal Design
http://www.ncsu.edu/project/design-projects/udi/
Connecting the Disability Community to Information and Opportunities
https://www.disability.gov/
Disability and Employment—Community of Practice
https://disability.workforce3one.org/page/home
National Collaborative on Workforce and Disability for Youth
http://www.ncwd-youth.info/
National Secondary Transition and Technical Assistance Center
http://www.nsttac.org/
United Nations Enable: Work of the United Nations for Persons with Disabilities
http://www.un.org/disabilities/

ADVOCACY ORGANIZATIONS

Alliance for Full Participation
http://www.allianceforfullparticipation.org/
The Arc: For People with Intellectual and Developmental Disabilities
http://www.thearc.org/
The Center for Self-Determination Home Page
http://www.centerforself-determination.com/
The Gray Center—Autism/Asperger's Resource site
http://www.thegraycenter.org
Job Accommodation Network (JAN)
http://www.jan.wvu.edu/
Kids Together Inc. (TM) disability, inclusion, rights, information & resources
http://www.kidstogether.org/index.htm
National Disability Rights Network
http://www.napas.org/
PACER Center
http://www.pacer.org/
PACER Center: Champions for Children with Disabilities, the Minnesota Parent Training and
Tools for Life, Georgia's Assistive Technology Act Program
http://www.gatfl.org
Virginia Department of Education resource site
http://www.imdetermined.org/

RESEARCH ON DISABILITY EMPLOYMENT AND REHABILITATION

American Association on Intellectual and Developmental Disabilities
http://www.aaidd.org/
American Network on Community Options and Resources (ANCOR)
http://www.ancor.org/
Association of University Centers on Disabilities
http://www.aucd.org/template/index.cfm
The National Technical Assistance and Research Center to Promote Leadership for Increasing
Virginia Commonwealth University Rehabilitation Research and Training Center
http://www.ntarcenter.org/

Indiana Institute on Disability and Community at Indiana University
http://www.iidc.indiana.edu/
Vocational Rehabilitation Service Models for Individuals with Autism Spectrum Disorders
http://autism.sedl.org/

DISABILITY SERVICES

APSE: Advancing Employment. Connecting People
http://www.apse.org/
National Association of State Directors of Developmental Disabilities Services
http://www.nasddds.org/index.shtml

DISABILITY NEWS

DBTAC-New England ADA Center—Student Videos
http://adaptiveenvironments.org/neada/site/student_videos
Disability and Employment—Community of Practice: Index
https://disability.workforce3one.org/
Disability Scoop—Developmental Disability News
http://www.disabilityscoop.com/
Disability World web-zine
http://www.disabilityworld.org/
Facing Life Head-On, host Brad Mattes—Home
http://www.facinglife.tv/
George Washington University HEATH Resource Center at the National Youth Transitions Center—Online Clearinghouse for
http://www.heath.gwu.edu/
One Place for Special Needs
Your place for disability resources, products, services and support
http://www.oneplaceforspecialneeds.com/
Real People, Real Jobs
http://www.realworkstories.org/
U.S. Department of Labor—ODEP: Offi ce of Disability Employment Policy—Publications—Soft Skills: The Competitive Edge
http://www.dol.gov/odep/pubs/fact/softskills.htm

DISABILITY-SPECIFIC INFORMATION

Asperger's Syndrome and Autism Spectrum DVDs, Videos, and Resources, Coulter Video
http://www.coultervideo.com
Down Syndrome Affiliates in Action
http://www.dsaia.org/
"Living with Autism in a World Made for Others," CNN.com
http://www.cnn.com/2007/HEALTH/02/21/autism.amanda/index.html
National Down Syndrome Society
http://www.ndss.org/
Ohio Center for Autism and Low Incidence
http://www.ocali.org
Transition Tool Kit Autism Speaks
http://www.autismspeaks.org/family-services/tool-kits/transition-tool-kit

EDUCATION AND CLASSROOM TOOLS

Building the Legacy: IDEA 2004
http://idea.ed.gov/
Casey Life Skills
http://www.caseylifeskills.org/
Disability Resources for Inclusion Training Resource Network, Inc.
https://trn-store.com/home
Disability Rights Laws
http://www.humancentereddesign.org/neada/disabilityrights/Welcome.html
Do2learn: Educational Resources for Special Needs
http://www.do2learn.com/picturecards/printcards/2inch/2inches.htm
DO-IT
http://www.washington.edu/doit/
Drive of Your Life—Indiana University career exploration
https://www.driveofyourlife.org
International Encyclopedia of Rehabilitation
http://cirrie.buffalo.edu/encyclopedia/en/
PictureSET
http://www.setbc.org/pictureset/
The Youthhood—Understanding Job Training
http://www.youthhood.org/jobcenter/lw_training.asp
Vocational Information Center: Career and Technical Education Resources
http://www.khake.com/index.html
Welcome to AccessIT
http://www.washington.edu/accessit/index.html
Welcome to Discovery Education Discovery Education
http://discoveryeducation.com
Welcome to TransCen, Inc.
http://www.transcen.org/
Whatdotheydo.com: The Best Search Links on the Net
http://www.whatdotheydo.com
Zarrow Center for Learning Enrichment—The University of Oklahoma
http://www.ou.edu/content/education/centers-and-partnerships/zarrow.html?rd=1

Index

Page numbers followed by *f* indicate figures; those followed by *t* indicate tables.

235